EARLY CHILDHOOD EDUCATION SERIES
Sharon Ryan, Editor

(continued)

DEFENDING CHILDHOOD

Keeping the Promise of Early Education

Beverly Falk

EDITOR

Linda Darling-Hammond

FOREWORD

TEACHERS
COLLEGE
PRESS

Teachers College, Columbia University
New York and London

KH

Published by Teachers College Press, 1234 Amsterdam Avenue, New York, NY 10027

Copyright © 2012 by Teachers College, Columbia University

Library of Congress Cataloging-in-Publication Data

Defending childhood : keeping the promise of early education / edited by Beverly Falk.
    p. cm.—(Early childhood education series) Includes bibliographical references and index. ISBN 978-0-8077-5310-1 (pbk.)—ISBN 978-0-8077-5311-8 (hardcover)
    1. Early childhood education—United States. 2. Child development—United States. I. Falk, Beverly. LB1139.25.D44 2012
    372.210973—dc23

                                                                2011042488

ISBN 978-0-8077-5310-1 (paper)

ISBN 978-0-8077-5311-8 (hardcover)

Printed on acid-free paper

Manufactured in the United States of America

19 18 17 16 15 14 13 12   8 7 6 5 4 3 2 1

4/15/13

Contents

Foreword

It has been said that the measure of a nation is how it treats its most vulnerable citizens. By that measure, there is a crisis in the United States, especially with respect to our children.

We live in a nation that is on the verge of forgetting its children. The United States now has a far higher poverty rate for children than any other industrialized country (nearly 25%, almost double what it was 30 years ago); a more tattered safety net—more who are homeless, without health care, and without food security; a more segregated and inequitable system of public education (with a 10:1 ratio in spending across the country); a larger and more costly system of incarceration than any country in the world (the United States has 5% of the world's population and 25% of its inmates) and one that is now directly cutting into the money we should be spending on education; a defense budget larger than that of the next 20 countries combined; and greater disparities in wealth than any other leading country (the wealthiest 1% of individuals control 25% of our country's resources).

While there is an intensified interest today in how education can prepare young people for the 21st century, the media, politicians, and policy makers too often focus their attention on testing and accountability, using international test score comparisons to bemoan our students' lack-luster performance in relation to the students of other high-performing countries. Yet there is little talk about what high-performing nations—like Finland, Singapore, and Canada—actually do. They ensure that all children have housing, health care, and food security; they fund schools equitably; they invest in high-quality preparation, mentoring, and professional development for teachers and leaders; they organize a curriculum around problem-solving and critical-thinking skills; and they test students rarely, relying instead on assessments (often developed and scored by teachers) that include research projects, scientific investigation, and other intellectually challenging work, all of which are used to inform and support teaching, not to rank and sort teachers or schools.

More about these strategies for how to support children's development, teaching, and schooling can be learned from reading this book.

Introduced in the context of the challenges to childhood presented by our contemporary society, the authors of each chapter—a cross-disciplinary group of extraordinary educators and scholars—share knowledge from their various disciplines about how educators and schools can best negotiate and mediate these forces to defend our society's youngest citizens and their families from influences that undermine optimal growth. Their writings provide new insights about children's development from neuroscience and psychology, as well as emerging understandings about the impact on development of cultural and linguistic diversity, poverty, families and communities, and the media. Additionally, the authors explain effective strategies and approaches for how to support learning, offering us images of what an equitable and just system of education could look like if our collective resources and will were to be harnessed toward these goals.

Although research confirms the importance of the early years in setting the foundation for lifelong learning, too often this critical period of life is given short shrift in discussions and proposals for how to improve students' educational outcomes. And all too often, politicians and policy makers make educational decisions without the benefit of knowledge from those experts who know the issue best.

Herein lies the importance and the opportunity that is presented by this book. In its pages, politicians, policy makers, educators, parents, and other readers can learn about research and successful strategies that illustrate what can be done to ensure that our young people develop into the informed, active, thinking citizens we want and need for our future. Readers will find explanations of how to nurture optimal learning, family and community supports, investments in professional learning, and equitable funding for public education.

We also learn that education is about opening minds to inquiry and imagination, that teaching is about enabling learners to make sense of their experience, to use knowledge for their own ends, and to learn to learn, rather than about spending precious childhood years simply preparing for standardized tests. These pages make clear that the way to foster effective teaching is not with curriculum mandates and pacing guides but with professional learning opportunities that prepare expert educators to take advantage of and create teachable moments. Finally, we learn why the problems of the poor cannot be solved by blaming the teachers and schools who seek to serve them, calling the deepening levels of severe poverty an "excuse," rewarding schools that keep out and push out the highest-need students, or threatening those who work with new immigrant students still learning English and the growing number of those who are homeless, without health care or food security.

The authors of this book share this knowledge in the hope that it will strengthen our collective commitment to support more exciting and empowering schools for children; more useful and appropriate assessments of learning; and more just and humane policies to guide an educational system that is focused on learning, not on selecting and sorting, rewarding and punishing. In these ways, this book contributes to efforts to build a more just and equitable democracy—one that provides for all children what, as the great educational philosopher John Dewey put it, the best and wisest parent wants for his or her child.

Linda Darling-Hammond
Stanford University
October, 2011

Acknowledgments

I am so grateful to the extraordinary educators and scholars who have participated in this project. It has been an honor to collaborate and learn from them about how to defend childhood and move toward realizing the promise of early education. Thank you Todd A. Grindal, Christina Hinton, and Jack P. Shonkoff; Jessa Reed, Kathy Hirsh-Pasek, and Roberta M. Golinkoff; Sonia Nieto; Barbara Bowman and Aisha Ray; Valerie Polakow; Delis Cuéllar and Eugene E. García; Nancy Carlsson-Paige; George Madaus and Terrence Lee-St. John; Robert L. Selman and Janet Kwok; Mara Krechevsky, Ben Mardell, Tiziana Filippini, and Howard Gardner; Edward Zigler and Matia Finn-Stevenson; and James J. Heckman.

Special thanks to Linda Darling-Hammond, my mentor and friend, whose life's work has been devoted to building a high-quality profession of teaching and a system of education that provides opportunities for all children to grow and develop to their fullest potential. My life has been enriched by her knowledge, her courage, her commitment to social justice, as well as her unfailing personal support.

Thank you to Teachers College Press editor Marie Ellen Larcada, for believing in the worthiness of this book, for providing me with a home for it, and for offering continuous encouragement and support. Many thanks also to other staff members at Teachers College Press and particularly Wendy Schwartz, who attended to all the myriad details in ensuring that the collective message of this book came across as intended and that all of the information provided is accurate and accessible.

And to my family, who inspire and inform all that I do, I offer my deepest gratitude for all the encouragement, understanding, tolerance, and love that they so generously gift to me each day.

On behalf of all of the participating authors of this volume, I dedicate this book to a future that ensures all children receive the opportunities they need to realize their potentials, their hopes, and their dreams and to become citizens who will continue our collective struggle of building a more equitable and just society.

DEFENDING CHILDHOOD

Keeping the Promise of Early Education

Introduction

Beverly Falk

Children are the living message we send to a time we will not see.

—Neil Postman, 1982

The world in which children are growing up today is global, competitive, and technological; it is a world that is creating altered expectations for what they can and should be able to do. Schooling is changing, family structures are changing, and how children spend their out-of-school time is changing. While some of these changes are simply the inevitable consequence of the forward march of time, many represent dangers to childhood, contradicting long-held understandings about learning and development.

A recent explosion of research from the neurobiological, behavioral, and social sciences has illuminated new knowledge about how children learn. In addition to affirming that children and their families, in order to thrive, need access to the basic necessities of life—homes, jobs, good health and nutrition, quality child care, and education— the research also confirms that children's educational environments need to be caring and have lots of opportunities for active, exploratory, child-initiated experiences responsive to their learning styles, interests, and needs. New findings leave no doubt that children, if nurtured in these ways, develop greater language skills, better social skills, more empathy, more imagination, more self-control, and higher levels of thinking than those who have not had such opportunities (Shonkoff & Phillips, 2000).

The need for all children to develop these skills and dispositions is greater now than ever before. This book examines some of the reasons why, as well as some areas of concern that need to be addressed in order to ensure that children obtain them. It presents what is known about how children learn, explaining the importance of the early childhood years and the long-term implications of how these years are affected by societal changes and evolving educational policies.

1

To set the context for this discussion and underscore the urgency of the need to support children's optimal development as well as defend them from societal harms, I introduce the issues below.

THE KNOWLEDGE EXPLOSION

We are living in exponentially changing times. Change is happening at such a rapid pace that it is projected that the careers of most of today's kindergartners have not yet even been invented. More knowledge is being generated in 1 year than was produced in the previous 5,000. New technical information is doubling every 2 years. It is also estimated that in the future, as new technologies rapidly become outmoded, people will have many different jobs throughout their lives, rather than only one career (Fisch & McLeod, 2010). Preparing children for this reality means that they must know more than just basic facts and skills. They need to be able to think critically and analytically, to creatively pose as well as solve problems, and to be innovative as well as adaptive to rapidly changing conditions and contexts.

In past generations, it was possible to earn a living in at least some sectors of the economy without graduating from high school or from college. Today's young people have much fewer options. Many jobs are being shifted to other countries or are disappearing altogether. Fewer jobs at a living wage are available for those without a college diploma; even fewer opportunities exist for those who do not graduate from high school. And the difference in lifetime income is dramatic between those who complete school and those who do not. Now more than ever, a quality education is essential for the economic survival of all citizens.

CHANGING DEMOGRAPHICS AND ECONOMICS

Our nation's demographics are rapidly changing. While minorities currently make up over 40% of our populace, this number is expected to increase to over 50% by 2050. Right now, about one of every five students is Hispanic; one in seven is Black; and one in five speaks a language at home other than English (Santa Cruz, 2010). A disproportionate number of these students live in urban, low-income communities. With the child poverty rate in the United States hovering around 20%—the 4th highest of OECD nations (Ranking America, 2010)—millions of children are now experiencing the cumulative stresses of poverty. The schools they attend are more likely than those attended by their more affluent, generally White, peers to employ higher proportions of unqualified or inexperienced teachers, to suffer from poorly maintained and overcrowded facilities, to have insufficient instructional resources and materials, and to emphasize "basic skills" at the expense of more challenging curricula (Kozol, 2005). And if these unequal conditions continue, as our population becomes more diverse, greater numbers of children will not get access to the educational supports that they need. Disparities will continue to grow in young children's health, well-being, and developmental outcomes (Ladson-Billings, 2006).

WHO IS CARING FOR THE CHILDREN?

Increasingly, families with young children in the United States struggle to balance family and workplace responsibilities. More women are working outside of the home and more children are being raised in single-parent families than has ever before been the case. As a result, more children are spending increasing amounts of time in care situations outside their homes. Despite research that points to the critical importance of quality care in the early years, access to it remains limited, especially in low-income communities.

Our nation's prenatal supports, parental leave, and child care policies lag far behind those of other countries. Our infant mortality rate is the second worst in the developed world; only Latvia exceeds it. We don't do much better with maternity and parental leave: Of 168 nations in the world, the United States is one of only five countries (including Lesotho, Papua New Guinea, Swaziland, and Australia) that do not provide some form of paid leave (Save the Children, 2009).

In contrast, other countries have comprehensive services that help balance work with family life: For example, Canada offers 14 months of paid maternity leave and Sweden offers 16 months of parental leave at 80% pay. The Scandinavian countries have child care for any who need it starting in the first year of life; providers are highly skilled pedagogues and families pay only a small percentage of the actual costs (Daycare Trust, 2005).

Unlike these other countries, the United States has no comprehensive system of supports for families in the child rearing years. Instead, we have a hodgepodge of services offered by for-profits, not-for-profits, family day care, and kith-and-kin care (care provided by informal arrangements of family and friends). Teachers who work in these settings are frequently undereducated and underpaid. Programs vary so widely in content, organization, and quality that children and families often do not experience the benefits that high-quality care can offer. This nonsystem is compromising children's school readiness. Too many children begin elementary school unable to take full advantage of its learning opportunities. The figure is estimated to be about 35%; some suggest that for children who are poor, the figure is closer to 50 or 60% (Perkins-Gough, 2007).

While there has been progress over the last 50 years in garnering support for quality care (due in part to studies of federal Head Start and other similar programs, which reveal long-lasting positive effects of quality early schooling), there simply are not enough programs available to accommodate those who are in need of such services. This situation is becoming even worse as economic hardships increase and fewer families are able to afford available options. Increasing numbers of young children are thus losing out on experiences that could provide them with an opportunity to get a strong start.

LOOKING TO SCHOOLS TO SOLVE THE PROBLEMS

A popular response to these changes in our nation—the knowledge explosion, our changing demographics, and our nation's evolving economic and family structures—has been to look to schools to solve the problems. The main focus, however, has been on student outcomes (viewed through the lens of standardized tests), with little attention paid to the inputs that provide communities and schools with the resources they need to actually carry out improvement initiatives.

Inappropriate Expectations Lead to Inappropriate Teaching

Schools' increasing focus on tougher standards, measured by tests and enforced by sanctions, dominates much of what goes on in schools. Because the tests are predominantly multiple-choice and focus on the recall of isolated skills, they in turn drive the curriculum to focus on facts and lower order thinking. This is happening in younger and younger grades. Policies that mandate yearly tests and then apply sanctions and rewards based on their outcomes, make it difficult in elementary through high schools to do much more than teach to the test. Even at the kindergarten level, a growing number of states administer standardized tests to young children, using the results to evaluate the students as well as to judge the programs they are in (Armstrong, 2006; Jacobson, 2007).

In contrast, tests in other countries (especially those in Finland, Canada, Singapore, China, and Japan, countries that are noted for their students' academic achievement) focus on higher order skills: critical thinking, defending ideas, and applying knowledge to solve real-world problems. These assessments, which examine students' learning through projects, math and science investigations, writing, and other authentic products, demonstrate how children are able to understand and apply what they have learned. They give teachers timely information to guide instruction. Unlike machine-scored standardized tests, which often take months for scores to be reported, these observational and performance assessments are generally evaluated by teachers who can use the information immediately. In addition, these assessments are not used to rank schools or to deny promotion or graduation to students. Rather, they are used to help students improve, to evaluate curricula, and to guide professional learning (Darling-Hammond, 2005).

A growing body of research has shown that the more stakes become attached to tests, the more the curriculum is narrowed to what is tested and the more subject area knowledge becomes fragmented (Hout & Elliott, 2011). As a result of increased testing, K–12 classrooms all over the nation are spending more time on language arts and math, while less is spent on other areas of learning, such as science, history, physical education, and the arts (Jennings & Rentner, 2006; Kroger, Campbell, Thacker, Becker, & Wise, 2007; U.S. Department of Education, 2007). But it is not only in these grades that test preparation activities are dominating the teaching and learning environment. They are also trickling down into early childhood classrooms. Out of a belief that early test preparation will better prepare young children for tests they will have to take in later grades, teachers in settings for younger and younger children are increasingly using more testlike activities that emphasize mastery of symbols and skills, despite the fact that many children of this age have not even developed a capacity to comprehend such abstractions (Elkind, 2001; National Association for the Education of Young Children, 1987).

The Disappearance of Play and Active Learning from Classrooms

Throughout the nation it is becoming harder and harder to find classrooms for young children that offer opportunities for the active, play-based experiences known to be needed for them to learn best. In many settings, long-held staples of early education—block play; make-believe play; work with manipulative materials; investigations of sand, water, and other scientific phenomena; cooking; art; writing; music and movement; story time; trips; even rest time and recess are fast disappearing from classrooms (Miller & Almon, 2009). These are being replaced with sedentary, paper-and-pencil work. This transformation is happening in schools everywhere, but it is especially prevalent in low-income communities, where it is often assumed that greater time spent on test prep is needed to ensure that the children will not lag behind their more well-resourced peers (Nichols, Glass, &

Berliner, 2006). Everything we know about how children learn, however, suggests that depriving them of active, play-based experiences is harmful—for academic as well as social-emotional reasons (National Association for the Education of Young Children, 2003; National Association of School Psychologists, 2005). And it may be even *more* harmful to young children who experience the multiple stresses that can accompany poverty and who, therefore, are most at risk. As the American Academy of Pediatrics has warned, free and unstructured play is not only healthy, but essential for helping children reach important social, emotional, and cognitive developmental milestones as well as helping them manage stress and become resilient (Ginsberg, 2007).

Ironically, as play and active learning disappear in schools in the name of preparing children for tests and academic success, more and more of them are actually experiencing failure. Increasingly, children are being held over in their grade or diagnosed with learning disabilities. Also on the rise are diagnoses of hyperactivity as well as reported incidences of frustrated and aggressive behaviors (Miller & Almon, 2009). These phenomena are the result, many suggest, not of problems within the children themselves, but rather of the children's reactions to the inappropriate expectations and play-deprived environments described above.

PROBLEMS WITH OUT-OF-SCHOOL TIME

As expectations inside of schools change, children's lives outside of schools are changing too. Some have schedules so filled with structured activities that they have little time for play or open-ended explorations. Others spend long stretches of time indoors, using mobile devices or sitting in front of TVs, video games, or computers. And while this technology has a positive side—offering unprecedented opportunities to learn in new ways and get exposed to new information—it is worrisome because these sedentary activities are replacing physical activity, play, and other opportunities for children to use their imagination and creativity.

TENSIONS BETWEEN WHAT WE KNOW AND WHAT WE DO: ABOUT THIS BOOK

The conditions presented in this brief introduction are discussed in greater detail in the rest of this book. Each chapter presents knowledge, experiences, and suggestions, from the perspective of a different discipline, about what can be done to protect childhood in the face of contemporary challenges.

Part I focuses on what is known about learning and development. Chapter 1, by Todd A. Grindal, Christina Hinton, and Jack P. Shonkoff, shares new understandings from neuroscience about the development of the architecture of the brain and the implications of these understandings for teaching and learning.

Chapter 2, by Jessa Reed, Kathy Hirsh-Pasek, and Roberta M. Golinkoff, explains what the field of developmental psychology has to say about the importance of play and active learning in the development of children and the implications of these understandings for teaching.

Chapter 3, by Sonia Nieto, discusses what is known from cultural studies about how community and culture impact children's learning and development.

Chapter 4, by Barbara Bowman and Aisha Ray, presents ecological research about the role that families and communities play in supporting children's learning.

Part II presents an in-depth exploration of the dangers to childhood posed by our culture. It offers recommendations for how educators and schools can best support children, their families, and their communities to access their resources and be resilient in the face of risks.

Chapter 5, by Valerie Polakow, explains the impact of poverty on the care of young children and their families and what needs to be done to create social supports that promote equality and quality services for all.

Chapter 6, by Delis Cuéllar and Eugene E. García, discusses the immigrant experience and the challenges faced by families and schools in supporting development for young children from diverse backgrounds.

Chapter 7, by Nancy Carlsson-Paige, explores the impact of the media and technology on children and how its negative influences can be minimized while enhancing its positives for young children's development.

Chapter 8, by George Madaus and Terrence Lee-St. John, demonstrates how high-stakes testing and accountability practices negatively impact children and their learning and what effective alternatives exist to these practices.

Part III puts forth theories of action and recommendations for how to advocate for and build a system of supports to ensure the optimal growth and education of all children.

Chapter 9, by Robert L. Selman and Janet Kwok, discusses how educators and schools can use literature to help children develop social awareness and engagement competencies as a way to reduce risks to their health, promote social relationships, and enhance academic performance.

Chapter 10, by Mara Krechevsky, Ben Mardell, Tiziana Filippini, and Howard Gardner, presents teaching strategies that nurture children to be educated in creative and intellectually engaged ways.

Chapter 11, by Edward Zigler and Matia Finn-Stevenson, describes a schoolwide model that fosters 21st-century skills while providing for the needs of the whole child.

Chapter 12, by James J. Heckman, offers a compelling economic argument for societal investing in young children.

And finally, in the Conclusion, I offer my suggestions for policies and practices of an equitable educational system that supports the learning and development of all children and prepares them for the challenges of sustaining our democracy.

Collectively the authors who have contributed to this volume make the case for play and active experiential learning to remain central in the lives of young children; for the development of expectations (standards) in schools that are appropriate to what is known about children's developmental progressions; for teaching and assessments that foster children's creativity and imagination and nurture the varied ways that they learn; and for school and societal structures that ensure equitable supports for all children's optimal physical, social, and emotional development.

TURNING KNOWLEDGE INTO ACTION

Much knowledge now exists about development and learning. Our challenge and responsibility as a nation is to turn this knowledge into action. Other countries, most especially those with high-performing students, have already been far more successful than we in establishing policies, practices, and resource allocations to support the well-being of their children and families. Our country has much to learn from these places—and much to learn from the authors in this book, who offer their insights about what we can do to defend childhood and ensure that all of our youngsters—our most vulnerable citizens— get access to the supports they need to be healthy, knowledgeable, critical thinkers, who realize their potentials and actively contribute to the development of a vibrant democracy.

REFERENCES

Armstrong, T. (2006). *The best schools: How human development research should inform educational practice.* Washington, DC: Association for Supervision and Curriculum Development.

Darling-Hammond, L. (2005). Teaching as a profession: Lessons in teacher preparation and professional development. *Phi Delta Kappan, 87*(3), 237–240.

Daycare Trust. (2005). *Learning with other countries: International models of early education and care.* London: Author.

Elkind, D. (2001). Much too early. *Education Next, 1*(2), 9–15.

Fisch, K., & McLeod, S. (2010). Did you know: Globalization and the information age. Retrieved from http://www. youtube.com/watch?v=jp_oyHY5bug&feature=related

Ginsberg, K. (2007). The importance of play in promoting healthy child development and maintaining strong parent-child bonds. *Pediatrics 119*(1), 182–191.

Hout, M., & Elliott, S. W. (Eds.). (2011). *Incentives and test-based accountability in education.* Washington, DC: National Research Council.

Jacobson, L. (2007). Preschool: First findings from the preschool follow-up of the Early Childhood Longitudinal Study-Birth Cohort. *Education Week, 27*(11), 5.

Jennings, J., & Rentner, D. S. (2006). Ten big effects of the No Child Left Behind Act on public schools. *Phi Delta Kappan, 88*(2), 110–113.

Kozol, J. (2005). *Shame of the nation: The restoration of apartheid schooling in America.* New York: Random House.

Kroger, L. E., Campbell, H. L., Thacker, A. A., Becker, D. E., & Wise, L. L. (2007). *Behind the numbers: Interviews in 22 states about achievement data and the No Child Left Behind Act policies.* Washington, DC: Center on Education Policy.

Ladson-Billings, G. (2006). From the achievement gap to the education debt: Understanding achievement in U.S. schools. *Educational Researcher, 35*(1), 3–12.

Miller, E., & Almon, J. (2009). *Crisis in the kindergarten: Why children need to play in school.* College Park, MD: Alliance for Childhood.

National Association for the Education of Young Children. (1987). *Standardized testing of young children 3 through 8 years of age.* Washington, DC: Author.

National Association for the Education of Young Children & National Association for Early Childhood Specialists in State Departments of Education. (2003). *Early childhood curriculum, assessment, and program evaluation* [Online joint position statement]. Retrieved from http://www.naeyc.org/about/positions/pdf/pscape.pdf

National Association of School Psychologists. (2005). *NASP position statement on early childhood assessment* [Online document]. Bethesda, MD: Author. Retrieved from http://www.nasponline.org/information/pospaper_eca.html

Nichols, S., Glass, G., & Berliner, D. (2006). High-stakes testing and student achievement: Does accountability pressure increase student learning? *Education Policy Analysis Archives, 14,* 1. Retrieved from http://epaa.asu.edu/ojs/article/view/72

Perkins-Gough, D. (2007). Giving intervention a head start: A conversation with Edward Zigler. *Educational Leadership, 65*(2), 8–14.

Postman, N. (1982). *The disappearance of childhood.* New York: Vintage/Random House.

Ranking America. (2010). *The U.S. ranks 4th in child poverty.* Retrieved from http://rankingamerica.wordpress.com/2010/01/13/the-u-s-ranks-2nd-in-child-poverty/

Santa Cruz, N. (2010, June 10). Minority population growing in the United States, census estimates show. *Los Angeles Times.* Retrieved from http://articles.latimes.com/2010/jun/10/nation/la-na-census-20100611

Save the Children. (2009). *State of the world's mothers 2009: Investing in the early years.* Westport, CT: Author.

Shonkoff, J. P., & Phillips, D. A. (Eds.). (2000). *From neurons to neighborhoods: The science of early childhood development.* Washington, DC: National Academy Press.

U.S. Department of Education, National Center on Education Statistics. (2007). *Changes in instructional hours in four subjects by public school teachers of grades 1 through 4.* Retrieved from http://nces.ed.gov/pubsearch/pubsinfo. asp?pubid=2007305

Part I

HOW CHILDREN GROW AND DEVELOP: IMPLICATIONS FOR TEACHING

CHAPTER 1

The Science of Early Childhood Development

Lessons for Teachers and Caregivers

Todd A. Grindal, Christina Hinton, and Jack P. Shonkoff

You may not remember cuddling with your mother as an infant, listening to dinner table conversations as a toddler, or playing with blocks as a preschooler—but your brain and body do. As young children interact with their families and communities, these experiences affect gene expression and literally shape the architecture of their developing brains. Though these gene-environment interactions continue throughout life, early influences set the trajectory for later development. In this way, early experiences establish a foundation for lifelong learning and health.

As any teacher will attest, children do not arrive on the first day of kindergarten as "blank slates." After 5 years of early childhood experiences, some children arrive ready to read, calculate, and participate in structured activities, while others struggle to identify letters and numbers or follow simple instructions (Hart & Risley, 1995). These initial differences create challenges for teachers and caregivers—and they are powerful predictors of later school achievement, economic productivity, and a lifetime of physical and mental health (Knudsen, Heckman, Cameron, & Shonkoff, 2006).

Most teachers and other early childhood caregivers recognize that children's early experiences play a powerful role in shaping later life outcomes. However, they are subject to a dizzying array of advice about how to best support positive development. For example, the American Academy of Pediatrics strongly urges parents and other caregivers to limit the amount of time that infants and toddlers spend in front of screens, while advertisers insist that children will fall behind without the aid of "educational" television and computer programs. Friends and grandparents are also eager to offer recommendations on how to raise healthy young children and much of this guidance is often contradictory. Amid this cacophony of conflicting advice, many early childhood caregivers struggle to distinguish well-intentioned opinion from sound science.

This chapter provides a succinct overview of the core science of early childhood development and incorporates key concepts that emerge from decades of neuroscience research (Shonkoff, 2010; Shonkoff & Phillips, 2000). Three particularly important messages are highlighted: Brains are constructed from the bottom up; emotional experiences are built into the architecture of the brain; and nurturing relationships are crucial to healthy development. Based on this science, early childhood caregivers are advised to engage children as active learners from the day they are born, pay close attention to all dimensions of development, and take care of themselves so that they can develop and maintain stable, responsive relationships with the children in their care.

THE SCIENCE OF EARLY CHILDHOOD DEVELOPMENT

Brains Are Constructed from the Bottom Up

Brains are built over time. The first signs of brain development are detectable just 3 weeks after conception. From that moment until the end of our lives, our brains continue to adapt in response to experience. The development of a brain can be compared to the construction of a house. The home-building process begins with a blueprint that maps out the basic materials and sequence of the project, which are then often modified "on the job" as the actual construction proceeds. In a similar fashion, genes provide a blueprint that maps out the brain's basic organization and connectivity patterns, which are then adapted to environmental influences over time. Thus, just as the successful transformation of a blueprint into a completed house depends on having the right materials, the genetic blueprint for brain development relies on the impact of appropriate experiences. Young children's brains are built as they interact with the world around them, and the brain is designed genetically to develop in response to both expected and unanticipated experiences. For example, the ability to process and discriminate visual images develops in response to opportunities to use their eyes. Similarly, acquiring the ability to understand

and produce language depends on children's early interactive engagement with people who speak to them in words and phrases.

The brain is made up of billions of specialized nerve cells (called neurons) and supporting structures (that originate from glial cells). As young children interact with the world around them, their experiences shape connections among neurons following a well-described pattern of proliferation followed by selective pruning ("use it or lose it"). That is, connections that are most active are strengthened and stabilized, while those that are least active are weakened and eventually eliminated (Kaczmarek, 1997). For example, as a child learns to play the violin, appropriate neuronal connections are gradually cued up and "tuned." As he or she practices that skill, the neuronal connections underlying finger dexterity in the left hand are activated and the associated activity strengthens these connections. Consequently, the brain areas representing the fingers of the left hand are larger in violinists than in nonmusicians (Elbert, Pantev, Wienbruch, Rockstroh, & Taub, 1995). Similarly, the neuronal connections recruited for processing musical notes are reinforced through practice, with the result that the brain areas representing musical tones are also larger in violinists than in nonmusicians (Pantev et al., 1998). This is just one example of the many ways in which the brain adapts to reflect experience over time.

Though this process of adaptation continues throughout life, the brain is particularly responsive to experiences in early childhood. As noted above, these first few years are associated with rapid overproduction of neural connections called synapses. In fact, in the time it took you to read this sentence, the average infant brain produces more than 700 new synapses. As children grow and interact with their environment, the total number of connections is gradually reduced as experiences sculpt a young child's brain to fit the needs of his or her environment. The complex neural circuitry that supports the breadth and depth of adult capabilities is built from the bottom up. A young child's lower level neural circuits, such as those for sensory capacities like vision and hearing, are shaped earliest. Higher level networks, such as those supporting complex cognitive functions, follow in a hierarchical fashion. In this way, early experiences shape the neuronal circuitry that forms the foundation of later learning and health.

Emotional Experiences Are Built Into the Architecture of the Brain

Virtually all early childhood caregivers feel a responsibility to provide nutritious food and opportunities for regular exercise to help the children in their care develop healthy bodies. Similarly, most caregivers recognize the importance of providing children with cognitive stimulation, such as through books and toys, to support the development of their language and thinking skills. That said, there is a fair amount of disagreement in some circles about the proper role of non-family caregivers in shaping children's emotional development. Some believe that all caregivers should nurture every dimension of children's well-being. Others argue that emotional development should be the responsibility of the family and consider the involvement of school and other formal institutions as an encroachment on family life.

From the perspective of neuroscience this debate is no longer relevant. Abundant evidence indicates that emotional development is inextricably intertwined with cognitive abilities and physical well-being (Hinton, Miyamoto, & Della-Chiesa, 2008). Neuroscientists conceptualize learning and health as multifaceted and view the cognitive, physical, and emotional dimensions of development as highly interrelated functions that evolve within the increasingly integrated circuitry of the maturing brain (Damasio,1994). The brain itself is organized into assemblies of neurons with specialized properties and functions. A stimulus elicits a network response of various assemblies to produce an experience. Particular components of this experience can be assigned a label, such as cognitive or emotional, but sharp distinctions among them are conceptual rather than practical.

The emotional dimensions of experience are built into the architecture of the brain. In fact, bonding and positive emotional interactions are critical for nurturing brain development. In the metaphor of building a house, positive emotional interactions could be thought of as the cement that holds the foundation of a house together. Without them, the house would be shaky regardless of how many other materials are available.

Persistent negative experiences are potentially toxic for the developing brain. This does not mean that children can, or should, be shielded from all sources of stress. Many of the stressors young children experience, such as receiving a vaccination from a pediatrician, are quite tolerable. Moreover, some stress can even be positive. For example, separation from their parents on the first day of a new preschool program may lead to tears and frustration (for children and parents alike) but it can also help children develop self-confidence and independence. On the other hand, chronic or traumatic experiences, such as homelessness, unremitting poverty, abuse, or neglect can have severe and long-lasting consequences on children's brain development (United Nations, 2006).

This toxic stress response gets "under the skin" and into the biology of the body. The circuits in the brain and other organ systems that regulate the response to stress develop in early childhood and are influenced by experience. When young children experience adversity, their heart rate increases, their blood pressure rises, and their bodies release hormones such as adrenaline from the sympathetic-adrenomedullary system, and cortisol from the hypothalamic-pituitary-adrenocortical system. If this response is evoked repeatedly from traumatic or chronic stressors, over time the increased levels of cortisol and adrenaline can disrupt the development of neural systems involved in regulating certain learning and memory processes (National Scientific Council on the Developing Child, 2005, 2010). The internal chemicals produced in response to these stressors can also have a "wear and tear" or "weathering" effect on the body's health over time and lead to increased susceptibility to depression, heart disease, asthma, or diabetes, among many other impairments (Danese et al., 2009).

The biological effects of chronic and traumatic experiences can also have corresponding behavioral consequences. Children who experience these sorts of stressors may have difficulties recognizing emotions, adapting to new situations, and forming and maintaining healthy relationships. For example, children who experienced physical abuse have been found to identify neutral facial expressions as angry much more often than children who have not experienced abuse, which suggests that they are more likely to perceive people as threatening (Pollak, Cicchetti, Hornung, & Reed, 2000). With this defensive stance, they may struggle to form close relationships with both peers and adults.

The good news is that the negative impacts of stress can be buffered by the presence and reassurance of a supportive caregiver. Thus traumatic experiences can be tolerable when children have a stable, loving relationship with at least one caring adult to help them cope. Teachers and other early childhood caregivers can provide these buffers and play a critical role in nurturing healthy development in the face of traumatic or persistent stress.

Nurturing Relationships Are Crucial to Healthy Development

Human infants are born completely dependent upon adults. They remain vulnerable for a long period of time with very limited ability to obtain food or protect themselves from dangers in the environment for the first several years of life. They can only survive and thrive when at least one adult is dedicated to their care. As Bronfenbrenner (1988) suggests, "In order to develop normally, a child needs the enduring, irrational involvement of one or more adults in care and joint activity with that child. In short, someone has to be crazy about that kid" (p. 145).

Infants and their caregivers engage in ongoing "serve-and-return" interactions in which they exchange a continuous flow of sounds, expressions, and gestures. A caregiver smiles and a baby smiles back. A baby cries and a caregiver offers safety and comfort. This comes naturally to most caregivers, but sometimes because of illness or difficult circumstances these sorts of interactions are derailed. In such circumstances, the absence of consistent, responsive communication with a loving caregiver has substantial consequences for the architecture of a young child's developing brain.

Research with children reared in orphanages provides an extreme example of this point. In some institutions, children's lives are characterized by highly regimented schedules, relatively limited cognitive and sensory stimulation, and few opportunities for consistent interaction with warm, responsive caregivers. By the age of 5, these institutionally reared children, on average, have lower IQ scores and higher rates of behavioral disorders than children who were adopted from these settings (Nelson & Sheridan, 2011). Moreover, this early deprivation seems to have persistent consequences even after the children are relocated to more favorable and nurturing environments. For example, more than 6 years after being adopted, children who spent as little as 8 months of their early childhood years in these depriving institutions demonstrate higher levels of the potentially damaging stress hormone cortisol than children who were not institutionalized during their early childhood years (Gunnar, Morison, Chisholm, & Schuder, 2001).

While few children in the United States today spend their early years in institutionalized settings, many grow up in circumstances in which their caregivers struggle to engage in regular, responsive, serve-and-return interactions. For example, nearly one out of every eleven U.S. infants spends his or her first year with a mother who experiences major depression. This condition limits a mother's capacity to respond to the constant needs of her young child, which can have adverse consequences for neurological development, as children who have severely depressed mothers demonstrate elevated levels of potentially damaging stress hormones. As they get older, these children are also more likely to develop depression or emotional disorders themselves (National Scientific Council on the Developing Child, 2009).

Extensive research on maternal depression demonstrates that young children are not immune to the struggles of the adults who provide their care. When adults experience stressors such as financial instability or racial discrimination, the children in their care can also suffer consequences. These adult stressors limit caregivers' capacity to engage children in the sort of contingent reciprocity that is crucial for healthy brain development. Thus meeting the needs of young children inherently involves caring for the adults in their lives as well.

IMPLICATIONS OF BRAIN DEVELOPMENT FOR TEACHERS AND CAREGIVERS

Although parents have the greatest influence on their children's development, providers of early care and education also have important impacts. Through their ongoing interactions they make hundreds of decisions that can affect children's cognitive, emotional, and physical well-being—and the science of early childhood development can help inform these decisions. We propose three guiding principles for caregivers of young children that are grounded in a strong evidence base: (1) Engage children as learners from the day they are born; (2) nurture emotional health along with physical and cognitive development; and (3) take care of yourself, the caregiver, so that you can build and sustain stable, caring relationships with the children in your care.

Engage Children as Learners from the Day They Are Born

Children are born ready to learn and the developing architecture of their brains is influenced by the experiences they have in the first years of life. These initial connectivity patterns shape early trajectory patterns for all later learning and health. Caregivers should therefore ensure that young children have the experiences that are necessary to support a successful developmental process. This does not at all mean attempting to cram every young child's days with a maximum amount of highly structured, academically focused stimulation. Rather, caregivers should provide children with safe, stimulating, child-friendly environments in which they can explore the world around them in a way that respects their individuality.

Because the brain develops rapidly in the first few years of life, early childhood is a period with tremendous potential for opportunity but also a time of considerable risk. Since early experience shapes brain architecture both for better and for worse, traumatic or severely impoverished environments can disrupt developing brain circuits and have serious lifelong consequences. Therefore, caregivers should intervene quickly when young children's needs are not being met. In simple terms, early intervention is generally more successful than later remediation.

Nurture Emotional Health Along with Physical and Cognitive Development

Emotional well-being is inextricably interrelated with physical health and cognitive development. It is impossible to target any of these dimensions in isolation from the others. Like nails and wood in a house, emotional and cognitive development work together to create a sturdy structure. Parents and providers of child care and early education should therefore actively support children's emotional as well as cognitive and physical well-being.

Learning to manage feelings is one of the most critical and challenging tasks of early childhood. Children who struggle to understand and control their emotions often also struggle to make friends with their peers and engage with their caregivers. These relational challenges can lead to a multitude of negative outcomes later in adolescence and adulthood. Caregivers therefore need to support young children's development of the capacity to regulate their emotions and behavior. Too many early childhood programs give up too quickly on children with challenging behaviors, as estimates indicate that preschool children are expelled from school at nearly three times the rate of kindergarten–12th-grade students (Gilliam, 2005). Just as early childhood programs would not reject students who struggle to identify their letters or numbers, they should not dismiss children who have emotional difficulties or behavior problems. Supporting children's emotional development should be a core aspect of any early childhood program's educational agenda.

Young children can experience profound and deep emotions as well as serious mental health problems. The notion that a child can easily shrug off significant abuse, neglect, or other types of adversity is not at all supported by credible evidence. Science tells us that these experiences can actually affect gene expression and shape the physical structure of a child's brain. Caregivers should intervene immediately to help our most vulnerable children cope with these kinds of stressors. While some caregivers may worry that labeling children with mental health needs could bring potentially damaging stigma, the failure to identify a serious problem can deprive a troubled child of years of effective treatment. The developing brain is particularly responsive to evidence-based interventions and early prevention is generally more effective than later remediation.

Take Care of the Caregiver

The serve-and-return relationship between caregivers and young children is essential for healthy development. Therefore, when caregivers struggle, children are at risk. Safety instructions on an airplane ask adults to secure their own oxygen masks before helping children because an adult who is struggling to breathe cannot attend to the needs of a child. This directive provides a metaphor for many aspects of effective child rearing. Adults need to make sure to take care of themselves so that they are able to meet children's needs. Parents and other caregivers of young children who are stressed or depressed often struggle to provide the positive serve-and-return interactions that are so important for healthy child development. The science is clear that a stable, secure relationship with an adult caregiver can buffer young children from the long-term consequences of traumatic events or chronic adversity.

Early childhood caregivers should therefore monitor and maintain their own and their colleagues' mental health. This is of course easier said than done. Longstanding social and institutional barriers continue to limit access and effective utilization of much needed mental health services. Nevertheless, as caregivers and policy makers recognize that adult mental health is a critical component of a child's well-being, these barriers hopefully will lessen over time.

CONCLUSION

Conscientious parents and caregivers confront a host of tough questions. What can I do to ensure that my child is confident and happy? How can I help my child learn to read? What are the most important features of an effective early education program? The answers to these kinds of questions are influenced by a broad variety of cultural values, family traditions, and personal beliefs—and reasonable people can disagree about the "best way" to handle a range of everyday challenges.

Although successful caregiving is much more of an art than a science, there is a strong and growing scientific knowledge base that can inform sound decision making. Science tells us that early experiences shape brain development in ways that can influence a lifetime of learning, behavior, and health. It also helps us understand that children are affected by both the well-being and the struggles of their caregivers. The evidence is clear that children benefit from stable relationships with caring adults who engage them as learners from the moment they are born and pay close attention to all aspects of their development. Early childhood caregivers have both a tremendous opportunity and important responsibility to shape young minds and bodies. Better understanding of the science of early childhood and early brain development can help caring adults provide the kinds of environments and experiences that will increase the likelihood that the children they care for will grow up to be the responsible citizens, productive workers, and successful parents of the next generation.

REFERENCES

Bronfenbrenner, U. (1988). Strengthening family systems. In E. F. Zigler & M. Frank (Eds.), *The parental leave crisis: Toward a national policy* (pp. 143–160). New Haven, CT: Yale University Press.

Damasio, A. R. (1994). *Descartes' error: Emotion, reason, and the human brain.* New York: Putnam.

Danese, A., Moffitt, T., Harrington, H., Milne, B., Polanczyk, G., Pariante C., Poulton, R., & Caspi, A. (2009). Adverse childhood experiences and adult risk factors for age-related disease. *Archives of Pediatrics and Adolescent Medicine, 163*, 1135–1143.

Elbert, T., Pantev, C., Wienbruch, C., Rockstroh, B., & Taub, E. (1995). Increased cortical representation of the fingers of the left hand in string players. *Science, 270*(5234), 305–307.

Gilliam, W. S. (2005). *Prekindergarteners left behind: Expulsion rates in state prekindergarten systems.* New Haven, CT: Yale Child Studies Center.

Gunnar, M., Morison, S., Chisholm, K., & Schuder, M. (2001). Salivary cortisol levels in children adopted from Romanian orphanages. *Development and Psychopathology, 13*(3), 611–628.

Hart, B., & Risley, T. (1995). *Meaningful differences in the everyday experience of young American children.* Baltimore: Paul H Brookes.

Hinton, C., Miyamoto, K., & Della-Chiesa, B. (2008). Brain research, learning and emotions: Implications for education research, policy and practice. *European Journal of Education, 43*(1), 87–103.

Kaczmarek, L. (1997). *The neuron.* New York: Oxford University Press.

Knudsen, E., Heckman, J., Cameron, J., & Shonkoff, J. (2006). Economic, neurobiological and behavioral perspectives on building America's future workforce. *Proceedings of the National Academy of Sciences, 103*, 10155–10162.

National Scientific Council on the Developing Child. (2005). Excessive stress disrupts the architecture of the developing brain (Working Paper No. 3). Retrieved from http://www.developingchild.harvard.edu

National Scientific Council on the Developing Child. (2009). Maternal depression can undermine the development of young children (Working Paper No. 8). Retrieved from http://www.developingchild.harvard.edu

National Scientific Council on the Developing Child. (2010). Persistent fear and anxiety can affect young children's learning and development (Working Paper No. 9). Retrieved from http://www.developingchild.harvard.edu

Nelson, C., & Sheridan, M. (2011). Lessons from neuroscience research for understanding causal links between family and neighborhood characteristics and educational outcomes. In G. Duncan & R. Murnane

(Eds.), *Whither opportunity? Rising inequality and the uncertain life chances of low-income children.* New York: Russell Sage Foundation Press.

Pantev, C., Oostenveld, R., Engelien, A., Ross, B., Roberts, L. B., & Hoke, M. (1998). Increased auditory cortical representation in musicians. *Nature, 392*(6678), 811–814.

Pollak, S. D., Cicchetti, D., Hornung, K., & Reed, A. (2000). Recognizing emotion in faces: Developmental effects of child abuse and neglect. *Developmental Psychology, 36,* 679–688.

Shonkoff, J. P. (2010). Building an enhanced biodevelopmental framework to guide the future of early childhood policy. *Child Development, 81*(1), 343–353.

Shonkoff, J. P., & Phillips, D. A. (Eds.). (2000). *From neurons to neighborhoods: The science of early childhood development.* Washington, DC: National Academy Press.

United Nations. (2006). *Report of the independent expert for the United Nations study on violence against children.* New York: Author.

CHAPTER 2

A Tale of Two Schools

The Promise of Playful Learning

Jessa Reed, Kathy Hirsh-Pasek, and Roberta M. Golinkoff

Brookfield Elementary: "Flight" is the curriculum topic. Kindergartners dutifully sign their names to enter the paper airplane "factory" in their classroom. The morning begins with circle time as children intently listen to a story about Amelia Earhart's solo flight across the Atlantic. The ensuing discussion is populated with vocabulary words like *aviator* and *pioneer*. Paper airplane stations dot the room, challenging young designers to fold rectangles into three-dimensional shapes that will stay afloat and sail across the room. Writing, reading, and arithmetic, coupled with art projects and social studies, form the flight-oriented curriculum. Children's imagination and motivation soar as students work together.

Winsor Elementary: Just 1 mile away across City Avenue, the curriculum topic is also "flight." Here kindergartners are seated in rows, quietly listening (and fidgeting) as their teacher uses the scripted lesson plan. For the next 45 minutes, they see the letter *a*, point to the letter *a*, and recite: "Aaay . . . aaay . . . aaay." The teacher next reads a storybook about Amelia Earhart but stops repeatedly to ask the children to say key words like *aviator* and recite their definitions. Worksheets for math are next as children stay seated and silent. Sitting on the floor—not allowed. Veering from the script—frowned upon. Lessons are geared to the test several months from now in May. There is no time for recess, none for art or music, and imagination is never in play.

These schools could not be further apart philosophically. While both infuse the curriculum with content in literacy and math, the first utilizes *playful learning* as a pedagogical approach while the second uses what is often called *direct instruction*. Playful learning is a developmentally appropriate practice that engages children in their education, nesting learning within a meaningful context. In stark contrast, direct instruction is more teacher-directed and compartmentalized, with little room for children's individual responses. Reading and writing are often considered different and unrelated subjects, not even loosely connected to mathematics. Kindergartners in Winsor Elementary will *learn to read*, but research suggests that by third or fourth grade, difficulties may arise when they are *reading to learn* (Chall & Jacobs, 2003). In these pages, we argue that effective learning will come from schools that offer a rich curricular program delivered within a playful pedagogy.

PLAY AND LEARNING

This tale of two schools is a signpost for the current trend in education (e.g., Hirsh-Pasek, Golinkoff, Berk, & Singer, 2009; Miller & Almon, 2009), representing the philosophical tug-of-war that has emerged regarding best practices for early childhood education. The constructivist approach to education, championed by Vygotsky, Piaget, Dewey, Montessori, Bruner, and others, emphasizes the learner's active role in creating meaning and drawing connections to foster not only knowledge but also a growing sense of self. In contrast, a direct instruction pedagogy necessitates a passive recipient, a role to which children are reluctantly resigned. The science is clear. Free play promotes better physical and mental health (Burdette & Whitaker, 2005), and playful learning is related to better outcomes in social and academic ability—in reading, spatial learning, and mathematics (for a review, see Hirsh-Pasek et al., 2009). How then, did play get divorced from learning?

The divorce proceedings began when play lost ground to direct instruction. This didactic focus in preschools comes from two main sources. The first is a societal misconception—about brain growth—and about what it takes for children to succeed in school. Parents feel pressure to accelerate and augment children's learning (Hirsh-Pasek & Golinkoff, 2003). Often exaggerated information suggests that brain development is more or less over by age 5 (e.g., Bruer, 1999; Silberg, 2000). Further, claims about "brain-based" education litter the Internet with over 174,000 hits even though scientific studies that directly link brain research and educational practice largely lag behind these claims (Hirsh-Pasek & Bruer, 2007; Stern, 2005). The onus is on parents to do everything they can to nurture their children's intelligence as early as possible. Preschool directors often feel the pressure to succumb to requests for worksheets and to drop less unstructured, "time-wasting" play. A recent survey of schools in Los Angeles suggests that fully 25% of the schools now have no time for play amidst the academic roster (Miller & Almon, 2009).

Secondly, the achievement gap paired with our national focus on educational accountability motivated our razor-sharp focus on instilling specific skill sets. This "sense of urgency" (Nicolopoulou, 2010, p. 2) has resulted in the almost-exclusive use of direct instruction, sacrificing a commitment to engaged learning and to the curiosity that develops during playful learning.

It is well known that intervening during the preschool years can reduce the "achievement gap" (Ramey & Ramey, 1999; Schweinhart, 2004). There is virtual consensus that preschool children benefit from learning *content* and that academic advancement is cumulative. The roots of children's competencies begin in infancy and early childhood. By way of example, toddlers' oral language skills not only predict how well they will communicate in school, but also how well they will learn their ABCs and understand written texts (Dickinson & Freiberg, 2009; NICHD, 2005; Scarborough, 2001; Storch & Whitehurst, 2001). Learning to count and mastering concepts related to numbers (e.g., "big" and "small") are also critical to later mathematical understanding and to flexible problem solving (Baroody & Dowker, 2003).

Self-regulation skills also scaffold school success (e.g., Ponitz, Mc-Clelland, Matthews, & Morrison, 2009; Raver, 2002). When children play a game of Simon Says, they must remember to follow only those instructions that are preceded by the two magic words and inhibit their impulse to act otherwise. These abilities—to plan, to monitor, to inhibit one's natural impulses—are referred to as self-regulation, effortful control, and executive function (e.g., Blair, 2002; Carlson, 2005; Diamond, Barnett, Thomas, & Munro, 2007). Rimm-Kaufman, Curby, Grimm, Nathanson, and Brock (2009) find that children with higher levels of self-regulation at the beginning of kindergarten are rated higher by teachers on levels of adaptive classroom behavior. Evans and Rosenbaum (2008) report that the link between families' income and academic achievement in fifth grade is mediated by children's self-regulation skills at 4.5 years, even when controlling for cognitive development at 15 months, as well as prior variables such as ethnicity, gender, and maternal education. Training in emotion regulation that helps children control their behavior and plan effectively is related to both academic outcomes and social gains (Diamond et al., 2007; Ogan & Berk, 2009). These facts alone compel us to design curricula for preschoolers that expose children to language, literacy, early number, *and* social skills.

Recently, a large survey of six longitudinal data sets from Britain and the United States examined precursors for school readiness. Using meta-analyses, across literally thousands of children, they concluded that mathematics, emergent literacy scores, and attentional skills were the best predictors of later academic success. These results held for children regardless of gender or socioeconomic class (Duncan et al., 2007). Thus we not only know that early education matters, but we are zeroing in on exactly the kinds of curricular goals that will align preschool education with later primary school outcomes.

Importantly, however, curricular goals that focus on *what* we teach but ignore the pedagogy of *how* we teach can go only half the distance in narrowing the achievement gap. This is a fertile area for research. Existing studies strongly suggest that we think about curricula that stress learning *via play*. A whole-child perspective enhances children's social, academic, and creative development, allows for accountability, and can easily align with pre-K–3rd-grade education (Bogard & Takanishi, 2005). That is, Brookfield Elementary teaches to a rich curriculum but does so in a way that is not only more playful, but also more meaningful and durable.

DEFINING PLAYFUL LEARNING AS THE PEDAGOGY FOR LEARNING

Playful learning is defined as both free play and guided play and encompasses a whole-child educational approach that promotes academic, socioemotional, and cognitive development (Fisher, Hirsh-Pasek, Golinkoff, Singer, & Berk, 2010; Hirsh-Pasek et al., 2009; Resnick, 2003; Singer, Golinkoff, & Hirsh-Pasek, 2006). Representing object play, pretend and sociodramatic play, and rough-and-tumble play, *free play* has been difficult to define because of this heterogeneity. The latest research suggests that play activities are fun, voluntary, flexible, have no extrinsic goals, involve the child's active engagement, and often contain an element of make-believe (Johnson, Christie, & Yawkey, 1999; Pellegrini, 2009; Sutton-Smith, 2001).

Guided play, on the other hand, fosters academic knowledge through play activities. Guided play can be defined through two characteristics (for a review, see Hirsh-Pasek et al., 2009). First, adults can enrich the environment with objects and toys that provide experiential learning opportunities infused with curricular content (e.g., Berger, 2008). In a Montessori classroom, for example, the well-chosen play materials enable children to discover and practice basic principles of math and reading (Lillard, 2005; see also Neuman & Roskos, 1992). Second, in guided play teachers enhance children's exploration and learning by commenting on children's discoveries, by coplaying along with the children, by asking open-ended questions about what children are finding, or by exploring the materials in ways that children might not have thought to do (Ash & Wells, 2006; Berk & Winsler, 1995; Callanan & Braswell, 2006; Copple, Sigel, & Saunders, 1979; Rogoff, 2003). For example, although the child initiates an action on a particular toy (e.g., hug a baby doll), the teacher may model ways to expand the child's repertoire (e.g., pretend to feed the doll, include the doll in a social routine such as a tea party). The new dimensions might then be incorporated into the child's spontaneous play activities. Importantly, Nicolopoulou, McDowell, and Brockmeyer (2006) argue, "although this is a structured and teacher-facilitated activity, it is simultaneously child-centered . . . the child is able to participate according to his or her own individual interests, pace, inclination and developmental rhythms" (p. 129).

Teachers play a unique role in guided play experiences. They can subtly intervene as play partners or curious onlookers, asking questions or making suggestions to help children when they have difficulty. As a result, both play and guided play can foster intrinsic motivation and learning in similar ways (e.g., Deci, 1992; Harter, 1992; Parker-Rees, 1997; Renninger, 1990; Schiefele, 1991). However, guided play may transform into adult-directed experiences when teachers or parents intervene too much. Shmukler (1981) found that when adults make suggestions and then let free play continue, children evidence their most creative play; however, when adults become too imposing, children stop playing altogether (see also Bonawitz et al., 2009; Dodd, Rogers, & Wilson, 2001). The success of guided play pedagogy hinges on several factors that include, among others, teachers' sensitivity to the line between child-centered learning activities and direct instruction. Teachers must continually evaluate and adapt their behaviors to foster learning yet not become overly intrusive (e.g., "hovering" over children's play activities, interjecting too much). It also includes teachers' acceptance of variability in children's answers (rather than demanding one correct response). Finally, there are individual differences and possibly socioeconomic status differences in the nature of and opportunities for free play and guided play that can influence when adult presence is more or less obtrusive (e.g., Dansky, 1980; Feitelson & Ross, 1973).

PLAYFUL LEARNING: PRESENTING THE EVIDENCE

According to the National Association for the Education of Young Children (NAEYC, 2006), "play provides a context for children to practice newly acquired skills and also to function at the edge of their developing capacities, to take on new social roles, attempt novel or challenging tasks, and solve complex problems that they would not (or could not) otherwise do" (p. 1). With a focus on children in pre-K to third grade, in the following sections we explore how different playful experiences promote learning in a host of areas including math/science, literacy, social understanding, and self-regulation. While many of these studies are correlational, there is also a growing literature that looks at playful learning in random assignment experiments (Bodrova & Leong, 2007; Lillard, 2005). The results from these studies are uniformly positive: Learning during free or guided play matches (or exceeds) that in direct instruction (Hirsh-Pasek et al., 2009) while also strengthening social well-being (Russ & Niec, 2011).

The Role of Play in Mathematics and Science

Research suggests that early mathematical thinking undergoes substantial development during the preschool and primary years (Clements & Sarama, 2007). Building blocks of mathematical knowledge emerge through self-directed, exploratory play activities and become further developed through playful learning (Ginsburg, 2006; Hirsh-Pasek et al., 2009).

Free Play. A landmark experiment conducted by Ginsburg, Pappas, and Seo (2001) examined the frequency of mathematic-related activities in 4- and 5-year-old children's free play (symbolic and object) in day care. Regardless of gender and ethnicity, over half of children's playtime was spent in some form of mathematics or science-related activity: 25% was spent examining patterns and shapes, 13% on magnitude comparisons, 12% on enumeration, 6% on dynamic change, 5% on spatial relations (e.g., height, width, location), and 2% on classifying objects. Sarama and Clements (2009) replicated these findings. Relatedly, in the domain of scientific reasoning, Schulz and Bonawitz (2007) found that children use play to disentangle ambiguities they find in the world and to test their incipient hypotheses about how things work (Bonawitz, Chang, Clark, & Lombrozo, 2008; Bonawitz, Fischer, & Schulz, 2008). When toddlers were given toys with ambiguous causal mechanisms, they engaged in exploratory play to determine how the toys worked (e.g., touching, moving levers on the object).

The frequency of math-related play has been linked to increases in mathematical knowledge and achievement (e.g., Ginsburg, Lee, & Boyd, 2008). Preschool children who participate in manipulative activities (e.g., block play, model building, carpentry) do better in spatial visualization, visual-motor coordination, and creative use of visual materials (e.g., Caldera et al., 1999; Hirsch, 1996). A longitudinal study by Wolfgang, Stannard, and Jones (2001) indicated that complexity of block play in preschool was significantly related to the number of math courses taken, number of honors courses taken, and mathematics grades achieved in junior and senior high school. Even when controlling for IQ and gender, the authors found that block play still accounted for significant portions of variability in math performance, suggesting that complex block play may be one mode in which children acquire rudimentary math knowledge.

Guided Play. Research also shows that the integration of math-related materials into children's early play environments promotes math relevant behaviors (e.g., Arnold, Fisher, Doctoroff, & Dobbs, 2002; Griffin & Case, 1996; Whyte & Bull, 2008). For example, Cook (2000) found that when preschoolers' pretend play was enriched by using artifacts emphasizing number symbols, children engaged in more talk and activity related to mathematical concepts. Similarly, Ness and Farenga (2007) found that children use spatial and geometric thinking when they are presented with shapes during spontaneous play activities. They explore geometric form through drawing, manipulation of blocks, and even by using language to explain their constructions. Ness and Farenga outline 13 space-geometry-architecture codes (e.g., symmetry, shapes, patterns, enumeration) to help teachers determine what types of problems children can perform during the given play activity. Fisher and colleagues also explored the impact of guided play and direct instruction on preschoolers' developing shape concepts (Fisher, 2010; Fisher, Ferrara, Hirsh-Pasek, Newcombe, & Golinkoff, 2010). Children were randomly assigned to a guided play, direct instruction, or control condition. In the guided play condition, they were encouraged to discover the "secret of the shapes." Experimenters facilitated children's discovery of shape properties by prompting exploration of the shapes and asking leading questions (e.g., "How many sides are there?"). Children were then asked to determine "real" triangles from nontypical triangles and nontriangles. In the direct instruction condition, the experimenter verbally described the "secret" (e.g., conceptual) shape properties and pointed out the properties while children watched. In the control condition, a story was read in place of the learning activity. Results from a shape-sorting task revealed that guided play and direct instruction—while equal in learning outcomes for simple, highly frequent shapes (e.g., circles)— were not equal for more complex shapes. Children in the guided play condition not only did better on hexagons and pentagons, but also remembered what they learned 2 weeks after the training (Fisher, 2010).

Taken together, research suggests that when children engage in free play and guided play activities, early mathematical and scientific concepts are strengthened and reinforced (see Baroody, Lai, & Mix, 2006; Seo & Ginsburg, 2004). Such knowledge becomes the foundation upon which more formal, higher order knowledge is built (e.g., a rudimentary concept of weight facilitates learning weight systems).

The Role of Play in Language and Literacy

Children naturally incorporate language into their play activities. In the toddler years they explore and practice components of the language system through private speech, word games, and complex language use in social play (e.g., Garvey, 1977; Hirsh-Pasek & Golinkoff, 1996, 2006; Roskos & Christie, 2001; Rowe, 1998; Zigler, Singer, & Bishop-Josef, 2004).

Free Play. The evidence suggests that free play activities relate to the development of language and literacy. Dramatic play, in particular, consists mostly of enacted narratives that naturally require instructional discourse between play partners (Nicolopoulou et al., 2006; Pellegrini & Galda, 1990). Specifically, children must convey their thoughts to their play partners, synthesize their individual thoughts into a shared play context, and integrate these components into a coherent story (e.g., Cloran, 2005). For example, a 4-year-old who wants to play "fairy princess" must communicate this idea to her partner, negotiate roles, and describe how props may be used for the setting (e.g., the swing set as castle; the flowers as her sparkling crown). Paramount in promoting early literacy, this decontextualized language emerges in pretend play, "where children must verbally move beyond the immediate conversational context to create and re-create events, analyze experiences, and share opinions and ideas" (Smith & Dickinson, 1994, p. 347). The narrative that children create in play builds a foundation for later literacy (e.g., Bruner, 1983; Dickinson, Cote, & Smith, 1993; Dickinson & Tabors, 2001; Pellegrini & Galda, 1990).

Several observational studies have focused on the roots of instructional discourse in symbolic play (Cloran, 2005; Lloyd & Goodwin, 1993; Tykkyläinen & Laakso, 2009). Sachs (1987) examined speech during a pretend play session among 46 same-sex dyads, ranging from 21–61 months of age, in a room containing doctor-theme toys as well as nondescript toys (e.g., fabric, hats, styrofoam, and dolls). Children engaged in a variety of communicative styles with one another, including directive statements (e.g., "Use this for a sling"), information requests (e.g., "Are you using that toy?" "Are you sick?"), and attentional requests (e.g., "Lookit").

Correlational research typically examines the relationship between the frequency of specific forms of literacy-related play activities and school readiness (Pellegrini & Galda, 1993; Pellegrini, Galda, Dresden, & Cox, 1991; Roskos & Christie, 2001). Bergen and Mauer (2000), for example, found that a higher rate of literacy-related play at age 4 (e.g., rhyming games and pretend reading to stuffed animals) predicted language and reading readiness in kindergarten. Kindergartners with increased rhyming and phonological awareness relative to their peers also had more diverse vocabularies, used more complex sentences, and were more likely to demonstrate their competencies in playful environments. Additionally, Dickinson and Moreton (1991) noted that the amount of time 3-year-olds spent talking with peers while pretending was positively associated with the size of their vocabularies 2 years later, after they had begun kindergarten.

Guided Play. Intervention studies also examine how embedding literacy materials within play settings increases the frequency of reading- and writing-related activities during free play (Christie & Enz, 1992; Christie & Roskos, 2006; Roskos & Christie, 2006; Saracho & Spodek, 2006). Neuman and Roskos (1992), for example, explored how the incorporation of literacy props (e.g., cookbooks in the designated "kitchen/house" space and business cards in the "office" corner) in 3- to 5-year-old children's free play environments increased literacy-related activities compared to a control group. At the intervention site, three theme-based play areas (kitchen, office, and library) were enriched with literacy objects. Children in the intervention group showed significantly higher rates of handling and reading of literacy materials as well as writing compared to those in the nonintervention school (e.g., touching materials, using materials during play activities, pretend writing). Other studies focused on how play activities influence emergent literacy skills, including storytelling, story acting, and journal writing (Nicolopoulou, 2005). Nicolopoulou, McDowell, and Brockmeyer (2006) reported that Head Start preschool children who engaged in storytelling and dramatization of their stories created longer, more complex storylines and more often used the third person in their narratives over time.

Pellegrini and Galda (1982) asked whether different types of play enhance story comprehension and recall in K–second grade children. Children were read a book and placed in one of three experimental conditions: (1) thematic-fantasy play, in which they acted out the story they had just heard, (2) discussion, in which they talked about the story; and (3) drawing, in which they drew pictures of the story. The three groups were then compared on their performance on both a story comprehension and a story recall task. Results indicated that children in the thematic-fantasy condition fared better on both tasks than children in the discussion and drawing conditions. Finally, experimental studies found thematic-fantasy play, compared to other less active play activities (e.g., puppet thematic play, coloring), promotes more complex narratives (Ilgaz & Aksu-Koç, 2005) and increased language recall (Marbach & Yawkey, 1980).

These findings lend credence to the belief that play and literacy development are inextricably intertwined. First, literacy activities increase when children's surrounding environment provides props or materials that naturally guide imaginative activities toward specific themes and learning outcomes (Christie & Roskos, 2006). Second, symbolic play and literacy appear to share similar mental processes (Nicolopoulou et al., 2006; Neuman & Roskos, 1992). Symbolic play, defined as make-believe play and storytelling, draw upon children's representational skills, in which "play . . . [is] story in action, just as storytelling is play put into narrative form" (Paley, 1990, p. 4). These studies thus provide an initial glimpse into how playful learning pedagogies can be integrated to support literacy as they were in Brookfield Elementary School described above.

The Role of Play in Social and Self-Regulatory Skills

Just as academic outcomes are critical for school readiness and success, so too are social skills, and here as well, play can enhance development. Through play, children re-create roles and situations that reflect their sociocultural world, where they learn how to subordinate desires to social rules, cooperate with others willingly, and engage in socially appropriate behavior (Berk, Mann, & Ogan, 2006; Hirsh-Pasek et al., 2009; Krafft & Berk, 1998; Saltz, Dixon, & Johnson, 1977; Vygotsky, 1978). Over time, these competencies are transferred to children's everyday behaviors, which foster a positive social environment that is conducive to learning and lifelong success (Brown, Donelan-McCall, & Dunn, 1996; Vygotsky, 1986).

Free Play. Theorists suggest that social play is a key factor in developing a sense of self-awareness and theory-of-mind (Ashiabi, 2007; Flavell, 1999; Lillard, 1993). *Theory-of-mind* refers to the developmental challenge of "seeing oneself and others in terms of mental states—the desires, emotions, beliefs, intentions, and other inner mental states that result in and are manifested in human action" (Wellman, Cross,

& Watson, 2001, p. 655). For example, in an innovative experiment, 14- and 18-month-old children watched as an adult savored broccoli and expressed disgust with cheese crackers, contrary to traditional children's tastes. In another condition, the adult matched the child's preference, delighting in the crackers but detesting the broccoli. When asked to give that same adult a snack, which food did the child select? When the adult shared the child's preferences, both the older and younger toddlers offered the crackers. When the adult initially preferred the broccoli, the 18-month-olds, but not the 14-month-olds, gave the vegetable to the adult (Repacholi & Gopnik, 1997).

Another developmental task is to recognize that one's beliefs may contradict reality, as captured through the classic false-belief task in which children watch as the following scene unfolds: After Maxi places his chocolate in the cupboard, his mother sneakily hides the chocolate in a drawer behind Maxi's back (e.g., Wimmer & Perner, 1983). In order to successfully report where Maxi will search for his chocolate, children must draw upon their theory-of-mind understanding and recognize that Maxi's beliefs will guide his actions, even if they conflict with reality. Through play activities (sociodramatic play, rule-based games, imaginative play), children become aware that they have desires and intentions that may not match those of others. For example, a child, unable to wait for his turn, grabs his playmate's truck and is greeted with a disgruntled tantrum. Startled, the boy forms a rudimentary notion that children have different goals and desires.

Pretend play is a conduit for theory-of-mind development in several distinct ways. First, discussing feelings and emotions during play activities with peers may prime children's perspective-taking ability, which, in turn, may promote positive peer relations (Brown et al., 1996; Hughes & Dunn, 1998). Second, talking about mental states (e.g., beliefs, desires, and so on) during pretend play may also advance children's theory-of-mind understanding (de Rosnay & Hughes, 2006).

Make-believe play also enhances effective emotion regulation. For example, high levels of sociodramatic play and conflict resolution themes in play narratives in preschool are positively related to children's effective emotional self-regulation (Fantuzzo, Sekino, & Cohen, 2004; Lemche et al., 2003; Smith, 2002). As early as 3 to 5 years of age, knowledge about emotions is related to friendly, considerate behavior, willingness to make amends after harming another, and constructive responses to disputes with age-mates (Brown & Dunn, 1996; Dunn, Brown, & Maguire, 1995; Garner & Estep, 2001).

An emerging literature indicates that play contributes vitally to children's self-regulation—advancing mastery over their own thinking, emotions, and behavior (see Berk et al., 2006). Vygotsky's (1978) view of make-believe play as a paramount early childhood context for the development of self-regulation served as the springboard for this line of research. In one study of 3- to 5-year-olds in two preschools, fantasy play emerged as the strongest correlate of children's use of private speech, including self-directed verbalizations aimed at both working out pretend characters' actions and guiding behavior during nonpretend tasks, such as solving puzzles (Krafft & Berk, 1998). Complex sociodramatic play in the block and housekeeping areas also positively predicted school-year gains in 3- and 4-year-olds' self-regulation during classroom cleanup periods (the extent to which they independently picked up materials)—a commonly used measure of socially responsible behavior (Elias & Berk, 2002). Measured as early as 3 to 5 years of age, other research shows that cognitive control predicts reading and math achievement from kindergarten through high school (Blair & Razza, 2007; Duncan et al., 2007; Gathercole, Tiffany, Briscoe, & Thorn, 2005).

Guided Play. What role do adults take in playful social learning? Ashiabi (2007) examined the role of teacher interaction in sociodramatic play and developing social skills. Findings suggest successful preschool practices for promoting social learning through play embrace a combination of free and guided play. Sociodramatic play in the classroom requires teacher observation, encouragement and support, and mediation of conflicts to guide these developing skills within a playful context. Others have found that a higher frequency of adult-initiated play activities with preschool children was associated with higher levels of prosocial behavior, lower levels of nonsocial behavior, and, among boys, greater peer acceptance in preschool (Ladd & Hart, 1992).

DIRECT COMPARISONS OF PEDAGOGICAL APPROACHES

There is a small but growing literature that compares guided play to more traditional learning environments like direct instruction. The results are compelling. One celebrated study compared the guided play approach used in the Montessori schools to a traditional inner-city school program in Milwaukee, Wisconsin (Lillard & Else-Quest, 2006). The results suggested that children in the Montessori school not only outperformed the others in reading and mathematics at age 5, but that these gains lasted in the primary school years at age 12. Testing the guided play program Tools of the Mind, Diamond et al. (2007) also report that inner-city children in the experimental condition with guided play had better executive function skills than those in matched randomly assigned classrooms using a direct instructional approach. These executive function capacities for attention and memory translated into better academic scores. Finally, the recent study by Fisher (2010) on early geometry offers a lab-based investigation of shape learning with 4- and 5-year-olds randomly assigned to free play, guided play, or direct instruction. Here the guided play condition afforded children advantages over the direct instruction condition.

Marcon (2002) also compared preschool models using guided play or direct instruction on a variety of academic, behavioral, and social measures. Children in sixth grade who had experienced child-initiated, guided play learning environments showed superior social behaviors, fewer conduct disorders, enhanced academic performance, and retention beyond children who had experienced didactic, direct instruction or mixed methods (didactic instruction and playful learning). Other researchers have documented similar gains in social and academic development of child-initiated learners over didactic learners (Burts, Hart, Charlesworth, & DeWolf, 1993; Lillard & Else-Quest, 2006).

Research on long-term social outcomes of playful learning comes from the now classic HighScope project (Schweinhart & Weikart, 1997; Schweinhart, Weikart, & Larner, 1986). By age 23, children who had attended play-based preschools were eight times less likely to need treatment for emotional disturbances and three times less likely to be arrested for committing a felony than those who went to preschools where direct instruction prevailed. To paraphrase Schweinhart, HighScope's director, direct instruction does not *cause* these problems. Rather, not giving children ample opportunity to develop socially is direct instruction's unintended side effect (Brown, 2009).

A TALE OF TWO SCHOOLS: THE REPRISE

Diane Ravitch, Assistant Secretary of Education under President George W. Bush, was among the architects of the 2001 No Child Left Behind Act, the U.S. government's legislated policy on education. In a surprising rebuttal of her former position, she published *The Death and Life of the Great American School System* (2010) in which she wrote, "As No Child Left Behind was implemented . . . it ignored such important subjects as history, civics, literature, science, the arts, and geography" (p. 16). The narrow focus on specific content, drilled during direct instruction, provides children only with passive input and cannot strengthen cognitive processes, such as the generation of ideas, flexibility, perspective taking, and language, that are reinforced during playful learning. Worse yet, this narrow focus does not even promote the learning of basic skills. As Ravitch argues, test scores have not measurably gone up since our reliance on direct instruction approaches.

Ravitch is not alone. In a recent cover story for *Newsweek* (July 10, 2010), Bronson and Merryman write about the Creativity Crisis, and authors/educators like Darling-Hammond (2010), Pink (2005), Gardner (2008), and Sternberg (2003) suggest that we need to focus as much on innovation and ingenuity as we do on basic skills. In the Google generation, facts can be easily assembled. Critical thinking and creative innovation have become the desired commodity.

It is in this light that we need to reassess schools like Brookfield and Winsor. In Winsor, the children will learn the facts—*just* the facts. Like the person who randomly buys products from the grocery store, the children in this classroom will have no recipes for putting together the information in new and useful ways. In stark contrast, when "flight" is learned within the context of a well-planned curriculum at Brookfield, the math lessons support the literacy instruction and the planes that fly around the school hallways are designed with explicit principles in mind. Playful learning and engagement contain just the ingredients that support this learning and make it flourish.

Many have written about the skill sets required for success in the 21st-century world, pinpointing creativity and critical thinking, among others. Culling from these sources (Cavanagh, Klein, Kay, & Meisinger, 2006; Edersheim, 2007; Galinsky, 2010; Gardner, 2008; Hirsh-Pasek et al., 2009; Sternberg, 2003), we have distilled a set of six skills that should be the core for a strong education. These "6 Cs" are collaboration, communication, content, critical thinking, creative innovation, and confidence.

Collaboration is critical today so that children can learn to work in teams to solve problems and in building communities of understanding. This social competence is the soup from which all else emerges (Tomasello, 2009) and is one that is nurtured through play. The second skill, *communication,* encompasses more than just form; it includes taking the listener's perspective— regardless of cultural differences— mastering rhetoric, writing, listening, and crafting an argument. To play efficiently, children must communicate effectively, using complex language to negotiate and to empathize (Kim & Kellogg, 2007; Pellegrini, 1983). A *content*-rich context for children's interactions with both peers and their environment stimulates another skill: *critical thinking.* When knowledge is abundant, we must selectively attend to and navigate through a sea of information. *Creative innovation* is the ability to link seemingly disparate facts, to envision the next YouTube, and to innovate for the problems of tomorrow. Finally, we need the *confidence* to test our new ideas and to take bold but calculated risks. Only by trying do we mix the creative with the possible. It is important to emphasize that although *content* is one of the core skills and is essential, it is not the only domain that educators must address in preparing children for success in school and in the workplace of tomorrow.

The 6 Cs allow us to imagine a school fashioned for our time rather than a school brought forth in the agricultural or industrial age. The 6 Cs allow us to imagine a school in which children work together and communicate about higher order goals that use content skills (geometry for plane design, stories about great pilots) rather than one that focuses on content as an end in itself. This school would look more like Brookfield than Winsor and would contain many opportunities for free play and playful learning. The children graduating from these schools are also more likely to do better in international tests that ask children to transfer what they learn to new instances and that examine higher level thinking. Creating such schools gives childhood back to children and can harness the power of play as we educate the next generation.

NOTE

This research was supported by Temple University's Center for Re-Imagining Children's Learning and Education that Hirsh-Pasek and Golinkoff codirect, by NICHD grant 5R01HD050199; NSF grant BCS-0642529; Spatial Intelligence Learning Center NSF grant SBE-0541957; and NIH grant 1RC1HD0634970-01.

REFERENCES

Arnold, D. H., Fisher, P. H., Doctoroff, G. L., & Dobbs, J. (2002). Accelerating math development in Head Start classrooms. *Journal of Educational Psychology, 92*, 762–770.

Ash, D., & Wells, G. (2006). Dialogic inquiry in classroom and museum: Action, tools, and talk. In Z. Bekerman, N. Burbules, & D. Silberman-Keller (Eds.), *Learning in places: The informal education reader* (pp. 35–54). New York: Peter Lang.

Ashiabi, G. S. (2007). Play in the preschool classroom: Its socioemotional significance and the teacher's role in play. *Early Childhood Education Journal, 35*, 199–207.

Baroody, A. J., & Dowker, A. (2003). *The development of arithmetic concepts and skills: Constructing adaptive expertise.* Mahwah, NJ: Erlbaum.

Baroody, A. J., Lai, M. L., & Mix, K. S. (2006). The development of young children's number and operation sense and its implications for early childhood education. In O. Saracho & B. Spodek (Eds.), *Handbook of research on the education of young children* (pp. 187–221). Mahwah, NJ: Erlbaum.

Bergen, D., & Mauer, D. (2000). Symbolic play, phonological awareness, and literacy skills at three age levels. In K. Roskos & J. Christie (Eds.), *Play and literacy in early childhood: Research from multiple perspectives* (pp. 45–62). Mahwah, NJ: Erlbaum.

Berger, K. (2008). *The developing person through childhood and adolescence* (8th ed.). New York: Worth.

Berk, L. E., Mann, T. D., & Ogan, A. T. (2006). Make-believe play: Wellspring for development of self-regulation. In D. Singer, R. M. Golinkoff, & K. Hirsh-Pasek (Eds.), *Play = learning: How play motivates and enhances children's cognitive and social-emotional growth* (pp. 74–100). New York: Oxford University Press.

Berk, L. E., & Winsler, A. (1995). *Scaffolding children's learning: Vygotsky and early childhood education*. Washington, DC: National Association for the Education of Young Children.

Blair, C. (2002). School readiness. *American Psychologist, 57,* 111–127.

Blair, C., & Razza, R. P. (2007). Relating effortful control, executive function, and false belief understanding to emerging math and literacy ability in kindergarten. *Child Development, 78,* 647–663.

Bodrova, E., & Leong, D. J. (2007) *Tools of the mind: The Vygotskian approach to early childhood education* (2nd ed.). Upper Saddle River, NJ: Prentice Hall.

Bogard, K., & Takanishi, R. (2005). PK–3: An aligned and coordinated approach to education for children 3 to 8 years old. *SRCD Social Policy Report, 19,* 415–429.

Bonawitz, E. B., Chang, I., Clark, C., & Lombrozo, T. (2008). Ockham's razor as inductive bias in preschoolers' causal explanations. *Proceedings of the 7th International Conference of Development and Learning*. Monterey, CA.

Bonawitz, E. B., Fischer, A., & Schulz, L. E. (2008). Training a Bayesian: Three-and-a-half-year-olds' reasoning about ambiguous evidence. *Proceedings of the 30th Annual Conference of the Cognitive Science Society*. Washington, DC.

Bonawitz, L., Shafto, P., Gweon, H., Chang, I., Katz, S., & Schulz, L. (2009). The double-edged sword of pedagogy: Modeling the effect of pedagogy on preschoolers' exploratory play. *Proceedings of the 31st Annual Conference of the Cognitive Science Society*. Amsterdam.

Bronson, P., & Merryman, A. (2010, July 10). The creativity crisis. *Newsweek.* Retrieved from http://www.newsweek.com/2010/07/10/the-creativity-crisis.html

Brown, E. (2009, November 21). The playtime's the thing. *The Washington Post*. Retrieved from http://www.washingtonpost.com/

Brown, J. R., Donelan-McCall, N., & Dunn, J. (1996). Why talk about mental states? The significance of children's conversations with friends, siblings, and mothers. *Child Development, 67,* 836–849.

Brown, J. R., & Dunn, J. (1996). Continuities in emotion understanding from 3 to 6 years. *Child Development, 67,* 789–802.

Bruer, J. (1999). *The myth of the first three years: A new understanding of early brain development and lifelong learning.* New York: Free Press.

Bruner, J. (1983). *Child's talk: Learning to use language.* New York: Norton.

Burdette, H. L., & Whitaker, R. C. (2005). Resurrecting free play in young children: Looking beyond fitness and fatness to attention, affiliation, and affect. *Archives of Pediatric Adolescent Medicine, 159,* 46–50.

Burts, D. C., Hart, C. H., Charlesworth, R., & DeWolf, M. (1993). Developmental appropriateness of kindergarten programs and academic outcomes in first grade. *Journal of Research in Childhood Education, 8,* 23–31.

Caldera, Y. M., McDonald Culp, A., O'Brien, M., Truglio, R. T., Alvarez, M., & Huston, A. C. (1999). Children's play preferences, construction play with blocks, and visual-spatial skills: Are they related? *International Journal of Behavioral Development, 23,* 855–872.

Callanan, M. A., & Braswell, G. (2006). Parent–child conversations about science and literacy: Links between formal and informal learning. In Z. Bekerman, N. Burbules, & D. Silberman-Keller (Eds.), *Learning in places: The informal education reader.* New York: Peter Lang.

Carlson, S. M. (2005). Developmentally sensitive measures of executive function in preschool children. *Developmental Neuropsychology, 28,* 595–616.

Cavanagh, R., Klein, D., Kay, K., & Meisinger, S. R. (2006). *Ready to work: Employers' perspectives on the basic knowledge and applied skills of new entrants to the 21st century U.S. workforce.* New York: The Conference Board, Corporate Voices, Partnership for 21st Century Skills, Society for Human Resource Management.

Chall, J. S., & Jacobs, V. A. (2003). Poor children's fourth grade slump. *American Educator, 27*(1). Retrieved from http://www.aft.org/newspubs/periodicals/ae/spring2003/hirschsbclassic.cfm

Christie, J., & Enz, B. (1992). The effects of literacy play interventions on preschoolers' play patterns and literacy development. *Early Education and Development, 3,* 205–220.

Christie, J., & Roskos, K. (2006). Standards, science, and the role of play in early literacy education. In D. Singer, R. Golinkoff, & K. Hirsh-Pasek (Eds.), *Play = learning: How play motivates and enhances children's cognitive and social-emotional growth* (pp. 57–73). New York: Oxford University Press.

Clements, D. H., & Sarama, J. (2007). Early childhood mathematics learning. In F. K. Lester (Ed.), *Second handbook of research on mathematics teaching and learning* (pp. 461–555). New York: Information Age.

Cloran, C. (2005). Contexts for learning. In F. Christie (Ed.), *Pedagogy and the shaping of consciousness: Linguistic and social processes* (pp. 31–65). London: Continuum.

Cook, D. (2000). Voice practice: Social and mathematical talk in imaginative play. *Early Child Development and Care, 162,* 51–63.

Copple, C., Sigel, I. E., & Saunders, R. (1979). *Educating the young thinker: Classroom strategies for cognitive growth.* New York: Van Nostrand.

Dansky, J. L. (1980). Cognitive consequences of sociodramatic play and exploration training for economically disadvantaged preschoolers. *Journal of Child Psychology and Psychiatry, 21,* 47–58.

Darling-Hammond, L. (2010). *The flat world and education: How America's commitment to equality will determine our future.* New York: Teachers College Press.

Deci, E. L. (1992). The relation of interest to the motivation of behavior: A self-determination theory perspective. In A. Renniner, S. Hidi, & A. Krapp (Eds.), *The role of interest in learning and development* (pp. 43–70). Hillsdale, NJ: Erlbaum.

De Rosnay, M., & Hughes, C. (2006). Conversation and theory-of-mind: Do children talk their way to socio-cognitive understanding? *British Journal of Developmental Psychology, 24,* 7–37.

Diamond, A., Barnett, W. S., Thomas, J., & Munro, S. (2007). Preschool program improves cognitive control. *Science, 318,* 1387–1388.

Dickinson, D. K., Cote, L., & Smith, M. W. (1993). Learning vocabulary in preschool: Social and discourse contexts affecting vocabulary growth. In C. Daiute (Ed.), *The development of literacy through social interaction* (pp. 67–78). San Francisco: Jossey-Bass.

Dickinson, D. K., & Freiberg, J. G. (2009, October 15). *Preschool language development and later academic success.* Paper presented at the Workshop on the Role of Language in School Learning: Implications for Closing the Achievement Gap, National Academies of Science, Menlo Park, CA.

Dickinson, D. K., & Moreton, J. (1991, April). *Predicting specific kindergarten literacy skills from three-year-olds' preschool experience.* Paper presented at the biennial meeting of the Society for Research in Child Development, Seattle, WA.

Dickinson, D. K., & Tabors, P. O. (Eds.). (2001). *Beginning literacy with language: Young children learning at home and school.* Baltimore: Brookes.

Dodd, A. T., Rogers, C. S., & Wilson, J. T. (2001). The effects of situational context on playful behaviors of young preschool children. In S. Reifel (Ed.), *Theory in context and out* (pp. 367–390). Play and culture studies, Vol. 3. Westport, CT: Ablex.

Duncan, G., Claessens, A., Huston, A., Pagani, L., Engel, M., Sexton, H., et al. (2007). School readiness and later achievement. *Developmental Psychology, 43,* 1428–1446.

Dunn, J., Brown, J. R., & Maguire, M. (1995). The development of children's moral sensibility: Individual differences and emotion understanding. *Developmental Psychology, 31,* 649–659.

Edersheim, E. H. (2007). *The definitive Drucker.* New York: McGraw-Hill.

Elias, C. L., & Berk, L. E. (2002). Self-regulation in young children: Is there a role for sociodramatic play? *Early Childhood Research Quarterly, 17,* 216–238.

Evans, G. W., & Rosenbaum, J. (2008). Self-regulation and the income-achievement gap. *Early Childhood Research Quarterly, 23,* 504–514.

Fantuzzo, J., Sekino, Y., & Cohen, H. L. (2004). An examination of the contributions of interactive peer play to salient classroom competencies for urban head start children. *Psychology in the Schools, 41,* 323–336.

Feitelson, D., & Ross, G. S. (1973). The neglected factor—play. *Human Development, 16,* 202–223.

Fisher, K. (2010). *Exploring the mechanisms of guided play in the development of children's geometric shape concepts* (Unpublished doctoral dissertation). Temple University, Philadelphia.

Fisher, K., Ferrara, K., Hirsh-Pasek, K., Newcombe, N., & Golinkoff, R. (2010, March). *Exploring the role of dialogic inquiry and exploration in guided play: An experimental study.* Paper presented at the biennial International Conference on Infant Studies, Baltimore.

Fisher, K., Hirsh-Pasek, K., Golinkoff, R. M., Singer, D., & Berk, L. E. (2010). Playing around in school: Implications for learning and educational policy. In A. Pellegrini (Ed.), *The Oxford handbook of play* (pp. 341–360). New York: Oxford University Press.

Flavell, J. H. (1999). Cognitive development: Children's knowledge about the mind. *Annual Review of Psychology, 50,* 21–45.

Galinsky, E. (2010). *Mind in the making: The seven essential life skills every child needs.* New York: HarperCollins.

Gardner, H. (2008). *Five minds for the future.* Boston: Harvard Business Press.

Garner, P. W., & Estep, K. M. (2001). Emotional competence, emotion socialization, and young children's peer-related social competence. *Early Education and Development, 12,* 29–48.

Garvey, C. (1977). *Play.* Cambridge, MA: Harvard University Press.

Gathercole, S., Tiffany, C., Briscoe, J., & Thorn, A. (2005). ALSPAC team: Developmental consequences of phonological loop deficits during early childhood: A longitudinal study. *Journal of Child Psychology and Psychiatry, 46,* 598–611.

Ginsburg, H. (2006). Mathematical play and playful mathematics: A guide for early education. In D. Singer, R. M. Golinkoff, & K. Hirsh-Pasek (Eds.), *Play = learning: How play motivates and enhances children's cognitive and social-emotional growth* (pp. 145–168). New York: Oxford University Press.

Ginsburg, H., Lee, J., & Boyd, J. (2008). Mathematics education for young children: What it is and how to promote it. *Social Policy Report, 22,* 1–23.

Ginsburg, H., Pappas, S., & Seo, K. (2001). Everyday mathematical knowledge: Asking young children what is developmentally appropriate. In S. L. Golbeck (Ed.), *Psychological perspectives on early childhood education: Reframing dilemmas in research and practice* (pp.181—219). Mahwah, NJ: Erlbaum.

Griffin, S., & Case, R. (1996). Evaluating the breadth and depth of training effects when central conceptual structures are taught. *Society for Research in Child Development Monographs, 59,* 90–113.

Harter, S. (1992). The relationship between perceived competence, affect, and motivational orientation within the classroom: Processes and patterns of change. In A. K. Boggiano & T. S. Pittman (Eds.), *Achievement and motivation: A social developmental perspective* (pp. 77–114). Cambridge, UK: Cambridge University Press.

Hirsch, E. (1996). *The block book.* Washington, DC: National Association for the Education of Young Child.

Hirsh-Pasek, K., & Bruer, J. (2007). The brain/education barrier. *Science, 317,* 1293.

Hirsh-Pasek, K., & Golinkoff, R. M. (1996). *The origins of grammar: Evidence from early language comprehension.* Cambridge, MA: MIT Press.

Hirsh-Pasek, K., & Golinkoff, R. M. (2003). *Einstein never used flashcards: How our children really learn—and why they need to play more and memorize less.* Emmaus, PA: Rodale.

Hirsh-Pasek, K., & Golinkoff, R. M. (2006). *Action meets word: How children learn verbs.* New York: Oxford University Press.

Hirsh-Pasek, K., Golinkoff, R. M., Berk, L. E., & Singer, D. G. (2009). *A mandate for playful learning: Presenting the evidence.* New York: Oxford University Press.

Hughes, C., & Dunn, J. (1998). Understanding mind and emotion: Longitudinal associations with mental-state talk between young friends. *Developmental Psychology, 34,* 1026–1037.

Ilgaz, H., & Aksu-Koç, A. (2005). Episodic development in preschool children's play-prompted and direct-elicited narratives. *Cognitive Development, 20,* 526–544.

Johnson, J. E., Christie, J. F., & Yawkey, T. D. (1999). *Play and early childhood development.* New York: Addison Wesley Longman.

Kim, Y., & Kellogg, D. (2007). Rules out of roles: Differences in play language and their developmental significance. *Applied Linguistics, 28,* 25–45.

Krafft, K. C., & Berk, L. E. (1998). Private speech in two preschools: Significance of open-ended activities and make-believe play for verbal self-regulation. *Early Childhood Research Quarterly, 13,* 637–658.

Ladd, G. W., & Hart, C. H. (1992). Creating informal play opportunities: Are parents' and preschoolers' initiations related to children's competence with peers? *Developmental Psychology, 28,* 1179–1187.

Lemche, E., Lennertz, I., Orthmann, C., Ari, A., Grote, K., Häfker, J., et al. (2003). Emotion regulatory processes in evoked play narratives. *Prax Kinderpsychol Kinderpsychiatr, 52,* 156.

Lillard, A. (1993). Pretend play skills and the child's theory of mind. *Child Development, 64,* 348–371.

Lillard, A. (2005) *Montessori: The science behind the genius.* New York: Oxford University Press.

Lillard, A., & Else-Quest, N. (2006). Evaluating Montessori education. *Science, 313,* 1893–1894.

Lloyd, B., & Goodwin, R. (1993). Girls' and boys' use of directives in pretend play. *Social Development, 2,* 122–130.

Marbach, E. S., & Yawkey, T. D. (1980). The effect of imaginative play actions on language development in five-year-old children. *Psychology in the Schools, 17,* 257–263.

Marcon, R. (2002). Moving up the grades: relationship between pre-school model and later school success. *Early Childhood Research and Practice, 4*(1).

Miller, E., & Almon, J. (2009). *Crisis in the kindergarten: Why children need to play in school.* College Park, MD: Alliance for Childhood.

National Association for the Education of Young Children (NAEYC). (2006). Developmentally appropriate practice in early childhood programs serving children from birth through age 8. Retrieved from http://www.naeyc.org/about/positions/dap3.asp

National Institute of Child Health and Development (NICHD) Early Child Care Research Network. (2005). Pathways to reading: The role of oral language in the transition to reading. *Developmental Psychology, 41,* 428–442.

Ness, D., & Farenga, S. J. (2007). *Knowledge under construction: The importance of play in developing children's spatial and geometric thinking.* Lanham, MD: Rowman & Littlefield.

Neuman, S. B., & Roskos, K. (1992). Literacy objects as cultural tools: Effects on children's literacy behaviors in play. *Reading Research Quarterly, 27,* 202–225.

Nicolopoulou, A. (2005). Play and narrative in the process of development: Commonalities, differences, and interrelations. *Cognitive Development, 20,* 495–502.

Nicolopoulou, A. (2010). The alarming disappearance of play from early childhood education. *Human Development, 53,* 1–4.

Nicolopoulou, A., McDowell, J., & Brockmeyer, C. (2006). Narrative play and emergent literacy: Storytelling and story-acting meet journal writing. In D. G. Singer, R. M. Golinkoff, & K. Hirsh-Pasek (Eds.), *Play = learning: How play motivates and enhances children's cognitive and social-emotional growth* (pp 124–144). New York: Oxford University Press.

Ogan, A., & Berk, L. E. (2009, April). *Effects of two approaches to make-believe play training on development of self-regulation in Head Start children.* Paper presented as part of the symposium, A Mandate for Playful Learning in Preschool: Presenting the Evidence, R. M. Golinkoff & K. A. Hirsh-Pasek (Chairs), At the biennial meeting of the Society for Research in Child Development, Denver, CO.

Paley, V. G. (1990). *The boy who would be a helicopter: The uses of storytelling in the classroom.* Cambridge, MA: Harvard University Press.

Parker-Rees, R. (1997). Learning from play: Design, technology, imagination, and playful thinking. *Proceedings of the International Conference on Design and Technology Education Research.* Retrieved from http://hdl.handle.net/2134/1458.

Pellegrini, A. D. (1983). Sociolinguistic contexts of the preschool. *Journal of Applied Developmental Psychology, 4,* 389–397.

Pellegrini, A. D. (2009). Research and policy on children's play. *Child Development Perspectives, 3,* 131–136.

Pellegrini, A. D., & Galda, L. (1982). The effects of thematic-fantasy play training on the development of children's story comprehension. *American Educational Research Journal, 19,* 443–452.

Pellegrini, A. D., & Galda, L. (1990). Children's play, language, and early literacy. *Topics in Language Disorders, 10,* 76–88.

Pellegrini, A. D., & Galda, L. (1993). Ten years after: A reexamination of symbolic play and literacy research. *Reading Research Quarterly, 28,* 163–175.

Pellegrini, A. D., Galda, L., Dresden, J., & Cox, S. (1991). A longitudinal study of the predictive relations among symbolic play, linguistic verbs, and early literacy. *Research in the Teaching of English, 25,* 219–235.

Pink, D. H. (2005). *A whole new mind.* New York: Riverhead Books.

Ponitz, C. C., McClelland, M. M., Matthews, J. S., & Morrison, F. J. (2009). A structured observation of behavioral self-regulation and its contributions to kindergarten outcomes. *Developmental Psychology, 45,* 605–619.

Ramey, S. L., & Ramey, C. T. (1999). Early experience and early intervention for children "at risk" for developmental delay and mental retardation. *Mental Retardation and Developmental Disabilities, 5,* 1–10.

Raver, C. C. (2002). Emotions matter: Making the case for the role of young children's emotional development for early school readiness. *Social Policy Report, 16*(3), 3–18.

Ravitch, D. (2010). *The death and life of the great American school system: How testing and choice are undermining education.* New York: Basic Books.

Renninger, K. A. (1990). Children's play interests, representation, and activity. In R. Fivush & J. Hudson (Eds.), *Knowing and remembering in young children* (pp. 127–165). New York: Cambridge University Press.

Repacholi, B. M., & Gopnik, A. (1997). Early reasoning about desires: Evidence from 14- and 18-month-olds. *Developmental Psychology, 33,* 12–21.

Resnick, M. (2003). Playful learning and creative societies. *Education Update, 8*(6).

Rimm-Kaufman, S. E., Curby, T. W., Grimm, K. J., Nathanson, L., & Brock, L. L. (2009). The contribution of children's self-regulation and classroom quality to children's adaptive behaviors in the kindergarten classroom. *Developmental Psychology, 45,* 958–972.

Rogoff, B. (2003). *The cultural nature of human development.* New York: Oxford University Press.

Roskos, K., & Christie, J. (2001). Examining the play-literacy interface: A critical review and future directions. *Journal of Early Childhood Literacy, 1,* 59–89.

Rowe, D. W. (1998). The literate potentials of book-related dramatic play. *Reading Research Quarterly, 33,* 10–35.

Russ, S. W., & Niec, L. N. (Eds.). (2011). *Play in clinical practice: Evidence-based approaches.* New York: Guilford Press.

Sachs, J. (1987). Preschool boys' and girls' language use in pretend play. In S. U. Philips, S. Steele, & C. Tanz (Eds.), *Language, gender, and sex in comparative perspective.* Cambridge, UK: Cambridge University Press.

Saltz, E., Dixon, D., & Johnson, J. (1977). Training disadvantaged preschoolers on various fantasy activities: Effects on cognitive functioning and impulse control. *Child Development, 48,* 367–380.

Saracho, O. N., & Spodek, B. (2006). Young children's literacy-related play. *Early Child Development & Care, 176,* 707–721.

Sarama, J., & Clements, D. H. (2009). *Early childhood mathematics education research: Learning trajectories for young children.* New York: Routledge.

Scarborough, H. S. (2001). Connecting early language and literacy to later reading (dis)abilities: Evidence, theory, and practice. In S. B. Neuman & D. K. Dickinson (Eds.), *Handbook of early literacy research* (pp. 97–110). New York: Guilford Press.

Schiefele, U. (1991). Interest, learning, and motivation. *Educational Psychologist, 26*, 299–323.

Schultz, L., & Bonawitz, E. B. (2007). Serious fun: Preschoolers engage in more exploratory play when evidence in confounded. *Developmental Psychology, 43*, 1045–1050.

Schweinhart, L. J. (2004). *The HighScope Perry Preschool Study through age 40: Summary, conclusions, and frequently asked questions.* Ypsilanti, MI: HighScope Educational Research Foundation.

Schweinhart, L. J., & Weikart, D. P. (1997). The HighScope preschool curriculum comparison study through age 23. *Early Childhood Research Quarterly, 12*, 117–143.

Schweinhart, L. J., Weikart, D. P., & Larner, M. B. (1986). Consequences of three preschool curriculum models through age fifteen. *Early Childhood Research Quarterly, 1*, 15–46.

Seo, K.-H., & Ginsburg, H. P. (2004). What is developmentally appropriate in early childhood mathematics education? Lessons from new research. In D. H. Clements, J. Sarama, & A. M. DiBiase (Eds.), *Engaging young children in mathematics: Standards for early childhood mathematics education* (pp. 91–104). Hillsdale, NJ: Erlbaum.

Shmukler, D. (1981). Mother-child interaction and its relationship to the predisposition of imaginative play. *Genetic Psychology Monographs, 104*, 215–235.

Silberg, J. (2000). *125 brain games for toddlers and twos: Simple games to promote early brain development.* Beltsville, MD: Gryphon House.

Singer, D. G., Golinkoff, R. M., & Hirsh-Pasek, K. (Eds.). (2006). *Play = Learning: How play motivates and enhances children's cognitive and social-emotional growth.* New York: Oxford University Press.

Smith, M. W., & Dickinson, D. K. (1994). Describing oral language opportunities and environments in Head Start and other preschool classrooms. *Early Childhood Research Quarterly, 9*, 345–366.

Smith, P. K. (2002). Pretend play, metarepresentation and theory of mind. In R. W. Mitchell (Ed.), *Pretending and imagination in animals and children* (pp. 129–141). Cambridge, UK: Cambridge University Press.

Stern, E. (2005). Pedagogy meets neuroscience. *Science, 310*, 745.

Sternberg, R. J. (2003). *Wisdom, intelligence, and creativity synthesized.* New York: Cambridge University Press.

Storch, S. A., & Whitehurst, G. J. (2001). The role of family and home in the literacy development of children from low-income backgrounds. In P. R. Britto & J. Brooks-Gunn (Eds.), *The role of family literacy environments in promoting young children's emerging literacy skills* (pp. 53–71). San Francisco: Jossey-Bass.

Sutton-Smith, B. (2001). *The ambiguity of play.* Cambridge, MA: Harvard University Press.

Tomasello, M. (2009). *Why we cooperate.* Cambridge, MA: MIT Press.

Tykkyläinen, T., & Laakso, M. (2009). Five-year-old girls negotiating pretend play: Proposals with the Finnish particle jooko. *Journal of Pragmatics, 42*, 242–256.

Vygotsky, L. S. (1978). *Mind in society: The development of higher mental processes* (M. Cole, V. John-Steiner, S. Scribner, & E. Souberman, Eds. and Trans.). Cambridge, MA: Harvard University Press. (Original work published 1930–1935)

Vygotsky, L. S. (1986). *Thought and language.* (A. Kozulin, Trans.). Cambridge, MA: MIT Press. (Original work published 1930, 1933, and 1935)

Wellman, H. M., Cross, D., & Watson, J. (2001). Meta-analysis of theory-of-mind development: The truth about false belief. *Child Development, 72,* 655–684.

Whyte, J. C., & Bull, R. (2008). Number games, magnitude representation, and basic number skills in preschoolers. *Developmental Psychology, 44,* 588–596.

Wimmer, H., & Perner, J. (1983). Beliefs about beliefs: Representation and constraining function of wrong beliefs in young children's understanding of deception. *Cognition, 13,* 103–128.

Wolfgang, C., Stannard, L., & Jones, I. (2001). Block play performance among preschoolers as a predictor of later school achievement in mathematics. *Journal of Research in Childhood Education, 15,* 173–181.

Zigler, E., Singer, D. G., & Bishop-Josef, S. J. (2004). *Children's play: The roots of reading.* Washington, DC: Zero to Three.

CHAPTER 3

Honoring the Lives of All Children

Identity, Culture, and Language

Sonia Nieto

Childhood has never been an easy time for some children, but it is becoming especially challenging in our current sociopolitical reality for particular segments of our population. Especially vulnerable are children who live in poverty and those whose race, culture, immigrant status, social class, and native language, among other differences, separate them from the so-called mainstream. These differences matter in how and to what extent children learn, not necessarily because they place students, to use the phrase in vogue, "at risk," but rather because how teachers, schools, and our society in general view such differences may jeopardize children even more. These children are my main concern in this chapter. Specifically, it is my intention to describe environments that might support rather than harm young children who exist on the margins of society with few resources and even less support from the institutions that should be concerned about them.

I begin with a demographic portrait of our society and especially of our most vulnerable children, a portrait that sets in bold relief the tremendous changes that have taken place in our society over the past several decades. I then describe some of the dangers—cultural and emotional, as well as others related to learning—that these children face, particularly in schools. Based on my research of many years with teachers and in schools, I then describe some of the strategies and approaches that have been most successful in honoring children's cultures, experiences, and identities. To demonstrate these, I use the words of teachers who are advocates for children and activists for social justice. I believe there are lessons to learn from teachers who have grappled with these matters, lessons that might lead to a less damaged and more joyful childhood for many children.

WHO ARE THE CHILDREN?

It is no surprise to anyone who has stepped inside an urban classroom in the past several decades that our public schools are now more racially, culturally, and linguistically diverse than ever before. Latinos and African Americans make up the largest segment of the non-White population in the nation. Of about 310,000,000 people living in the United States, over 48,000,000, the largest so-called minority group, are Hispanic (please note that the terms *Hispanic* and *Latino* will be used interchangeably in this chapter, depending on the reference cited), and nearly 38,000,000 are African American (U.S. Census Bureau, 2010). In addition, some segments of the population have grown much more rapidly than others. According to the Census Bureau, from 2000 to 2008, the number of Whites increased by only 6.4%, and African Americans, by 9.4%. At the same time, the largest increases by far were among Latinos, whose population grew by 33%, and Asians, by 28% (U.S. Census Bureau, 2008).

Currently, the number of foreign-born or first-generation U.S. residents has reached its highest level in U.S. history—56 million, or triple the number in 1970. The vast majority of immigrants before 1969 were from Europe, but that has changed a great deal: At present, more than half of all new immigrants are from Latin America, and 25% are from Asia. In 2009, just five countries accounted for 35% of all new legal residents to the United States: Mexico, China, the Philippines, India, and the Dominican Republic (Monger, 2010).

The increasing diversity in the nation is visible especially in urban areas. Some people, however, may be surprised to learn that our nation's suburban and rural areas, and consequently the schools in those areas, are also increasingly diverse. Although it is true that White students continue to outnumber students of color and English language learners in rural areas, the margin is getting smaller. As of 2007 the percentage of students of color (i.e., Hispanic, African American, Asian and Pacific Islander, Alaska Native, and American Indian) in rural schools was over 22%. And while English language learners (ELLs) continue to be more prevalent in urban areas (13.9%), the percentage of ELLs in rural areas has climbed to 2.4% (Provasnik et al., 2007). Moreover, there are some regions of the country where the cultural and ethnic diversity was traditionally either quite small or limited to particular groups, but that is no longer the case. For example, the southeastern United States, where the White and African American communities made up the great majority of residents, is now experiencing a tremendous increase in the Latino population, and in some areas, in the Asian and Pacific Islander population as well. For example, from 2000 to 2006, Arkansas saw a 69.3% increase in Hispanics, while the increases in Georgia (60%), North and South Carolina (about 58% each) and Virginia (40%) were also dramatic. In addition to the Southeast, tremendous increases in the Latino population are evident in the Northwest and Midwest (Pew Hispanic Center, 2006).

Language diversity has also increased enormously over the past several decades. The number and variety of languages spoken in the nation is over 380—from Arabic to Urdu and Punjabi to Yup'ik—although by far the largest percentage of people who speak languages other than English (over half) speak Spanish. In 2010 the U.S. Census Bureau reported that the number of people age 5 and older who spoke a language other than English at home had increased by 140% in the previous 30 years, currently reaching 20% of the entire population, while the nation's overall population grew by only 34% (Shin & Kominski, 2010). Naturally, this language diversity is also reflected in public school enrollments. There are over 5 million English language learners enrolled in grades pre-K through 12, about 10% of total public school student enrollment, and nearly 80% are Spanish-speaking (Jost, 2010).

The population of children of immigrant families is growing more rapidly than any other segment of the population, but nearly 80% of language-minority students were born in the United States (Hernandez, Denton, & Macartney, 2008). Needless to say, not all children of immigrant families are English language learners; many were fluent in English in their home countries, like Jamaica, and others learned English here. Likewise, not all English language learners are immigrants; some families have been here for a generation or more but continue to speak their native language at home.

In addition to issues of race, ethnicity, language, and immigrant status, social class is also a significant determinant of students' learning. More children than ever live in poverty, and this too has an impact on how students learn, and on how we protect, or do not protect, them. According to the National Center for Children in Poverty (Wight, Thampi, & Briggs, 2010), while 14,000,000 children live in poor families (that is, in families that live below the poverty line of $22,050 for a family of four), families living on double that amount also suffer the effects of poverty. Poverty affects families of different demographic groups differently. For example, while 26% of White children and 30% of Asian children live in poverty, the rates for African American and Latino children are much higher, 60 and 57% respectively. Also, 57% of children of immigrants live in poverty (National Center for Children in Poverty, 2010). In a comprehensively researched article on the effects of poverty on learning and achievement, David Berliner (2009) makes the argument that Out-of-School Factors (OSFs) caused by poverty place severe limits on what can be accomplished through educational reform efforts. These include scarce health care, low birth weight, lack of preschool education, inadequate housing, low level of parental education, high unemployment, drug and alcohol abuse, pollutants and toxic sites in poor communities, and many other factors. He points out that many OSFs are strongly correlated with class, race, and ethnicity. In addition, many children are segregated in schools by those very same characteristics. His conclusion is that to improve our nation's school achievement, a reduction in family and youth poverty is essential.

These, then, are the most vulnerable children in our society. How teachers and schools respond to them often determines whether they will succeed, both in school and in life.

FROM DEFICIT TO ASSET

Teachers and schools, even the most well-meaning among them, may place young children in jeopardy when they do not acknowledge children's backgrounds and realities. Given the immense variety of cultures, languages, and experiences with which young people arrive at school, educators need to understand how they experience school and how their backgrounds might affect their learning.

Although conventional wisdom used to be that cultural and language differences, referred to disparagingly as "cultural baggage," should be left outside the classroom door, more recently such thinking has been challenged. Children, especially young children, cannot be expected to do what even many adults cannot do, that is, to adapt instantly and effortlessly to a new cultural milieu. Children's family traditions, their cultural values, and their home languages are as much a part of them as are their names. That being the case, the most harmful thing a school can do is to ignore those cultural and linguistic experiences, or behave as if they did not exist. Children are, in effect, placed in danger when their identities are overlooked or when they are invisible in the classroom setting.

In too many cases children's very identities are defined as deficiencies. Even the term "children at risk" may classify children's race, ethnicity, or native language as risk factors rather than viewing them as assets that can be used in the service of their education. And while it is true that poverty does indeed place children at risk because it means they do not have access to the kinds of health care, housing, and other essential resources that more privileged children can take for granted, even in the poorest families there are strengths and talents, or "funds of knowledge," to use the term popularized by Norma Gonzalez and her colleagues (2005), that are often overlooked by teachers and schools.

Rather than viewing students' identities as deficits, it is far more productive to consider them as assets. That is, instead of defining students who speak a native language other than English as non-English speakers, why not think of them as "speakers of another language" or as "becoming bilingual"? Instead of thinking of immigrant children as foreign and somehow un-American, why not think of them as having cultural knowledge and experiences that can enrich U.S. classrooms and culture? Developing this mind-set requires a fundamental change in how we define culture and difference, but it is essential if we are to honor all children. This is an especially important shift for teachers, administrators, and teacher educators.

That children's language and culture matter in teaching and learning has been documented repeatedly and consistently. For example, a recent metareview of the benefits of bilingualism concluded that bilingualism is reliably associated with increased attentional control, working memory, metalinguistic awareness, and abstract reasoning, all of which, naturally, can contribute positively to academic success (Adesope, Lavin, Thompson, & Ungerleider, 2010). In terms of the benefits of affirming both language and culture, researchers Alejandro Portes and Ruben Rumbaut (2006) have found that immigrant youths who maintain ethnic ties have fewer problems of adjustment, including fewer mental health problems. In addition, their research discovered that students with limited bilingualism are far more likely to leave school than those who are fluent in both languages. My own research with young people (Nieto, 1994; Nieto & Bode, 2012) confirms the power of affirming students' language and culture. The conclusion is clear: Rather than an impediment to academic achievement, bilingualism and biculturalism can actually promote learning.

WHAT CAN TEACHERS AND SCHOOLS DO?

What follows are some strategies and ideas that teachers and schools can use to honor the cultures and identities of all children. But first a caveat: I want to make it clear that teachers and schools cannot by themselves change the situation for our most vulnerable children. For lasting and comprehensive change to happen, massive changes in institutional policies and practices not only in education but also in health care, housing, employment, and other areas need to take place. That will take a concerted effort on the part of policy makers and local, state, and federal government bodies. Teachers and other educators, in fact, many times work in climates that are hostile to vulnerable children: These climates include rigid so-called ability tracking that condemn students to uninspiring pedagogy and, in the future, to dead-end jobs; high-stakes tests that force teachers to "teach to the test" and strip them of their autonomy and creativity; and prescribed, monocultural, and insipid curricula that do little to excite students or teachers. If this is the case, it is unrealistic to expect teachers, administrators, or teacher educators alone to reverse the situation.

That being said, we cannot sit around and wait for policy makers and governments to catch up. In the meantime, teachers, schools, and teacher educators can do a great deal to honor all children and their families. The strategies and ideas that follow are not meant as recipes, but rather as recommendations that can be adjusted to fit particular contexts. They range from simple gestures to major projects, from individual classroom activities to collaborative endeavors, and from changes in personal values and commitments to institutional transformations that affect entire organizations.

Some of the strategies and ideas below can be implemented at several levels, although for purposes of simplicity, I have separated them according to the roles of teachers, administrators, and teacher educators.

Teachers

As the individuals who are most consistently and directly in contact with students, teachers have an immensely significant role. Whether teachers realize it or not, what they say and do carries a great deal of weight with their students, even the most seemingly uninterested among them.

Learn to Pronounce Students' Real Names. This is such a small thing but it can have a huge impact. In too many cases, teachers change children's names, often in an effort to make things easier for themselves and other students in the class. But a person's name is more than an assembly of letters; it says who one is and where one comes from. When a teacher changes Marisol to Marcy, or Tamami to Tammy, she is also sending a clear message about which identities matter and which do not. Certainly, learning to say the names of all students correctly—especially in middle and high school where teachers frequently see more than 100 students a day—takes some work, but the effort pays off in the long run. I should also mention that some immigrant families have already changed their children's names by the time they get to school, usually to make things easier for teachers. Even in those cases, I'd suggest speaking with parents and making it clear that you would like to learn the child's given name and would be happy to use it in the classroom. This open and respectful approach often leads to families changing their minds about having their child's real name used in the classroom.

Confront Your Own Biases and Preconceptions. We all have them. Biases are sometimes based on ignorance, other times on ingrained stereotypes, and still others on a lack of experience with diversity. Yet because we are reluctant to face them, educators sometimes continue to harbor preconceived notions about their students, their students' families, and their students' cultures. It takes a great deal of reflection and humility to come to terms with these things. A good example comes from Mary Ginley, a gifted teacher who has been in the classroom for 42 years. She was, in fact, the Massachusetts Teacher of the Year in 1999, a well-deserved honor. In spite of her excellence as a teacher—or perhaps because of it—Mary is a perfectionist and demands a great deal of herself. This was most evident in a journal she kept for a class she took with me about 15 years ago. At the time, she was working in an impoverished city in the Northeast, and the majority of her students were Puerto Rican and second- or third-generation immigrants from Ireland and other European countries. After an activity in class, she reflected in her journal,

> It's amazing how middle-class and narrow I can be—even when I'm trying to be sensitive to the needs of others. I suppose I'm one of those well-meaning teachers who devalues children without even realizing it. I have a lot to learn. (Ginley, 2010a, p. 104)

Later that same semester, at the end of her journal, she wrote about why she had returned to school. One reason was for the intellectual stimulation, and the other was because she wanted "to do it right." She asked:

> Why did the kids who failed to learn to read in my class, year after year, have last names like Vega, Lopez, and Rivera, while the kids who sailed

along were named Moriarty, Cavanaugh, and Schwartz? . . . The other reason I wanted to go back to school is to try to discover how to make school
successful for all kids—not just the Moriartys, Cavanaughs, Schwartzes,
and Ginleys—because so far, I haven't done it right. This course is helping; others will too. I know they will. (Ginley, 2010b, p. 183)

Learn Another Language. This is, of course, a major commitment
but, again, one that can have long-term benefits. When teachers make
a decision to learn a second language—usually the language spoken
by the majority of English language learners in their classroom—they
are also making a commitment to connect more deeply with students' culture. Alicia Montejo, a young woman who was interviewed
by teacher Stephanie Schmidt for *Affirming Diversity* (Nieto & Bode,
2012), mentioned a particular teacher, Mr. Thomas, who had learned
Spanish because he was married to a Dominican woman. She commented, "He talks to everybody in Spanish!" noting how much she
appreciated this. When asked what she would suggest to teachers, she
very quickly said, "To get to know my culture, I would tell teachers to
understand my language. Take a course or something; take courses"
(p. 250).

Language and culture are inextricably linked, as is clear in the
words of Bill Dunn, a teacher who decided to "come out of the closet"
as a Spanish speaker when he realized that, after 20 years in a school
with a growing number of Latino students, he was able to understand
almost everything they were saying in Spanish. In the journal that he
kept that semester, he explained:

> Like the risks involved in revealing a homosexual orientation, there are
> risks involved in acquiring a second language as well. Americans are partic-
> ularly poor at second-language acquisition; the dominant culture demands
> "English only." When you acquire a second language, you put yourself at
> odds with the dominant culture, and any time you go against the flow you
> have to be willing to take some heat for it. (Dunn, 2010, p. 170)

Learn as Much as You Can About Your Students. Really learning
about one's students means going out of the way to find out who they
are. Alicia López, a middle school Spanish teacher I interviewed for
a book on thriving teachers (who also happens to be my daughter),
spoke about how she writes a letter to her students at the beginning
of every year as a way to connect with them. She tells them about her
cultural background, where she grew up, about her family, about the
foods she likes to eat, and so on. Then she asks them, for their first
homework assignment, to write a letter to her, and she says, "I find
right away, that opens up how the students respond to me. I love get-

ting those letters and I can't wait to get home and read them. Then I keep them all year and I read them throughout the year." Alicia says that through the students' letters, she finds out where they live, what they like to do, how they identify, and much more. She keeps these things in mind so that, for example, when she does a unit on housing, she remembers to teach the word for *apartment*, rather than just assume that everyone lives in a house. She also makes sure to ask them if they speak any other languages because,

> I think it's important for other students to realize that this person is going to be learning her third language or her fourth language. It's also good for me to know. I can use that later on, to ask them, "So, how do you say apple in Swahili?" and I can bring those little pieces into class once in awhile. (Nieto, in press)

Get to Know the Families of Students. Most teacher preparation programs do little to teach prospective teachers how to work productively and respectfully with families, so this is a skill that most teachers need to learn on the job. Yet there is often an unspoken adversarial relationship between teachers and families, as if they had competing goals. Nothing could be further from the truth, but moving from discomfort to trust is not always easy. One way to begin bridging the gap between teachers and families is to make family visits in the context where families feel most comfortable, their homes. This is what Mary Cowhey, a teacher with whom I've collaborated for many years, does every year before the start of school. In a book of letters to Paulo Freire from a variety of teachers and others, she responded to his suggestion that teachers learn to "read" their students like a text. She wrote,

> I can't wait for the first day of school, and so I go out and read the students in their neighborhoods, their homes, with their families. That way I know where my students are coming from, literally. I know who their people are. I know the names their families call them. I know what they are proud of and what worries them. I begin to trust these families. My students and their families begin to trust me. (Cowhey, 2008, p. 13)

Family visits are easiest for teachers of young children, but for those who teach middle and high school students, it is difficult if not impossible because of the great number of students they teach. Fortunately, there are many other ways to connect with families, including writing a weekly newsletter, having a "coffee with Ms./Mr. ___," on a regular basis, or keeping in touch via phone or e-mail, especially to share class happenings and good news. Otherwise, families always expect to hear the worst when a teacher calls.

Learn About and Become Involved in the Community. Jason Irizarry (2009), in a study of teachers who were especially effective with urban students, found that those who lived in the community where they taught were more likely than others to develop close and meaningful relationships with their students, regardless of their own identities. In his study the students were overwhelmingly African American and Latino, while the teachers were White, African American, and Latino. Regardless of their backgrounds, all were what Irizarry called "culturally connected" because of their concerted efforts to become immersed in the life of the community.

Even if teachers do not live in the neighborhood or town where they teach, they can learn about, and take part in, community activities, particularly those that involve their students. This may mean going to the school's athletic events, accepting invitations to children's birthday parties and other family gatherings, going to community festivals and fairs, and attending religious services, among others. These are genuine ways in which to learn about a community, about its values and traditions, and by extension about the families of the students in the school. In addition, doing these things is a natural way to develop strong relationships not only with the students, but also with their families and other community members.

Administrators

The role of administrators—principals, assistant principals, curriculum directors, department heads, and others—is especially important in creating a climate of acceptance and respect in a school. For instance, in Mary Cowhey's school in Northampton, Massachusetts, all families are photographed at the beginning of the year and their photos are displayed in the school's hall entrance. There, one sees families of all sizes, colors, genders, and configurations. What more eloquent statement about a school's affirmation of diversity than this very public celebration of all kinds of families? This is just one of many strategies that are effective; I list below a few others.

Sponsor Picnics, Open Houses, and Exhibits. It is no accident that the most robust parent attendance in schools happens when their children are highlighted. Assembly programs, musical presentations, and other events that focus on children are always a great way to bring families into schools, and a nonthreatening way in which to entice them to become involved in other ways. A school that has an active calendar of events, with different kinds of activities to encourage different families, is an active school.

Dedicate a Room to Families. In one of the schools where I taught, there was a "Family Room" right next to the principal's office. Workshops ranging from child rearing to crafts and other topics were offered. It was also a room where family members could gather to learn about the latest school activities or simply to have a cup of coffee.

Sponsor Professional Development That Focuses in Authentic Ways on Diversity. It is too often the case that professional development skirts issues of diversity, race, and privilege because such topics are uncomfortable for many staff members. Other times, there is a perfunctory and superficial treatment of these topics, resulting in what has been called a "holidays and heroes approach" (Lee, Menkart, & Okazawa-Rey, 1998). Even when the topic is broached in a more nuanced way, it is often done through mandated professional development in which all staff members are herded into an auditorium to passively listen to an outside speaker. The result is frequently resentment on the part of teachers because they feel that they are being treated as less than intelligent, and as needing to be "fixed."

Instead, teachers are looking for more respectful professional development strategies that encourage their participation and dialogue. As Steve Gordon, a veteran teacher of 35 years in the Boston Public Schools and now retired, who took part in a yearlong inquiry group with some of his peers, wrote,

> I am not looking for prescriptions for teachers. I am not looking for narrow "silver-bullet" programs that script teacher behaviors using some quasi-scientific rationale, . . . I want to find ways to teach that embody the several theories and beliefs that I have come to believe are true and good, truths and knowledge that have consequence for educating urban children. (Gordon, 2003, p. 86)

In addition to inquiry, study groups, and collaborative research, schools can demonstrate that they value the diversity of their student population by sponsoring classes in the major language or languages spoken by the students, and making sure that teachers receive graduate or professional development credit for taking these classes.

Teacher Educators

Teacher educators have a significant role to play in preparing new teachers, and motivating practicing teachers, to view their role as not simply teaching content but more importantly as developing strong relationships with students that help them connect more meaning-fully with school.

Encourage Teachers, Administrators, and Other Prospective Educators to Confront Their Preconceptions, Biases, and Attitudes Concerning Their Students' Identities. Given the reality that the vast majority of teachers in the United States are White, while the majority of students in most urban areas and increasingly in some suburban and rural areas are students of color, teachers and other educators must learn to face and deal honestly with negative attitudes about diversity. Many times, these attitudes are subconscious. Teachers may believe that the behaviors based on such attitudes are in the best interests of their students. For example, teachers and administrators often ask immigrant parents to speak English at home with their children, believing that doing so will accelerate the learning of English by the children. Yet research on language acquisition refutes this claim (Adger, Snow, & Christian, 2002). Likewise, a teacher may be reluctant to broach issues of race and ethnicity in the classroom, in the belief that doing so may actually exacerbate racism. As a result, many students become the victims of the silence related to racism and discrimination (Pollock, 2008).

In a chapter for a recent book, my colleague Kathy McDonough and I reviewed the progress made in the past decade in preparing teachers for diversity (Nieto & McDonough, 2011). Although much more needs to be done, we found that a good number of colleges and universities are now taking on this challenge. One of the most prevalent ways that teacher preparation programs are doing so is by asking teachers to be introspective about their own identities and unearned privilege. In addition, class discussions, readings, field placements, and out-of-class assignments also can encourage more critical thinking on the part of prospective and practicing teachers.

Involve Practicing and Prospective Teachers in Meaningful Activities. People need time to reflect on new material and on ideas that may contradict some deeply held attitudes and perceptions. Consequently, in my own courses in multicultural education over the years, I used a great variety of pedagogical strategies to create an environment that I hoped was direct and yet supportive rather than accusatory and confrontational. These included not only whole-class discussions, but also many kinds of small-group work, debates and dialogues, out-of-class assignments, journaling, videos, and more.

Using a variety of methods and approaches meant that all my students could learn in ways that were meaningful for them. If they felt comfortable writing in their journals but not being very vocal in class, that was fine; in contrast, if they enjoyed a good debate on a "hot" topic, they could focus on that. This also helped create a climate in which practicing and prospective teachers learned not only about methods and curriculum, but where they were open to learning about their students.

Teacher educators, however, need to be careful not to perpetuate preconceived notions that fall into the deficit perspective by, for example, providing teachers with only partial or one-sided portraits of students of diverse backgrounds. Doing so can lead teachers to expect all students of the same background to be exactly the same in temperament, conduct, and ability. Instead, prospective and practicing teachers need to be provided with multidimensional and realistic portraits of students, portraits that also help shatter stereotypes about what it means to be from a particular group (Nieto & Bode, 2012). Instead, it is more important for teachers to learn something of the history of the group, why they came to this country, and what their hopes are. They can also learn, through direct interaction with families, about their everyday lives and cultural practices. These are far more authentic ways to learn about cultural differences than lists of supposed characteristics of students from particular groups.

FINAL THOUGHTS

The tremendous diversity in our public schools means that teachers and other educators have more responsibilities than ever before for their students. Not only do they need to learn a great deal about their students, but teachers and other educators also need to create learning environments that affirm who their students are while also teaching them about life outside their particular realities. In the words of Mary Ginley, the veteran teacher of 42 years mentioned earlier, "My philosophy has always been—start from where they are and go together to someplace else" (2010a, p. 103). This philosophy should guide all educators who want to affirm people of all backgrounds and make them part of the school culture: "To start from where they are" is to acknowledge and respect their identities and experiences rather than to wipe them out; and to "go together to someplace else" means to open up the world outside to them. This is, indeed, a good definition of education, and one that would honor all students.

REFERENCES

Adesope, O. O., Lavin, T., Thompson, T., & Ungerleider, C. (2010). A systematic review and meta-analysis of the cognitive correlates of bilingualism. *Review of Educational Research, 80*(2), 207–245.

Adger, C. T., Snow, C. E., & Christian, C. (Eds). (2002). *What teachers need to know about language.* Washington, DC: Center for Applied Linguistics.

Berliner, D. C. (2009). *Poverty and potential: Out-of-school factors and school success.* East Lansing, MI: Great Lakes Center for Education Research & Practice. Retrieved from http://www.greatlakescenter.org/

Cowhey, M. (2008). Reading the class. In S. Nieto (Ed.), *Dear Paulo: Letters from those who dare teach* (pp. 10–16). Boulder, CO: Paradigm.

Dunn, B. (2010). *Mi semestre de español:* A case study on the cultural dimension of second-language acquisition. In S. Nieto, *The light in their eyes: Creating multicultural learning communities* (10th ed., pp. 169–175). New York: Teachers College Press.

Ginley, M. (2010a). Start from where kids are at. In S. Nieto, *The light in their eyes: Creating multicultural learning communities* (10th ed., pp. 103–104). New York: Teachers College Press.

Ginley, M. (2010b). Why I went back to school. In S. Nieto, *The light in their eyes: Creating multicultural learning communities* (10th ed., p. 183). New York: Teachers College Press.

Gonzalez, N., Moll, L. C., & Amanti, C. (Eds.). (2005). *Funds of knowledge: Theorizing practices in households and classrooms.* Mahwah, NJ: Erlbaum.

Gordon, S. (2003). Is teaching rational? In S. Nieto, *What keeps teachers going?* (pp. 86–87). New York: Teachers College Press.

Hernandez, D. J., Denton, N. A., & Macartney, S. E. (2008). Children in immigrant families: Looking to America's future. *Social Policy Report, 22*(3), 3–22.

Irizarry, J. G. (2009). Representin': Drawing from urban youth culture to inform teacher preparation. *Education and Urban Society, 41*(4), 489–515.

Jost, K. (2010). Bilingual education vs. English immersion: Which is better for students with limited English? *CQ Researcher, 19*(43), 1029–1052.

Lee, E., Menkart, D., & Okazawa-Rey, M. (1998*). Beyond holidays and heroes: A practical guide to K–12 antiracist multicultural education and staff development* (2nd ed.). Washington, DC: Teaching for Change.

Monger, R. (2010). *Annual flow report: U.S. permanent legal residents: 2009.* Washington, DC: Department of Homeland Security, Office of Immigration Statistics.

National Center for Children in Poverty (NCCP). (2010). Ten important questions about child poverty and family economic hardship. Retrieved from http://www.nccp.org/faq.html#question5

Nieto, S. (1994). Lessons from students on creating a chance to dream. *Harvard Educational Review, 64*(4), 392–426.

Nieto, S. (in press). *From surviving to thriving: Finding joy in teaching students of diverse backgrounds.* Portsmouth, NH: Stenhouse.

Nieto, S., & Bode, P. (2012). *Affirming diversity: The sociopolitical context of multicultural education* (6th ed.). Boston: Allyn & Bacon.

Nieto, S., & McDonough, K. (2011). Placing equity front and center revisited. In A. Ball & C. Tyson (Eds.), *Studying diversity in teacher education* (pp. 361–382). Washington, DC: American Educational Research Association.

Pew Hispanic Center. (2006). *Statistical portrait of Hispanics in the United States.* Washington, DC: Author.

Pollock, M. (Ed.). (2008). *Everyday antiracism: Getting real about race in school.* New York: New Press.

Portes, A., & Rumbaut, R. G. (2006). *Immigrant America: A portrait* (3rd ed.). Berkeley: University of California Press.

Provasnik, S., KewalRamani, A., Coleman, M. M., Gilbertson, L., Herring, W., & Xie, Q. (2007). *Status of education in rural America* (NCES 2007-040). National Center for Education Statistics, Institute of Education Sciences, U.S. Department of Education.

Shin, H. B., & Kominski, R. A. (2010, April). *Language use in the United States: 2007.* American Community Survey Reports, ACS-12. Washington, DC: U.S. Census Bureau.

U.S. Census Bureau. (2008, August 14). *An older and more diverse nation by midcentury.* Retrieved from http://www.census.gov/newsroom/releases/archives/population/cb08-123.html

U.S. Census Bureau. (2010). *USA People Quick Facts.* Retrieved from http://quickfacts.census.gov/qfd/states/00000.html

Wight, V. R., Thampi, K., & Briggs, J. (2010). *Who are America's poor children? Examining food insecurity among children in the United States.* New York: National Center for Children in Poverty, Columbia University.

CHAPTER 4

Low-Income Families and Young Children's Development and School Success

Barbara Bowman and Aisha Ray

Families exert the most influence on children's development and learning because of the length of their involvement with their children and the strength of their attachment. However, many factors outside of the family also affect how families function and children develop and learn. As children negotiate the world of school, their challenges and opportunities are shaped by the interaction of home, school, and community, as well as by the larger context of the economy, laws, and public policies (Bronfenbrenner, 1995). Any and all of these factors may either support or subvert children's school achievement.

The United States has a long history of involving families, especially parents, in children's education. Generations of American parents have been exhorted to further their understanding of their child's development and be active in support of their children's schools. The Parent Teachers Association, founded in 1897, was explicitly designed to foster parent education and to encourage parental involvement in schools. The U.S. Children's Bureau, an arm of the federal government, was established in 1912 to conduct research and disseminate information about women and children. Child rearing advice, based on the science of child development, was a part of the mission of the department and played an important role in improving the health and well-being of children. Parent involvement also has a long history in early childhood programs. Parent education and support were integral to the Cooperative School movement established in 1916 and has since been a part of the traditional nursery (or play) schools and preschools. More recently, parent education, support, volunteering, and empowerment have been incorporated in the performance standards

for Head Start as well as in special education requirements. The primary target of these efforts has been economically marginalized families
and their children, including cultural, racial, and ethnic minorities.

Over the past century, as research on child development has
mushroomed, particular parenting practices have been identified that
are associated with positive educational outcomes for children. This
research has reinforced the commonsense understanding that parents
are an important factor in children's school achievement. Reports of
this research are found in books, magazines, and the media, and policy makers, schools, as well as parents themselves are eager to capitalize
on it. While this has led to fads (refusing vaccinations) and misinterpretations (classical music for infants), it has also promoted more attention to children's health and well-being.

Of particular interest to both the public and private welfare systems have been programs designed to change parenting practices for
low-income and minority parents. While many of these interventions
were supportive, such as information about sanitation in the 1920s,
some were abusive. Negative strategies, for example, have included
forced sterilization (presumably for genetic defects), exhortation and
blame (mandatory parenting classes), and punishments (denial of services). Despite the severity of some of these practices, there is little evidence that either the supportive or abusive ones significantly changed
child rearing in low-income communities.

Current concerns about the achievement gap have again focused
interest on changing low-income families to improve children's school
achievement. In the hope of disentangling the complicated ways in
which families mediate children's development and learning, in this
chapter we review the literature on families and young children's
school achievement and make recommendations for more effective
policies and practices.

THE RELATIONSHIP BETWEEN CHILD DEVELOPMENT AND EDUCATIONAL ACHIEVEMENT

Advances in neurobiological research have made it increasingly clear
that early experience is critical for development and school learning.
Scientists have pointed out that early childhood is a period when the
architecture of the brain is being shaped and failure to have the right
experiences, at the right time, and in sufficient quantity can stunt
development in ways difficult to correct later. The plasticity of the
brain during the first few years of life has made early intervention
in child rearing an attractive strategy to improve children's school

achievement. It is assumed that the young brain is particularly vulnerable to environmental influences (Knudsen, Heckman, Cameron, & Shonkoff, 2006; Shonkoff & Phillips, 2000). As neuroscientists have shown the importance of prior learning in shaping subsequent learning, the importance of an early start on school learning is indicated. By intervening early, it is expected that the architecture of the brain will be more supportive of the social and cognitive skills necessary for school (Duncan, Huston, & Weisner, 2009).

Experience is the trigger that enables children to organize their brains to support the challenges they meet. Shonkoff and Phillips (2000) pointed out that experience has two dimensions, *expectant* and *dependent*. Expectant dimensions are ubiquitous and similar for all children, like being kept sufficiently warm, dry, fed, and stimulated. In this sense, experiences awaken the genetic capabilities inherent in being human; children learn to love, use language, make categories, represent ideas, and regulate their bodies. These experiences go to the heart of development and chronic deprivation can compromise the ability of children to develop normally. Children whose development is compromised are likely to be poor school learners.

The dependent aspect of experience comprises the particular ways that caregivers implement ordinary caregiving: the ways the family reflects the personal, structural, and, cultural aspects of their collective lives. This dimension affects what and how children learn: what language they speak (English or Urdu), the motor skills in play (lacrosse or spear throwing), whom they should love (clan or tribe).

Parents and other caregivers in their interactions with children provide both dimensions of experience. Some children's development is retarded or disrupted because they do not have the "expectant" experiences necessary to support ordinary development. Other children have enough of the right kinds of experience to pull the triggers for typical development; however, what they have learned in family and community does not sufficiently prepare them for school where a discrete set of knowledge and behavior is privileged. Although developmentally competent, these children may have either learned strategies that school settings problematize, and hence their learning in school is jeopardized, or they have not had access to the knowledge necessary to learn in school.

It is frequently difficult to determine if children are at developmental risk for school achievement or if they are simply unprepared. It is important to distinguish between these two causes since developmental failure is a far more serious disadvantage and requires a much longer and more intensive remediation. Programs that fail to make this distinction often bring too few resources too late to children living in environments that significantly jeopardize development and assume deficits in developmentally capable children that they do not have. Nevertheless, school failure becomes a major disadvantage no matter what the cause.

RISKS FOR EDUCATIONAL ACHIEVEMENT

A number of forces inside and outside of the family affect the kinds of experiences children have and, therefore, their school achievement. Among the external factors negatively influencing families are poverty, lack of community resources, and poor schools. Important family factors that affect school performance are family structure, culture, and parent-child interactions. The effects of any of these conditions are not inevitable. As Werner (1990) pointed out, "Even in the most disorganized and emotionally impoverished homes, and beset with serious physical handicaps, some children appear to develop stable, healthy personalities and display a remarkable degree of resilience" (p. 54). Nevertheless, these factors are found frequently enough to suggest their relevance to school success.

Poverty

There is a significant body of research that correlates family income and children's development and academic performance, even when controlling for other risk factors that may be present in low-income families, such as low levels of parental education (Bradley & Corwyn, 2002; Brody & Flor, 1997; Duncan, Ludwig, & Magnuson, 2007). Poverty is implicated in children's development directly through malnutrition, poor health care, substandard housing, the quality of schools, and the availability, quality, and quantity of community resources. The effects of poverty are especially strong when they occur in early childhood and/or last for a long period (Brooks-Gunn & Duncan, 1997; Duncan et al., 2009; Morris, Duncan, & Clark-Kauffman, 2005). The extent and consistency of a poverty environment predict poorer outcomes for children. Also, the impact of social class on student achievement was found to be greatest in 29 countries with high per capita income, such as the United States (Heyneman & Loxley, 1983). This suggests that relative poverty may negatively affect children's experience as pervasively as more severe levels. The effects of poverty are transmitted to children by their families through caregiving practices and caregiver stress (McLoyd, 1990). The strain of living in poverty and dealing with too few resources is stressful in itself, but poverty also exacerbates other stressful conditions, such as poor mental health, neighborhood violence, and diminished self-esteem. When parental aspirations and expectations for achievement, their strategies for controlling child behavior, and their linguistic orientation (Powell, 1991; Sukhdeep & Reynolds, 1996) conflict with school requirements, it may translate into lower test scores and grades, high failure and dropout rates, early pregnancy, under- and unemployment, and crime.

Low-income parents are more likely to be depressed and less likely to use positive parenting behaviors (Gershoff, Aber, Raver, & Lennon, 2007; Yeung, Linver, & Brooks-Gunn, 2002), which may contribute to poorer verbal and behavioral outcomes for young children (Caughy, Nettles, & O'Campo, 2007; Kohen, Leventhal, Dahinten, & McIntosh, 2008; Plybon & Kliewer, 2001). Parental depression and stress also affect learning and emotion regulation (Chazan-Cohen et al., 2009). Additionally, the stress that low-income parents experience can even lessen the potential effects of interventions designed to improve the home environment to support child development (Bakermans-Kranenburg, van Ijzendoorn, & Juffer, 2003).

Low-income families also tend to live in neighborhoods in which other impoverished families are segregated. Chronically poor neighborhoods are less likely to have a positive child involvement climate, as measured by the level of social interaction and the willingness of neighborhood adults to intervene with or assist children (Caughy et al., 2007). While the neighborhood in which a family lives is highly confounded with socioeconomic status, research does indicate that neighborhoods play a role in influencing child outcomes separate from poverty (Bradley & Corwyn, 2002; Leventhal & Brooks-Gunn, 2000). The growing neighborhood-effects literature suggests neighborhood and community characteristics and processes, such as social control, trust, and institutional resources are important variables (Sampson, Raudenbush, & Earls, 1997).

Preschool children from neighborhoods with low cohesion (where parents report lower levels of helping and support among neighbors) have lower verbal ability scores than those in highly cohesive neighborhoods, even when controlling for socioeconomic status (Kohen, Brooks-Gunn, Leventhal, & Hertzman, 2002; Kohen et al., 2008). It seems community support can play an important role in supporting children's academic achievement and lends support to efforts to revitalize low-income communities.

Simply raising a family's income can mitigate some of the disadvantages for children living in poverty. Morris, Duncan, and Clark-Kauffman (2005) found that simply increasing the income of low-income families participating in welfare programs had a positive impact on the school achievement of preschool children. Seemingly, relieving even a little of the pressure of poverty permits parents to do more of the supportive things that lead to school achievement. A number of different models have been used to raise family income, from direct welfare payments, to tax rebates and employment programs. All have both positive and negative results. However, finding ways to increase family resources must be high on the list of objectives to ensure permanent changes in children's development and school success.

Lack of Community Resources: Environmental Mediating Factors

Living in an economically disadvantaged neighborhood does not necessarily have to result in poor child outcomes. Emory, Caughy, Harris, and Franzini (2008) found that positive neighborhood characteristics, such as high expectations and collective socialization, are more important predictors of children's performance on third-grade tests than is the extent of economic disadvantage in the neighborhood. Parents (and children) take on the characteristics of the people they live with; thus positive neighborhoods provide support for both generations. Obviously, efforts at community building and mixed-income communities offer advantages for families and can help reverse the effects of poverty on families and their young children.

Race

Income is closely correlated with race and ethnicity, making it difficult to isolate the effects of each on children's school achievement. In 2008, 59% of Latino and 60% of African American children lived in low-income families, compared to 27% of White children; that same year, 42% of Latino children and 25% of African American children under 18 lived with a mother who did not graduate from high school, while only 10% of White children did (Mather & Foxen, 2010). African American and Latino children are also significantly more likely than White children to face at least three family risk factors; Romero and Lee (2008) found that only 6% of White children in a sample of kindergartners faced high cumulative risk, compared to 38% of African American children and 28% of Latino children. The historic burden of poverty and poor education that is the heritage of many African Americans continues to negatively affect their educational attainment to today.

Low-Quality Schools

Low-income families want their children to achieve both in school and in life. Unfortunately, schools have not been in the forefront of providing the necessary opportunities and thus reproduce inequality. Ferguson (1991) found that differences in school quality accounted for between one quarter and one third of variation in test scores across Texas school districts, which suggests that much of the explanation of the achievement gap lies in the quality of the schools children attend.

School is a challenge for all children (Haith & Sameroff, 1996), but low-income and minority children are especially unprepared for the challenge. School failure is not related to a single factor, but in part is due to the discrepancy between what children know and can do in relationship to social and cognitive expectations of the school. African American, Native American, and Latino children, in particular, and low-income students in general, are likely to experience this difference.

Low-income families are more dependent on the school to provide school skills and knowledge than are their middle-class counterparts. Yet, on average, low-income children attend schools with low expenditures on instruction, which is correlated with lower test scores (Archibald, 2006). Low-income children also attend schools that are underresourced and staffed with less-qualified teachers (Clotfelter, Ladd, Vigdor, & Wheeler, 2006; Kozol, 1991; Orfield & Lee, 2005; Peske & Haycock, 2006), which has been shown to have a significant effect on child outcomes (Darling-Hammond, 2000). Not surprisingly, the positive effects of early childhood programs for poor children, such as Head Start, fade more quickly for minority children as they move on to attend low-performing schools (Currie & Thomas, 2000; Lee & Loeb, 1995).

Many poor parents are aware of the poor quality of the schools their children attend, but often do not have the power or skills to negotiate change or the income to move to neighborhoods with superior schools. Programs like Head Start encourage families to assume more responsibility for the quality of their children's schooling; however, many parents are unable to translate their experience in Head Start into effective community activism. In addition, public schools may not sufficiently encourage or support the engagement of families.

THE INFLUENCE OF FAMILIES ON CHILDREN'S ACHIEVEMENT

While low socioeconomic status, neighborhood and cultural characteristics, and family risks have an effect on children's development and school achievement, children from these families are not doomed to fail. There are many additional factors—factors within the control of parents—that are of equal or greater importance in determining a child's academic achievement. In the words of Melhuish and colleagues (2008), "what parents do is as important as who parents are" (p. 1162). Supportive characteristics of families include responsive parent-child interactions, the home learning environment, and parent expectations for academic achievement.

Protective factors enable vulnerable children to overcome risk and many of these come from within the family (Garmezy, 1991; Wang, Haertel, & Walberg,1993). Many studies show that the home environment created by parents can have a positive influence on children's outcomes (Clark, 1983; Melhuish et al., 2008; Wang et al., 1993). Wang et al. wrote, "The home functions as the most salient out-of-school context for student learning, amplifying or diminishing the school's effect on learning" (p. 278). Other research has found that the home learning environment has a greater influence on child achievement than either socioeconomic status or parents' education (Melhuish et al., 2008).

At-risk children are more likely to succeed when they have a positive relationship with a competent adult (Masten, Best, & Garmezy, 1990) and when family relationships contain warmth, affection, cohesion, commitment, and emotional support (Seccombe, 2002). Some research indicates that parents dealing with the stress of limited resources might actually utilize more positive parenting behaviors in an effort to make up for those circumstances (Gershoff et al., 2007). Father involvement has also been shown to be a protective factor for children who are at risk (Flouri & Buchanan, 2004).

Family Interactions

A central theme in current developmental literature is the importance of the first infant/caregiver relationships in shaping later development and learning. Many researchers see this first social relationship as setting the stage for later inter- and intrapersonal characteristics, and the parent-child relationship is often used as a predictive marker for social/emotional development. It is thought that the early caregiving relationships should have the following characteristics: reliable support that establishes confident security in the adult, responsiveness that strengthens a young child's sense of agency and self-efficacy, protection from harm and excessive fear, affection, opportunities to experience and resolve human conflict cooperatively, support for the growth of new skills and capabilities, reciprocal interaction with other children, and experience of being respected (Shonkoff & Phillips, 2000).

Research has shown that responsive and stimulating care (Burchinal, Peisner-Feinberg, Pianta, & Howes, 2002), responsive parenting (Landry, 2008), home social factors (Neitzel, 2009), and quality of mothers' engagement with children (Rodriguez et al., 2009) have a positive effect on children's development. Maternal supportiveness is positively correlated with child vocabulary, letter-word knowledge, and emotional regulation (Chazan-Cohen et al., 2009), and parent-child interactions that are responsive to the child's emotional and developmental needs have a positive impact on school readiness and social skills (Connell & Prinz, 2002). Some research on the effects of parental involvement in school points to the role played by the underlying enthusiasm and positive parenting practices of highly involved parents (Zellman & Waterman, 1998). Hao and Bonstead-Bruns (1998) suggested that educational achievement is related to increased parental expectations and high levels of engagement.

Qualities of caregivers that ensure normal brain and behavioral development and school readiness are the following: They encourage exploration; mentor basic skills; celebrate developmental advances; rehearse and extend new skills; protect child from inappropriate disapproval, teasing, and punishment; communicate richly and responsively; and guide and limit behavior (Ramey & Ramey, 1999).

Family Structure

Statistics suggest that family structure is a significant predictor of children's poorer educational outcomes. Certainly, single parents have less time and energy to devote to their children than two-parent families. However, there is strong evidence that the effects of living in a single-parent family are almost entirely due to the high correlation between single parenthood and poverty (Carlson & Corcoran, 2001; Entwisle & Alexander, 1995). Flouri and Buchanan (2004) argued that the level of parental involvement—for both mothers and fathers—is more important than family structure. This does not mean that the presence of a father has no impact on children's development and school achievement, only that negative effects may be ameliorated by greater family affluence. The amount and type of paternal involvement does seem to play a role in children's cognitive development, particularly in math (Black, Dubowitz, & Starr, 1999; Campbell, 1996). This suggests the importance of including fathers in involvement programs, whether they live in the home or not.

Parents' Education Level

Children of mothers with lower levels of education have poorer academic and social outcomes (Davis-Kean & Sexton, 2009) than children with better educated mothers. This is especially the case for children of mothers with less than a high school diploma compared to children of mothers with at least a bachelor's degree (Davis-Kean, 2005; Halle, Kurtz-Costes, & Mahoney, 1997). For example, Seccombe (2002) found that upon entering kindergarten, 38% of children with mothers who had not completed high school were proficient in recognizing letters, compared to 86% of children with mothers who had at least a bachelor's degree. Other studies show that children with more highly educated mothers score higher on reading and math tests (Campbell, 1996) and have better outcomes in the areas of vocabulary and letter-word identification (Hammer, Farkas, & Maczuga, 2010; Melhuish et al., 2008) and children's vocabulary (Rowe, Jacobson, & Van den Oord, 1999). Low parental education is also linked to low parental self-efficacy, which has been shown to have a negative impact on child cognitive outcomes (Seefeldt, Denton, Galper, & Younoszai, 1999).

Parents' education is an important component of socioeconomic status so it is not surprising to find it is also predictive of children's educational attainment. It is generally not possible to change parents' education level quickly or perhaps at all. However, some studies find that parents who are enrolled in school and parents whose work is seen as challenging provide role models for their children. This research supports program strategies that engage parents in additional schooling and as leaders in programs and in the community.

Family Ethnicity and Culture

There is some evidence that ethnicity, or culture, plays a role in child outcomes that is independent from income. Ethnicity is correlated with vocabulary in Head Start and reading ability in kindergarten (Hammer et al., 2010), and Halle, Kurtz-Costes, and Mahoney (1997) found that disparities in child cognitive development based on ethnicity (along with home language and maternal education level) begin to emerge as early as 9 months, and by 24 months this disparity has grown larger. This disparity has also been measured as children enter kindergarten, with findings that math achievement is 21% lower for African American children and 19% lower for Latino children compared to their White peers (Lee & Burkam, 2002). The achievement of middle-class African American children is also lower than that of middle-class Whites, while that of some low-income Asian American groups exceeds that of Whites.

Most parents learn to be parents informally; child-rearing practices are embedded in family traditions, and responsive to the life challenges of the community as perceived by the residents. Cultural patterns reflect the challenges people experience and their traditional ways of dealing with them. Long-standing cultural adaptations do not change quickly or easily. Therefore, many low-income children of color come from families and communities that have long experienced institutional barriers to school achievement and full participation in the civic life of the country. Family values and practices are embedded in socioeconomic contexts and cannot be expected to change without concomitant changes in other dimensions of daily living, including income, housing, and parents' social referencing groups' values and behavior. Halpern (1990) commented, "Parent support and education programs cannot be expected to alter basic parenting capacities and styles, acquired through a lifetime of experience in a particular familiar and social world, and often continually reinforced in the present. Nor can they alter families' basic life situation" (p. 305).

It is unfortunate that in many low-income communities, as stronger or more economically advantaged members may move out, the remaining community is in danger of becoming even less supportive of families. The remaining families and parents are less likely to have the skills and knowledge necessary to help their children with school skills and knowledge privileged in schools. Schools and other social institutions will need to intervene earlier and with more support if low-income, minority children are to compete in school on a level playing field.

Home Learning Environment

Aspects of the home learning environment, including structured play and amount and type of language used by caregivers, have a positive relationship with developmental outcomes (Chazan-Cohen et al., 2009; Payne, Whitehurst, & Angell, 1994; Reissland, Shepard, & Stephenson, 1999; Rush, 1998). Provision of age-appropriate and stimulating materials, while a challenge for low-income families, is also important (Rodriguez et al., 2009; Yeung et al., 2002). Provision of stimulating activities has been shown to mediate the negative effects of maternal depression on children (Zajicek-Farber, 2010).

The home literacy environment—which includes shared book reading, exposure to print, and other literacy and language-related activities and interactions—is of particular importance for child outcomes (Carter, Chard, & Pool, 2009; Hood, Conlon, & Andrews, 2008; Payne et al., 1994; Phillips & Lonigan, 2009). The quality of the home literacy environment has been shown to affect children's vocabulary in Head Start and reading ability in kindergarten (Hammer et al., 2010), and performance on early literacy and vocabulary measures (Rush, 1999). The home literacy environment is important even for children under age 3 (Rodriguez et al., 2009).

Unfortunately, however, low-income families in which parents have low levels of education and face financial stressors and time constraints are less likely to provide a stimulating home learning environment. A study of Head Start children's home literacy environments found that while play-related activities occurred almost daily, families did academically related activities just once or twice per week on average (Wasik & Hindman, 2010). However, interventions such as those designed to increase the amount of home reading have been shown to have significant effects for low-income children (Lonigan & White-hurst, 1998).

Programs that help parents learn how to promote child development and school readiness include the following characteristics: Parents read with their children, parents are less negative and more emotionally supportive with their children, and parents are more supportive of language and learning, including asking questions about readings (Haskins & Rouse, 2005).

Parent Expectations

Stereotypes persist that low-income families do not have high expectations for their children's academic achievement. Yet research indicates that low-income parents often have expectations for their child's school readiness that are equivalent to or even higher than those of higher income parents. One hypothesis is that the higher expectations reflect low-income parents' desire to prepare children for attending schools with insufficient resources (Piotrowski, Collins, Knitzer, & Robinson, 1994).

There is some evidence that parental expectations and their effect on child outcomes vary by ethnic and immigrant group. Davis-Kean and Sexton (2009) found that parental expectations were a predictor of outcomes for White, African American, and Asian American children, but not for Latino children. Other research shows that immigrant parents' educational expectations vary by ethnicity and by premigration educational status (Feliciano, 2006). Research about the effects of neighborhood characteristics on child outcomes indicates that living in a neighborhood that has high expectations for academic achievement has a positive impact on standardized test scores among third graders (Emory et al., 2008).

Home-School Relationships

Parental involvement can have a positive effect on child achievement (Jeynes, 2005; Sui-Chu & Willms, 1996). Even parental involvement in preschool and the early grades has been shown to have an effect lasting into middle school and high school (Flouri & Buchanan, 2004; Miedel & Reynolds, 1999; McWayne, Hampton, Fantuzzo, Cohen, & Sekino, 2004).

Several studies suggest that home-based parental involvement—such as talking about school with children, actively promoting learning, and helping with homework—has a greater effect on child outcomes than school-based involvement (McWayne et al., 2004; Sui-Chu & Willms, 1996). However, school-based parental involvement is also important.

Factors that can negatively affect the amount and type of parental involvement include parental stress or depression, single-parent status, and parents' education level (Kohl, Lengua, & McMahon, 2000). Some studies have found that low-income or ethnic minority parents are less involved than other parents (Kohl et al., 2000), while others have found no difference (Sui-Chu & Willms, 1996). There is evidence that educators can play a role in encouraging and supporting parental involvement. One study found that children in urban elementary schools performed better on state achievement tests when their schools were making a significant effort to increase family and community involvement (Sheldon, 2003). An intervention designed to teach parents of Head Start children how to support their children's mathematical development had a positive impact on their children's mathematical knowledge (Starkey & Klein, 2000). The parents, who would not otherwise have known how to help, were willing and able to do so once they received training and support. Research indicates that efforts to foster parent involvement should start as early as preschool and be comprehensive (Miedel & Reynolds, 1999; Reynolds, 1992).

Minority children are less likely than their White peers to experience outreach from the school to ease the transition to kindergarten (Lee & Burkham, 2002). Perhaps more important, research indicates that ethnic and cultural differences among parents—including African American (Cooper & Crosnoe, 2007), Latino (Espinosa, 1995), and immigrant (Carreon, Drake, & Barton, 2005) families—influence the type and amount of parental engagement.

Parents face a range of challenges and barriers to their school involvement. Lott (2001) refers to the "uphill battle" that low-income and minority parents face in being involved in their children's education. Stereotypes, assumptions, and lack of cultural awareness on the part of educators can lead to situations in which parents are frustrated and left feeling powerless by their attempts to become involved. Both parents and schools can play a role in resolving this problem. Parents can utilize community connections and social capital to better communicate to schools their concerns and priorities and to make sure their voices are heard. Educators can be aware of the beliefs and assumptions they may hold that negatively affect their interactions with low-income students and families, and make an effort to be more culturally aware and accepting of diverse approaches to parental involvement.

RECOMMENDATIONS FOR CHANGE

Changing educational outcomes for low-income minority children will not be easy. Poverty and generations of social and educational exclusion have supported ethnic and community patterns that make change difficult. Without changing the conditions of people's lives, it is hard to change established child rearing patterns. However, recent research suggests new strategies that can be brought to bear on the achievement gap.

Infant Programs

New research on the brain points to infancy as an important time for development. It is essential for infants and toddlers to be exposed to warm, sensitive, and supportive interpersonal environments. When parents are unable to supply such an environment, child care centers and homes can be used to augment family care and take some of the stress off parents. Such programs as Early Head Start and the Ounce of Prevention are prototypes of how such programs can be structured.

Recommendation: Fund more high-quality infant and toddler programs for parents under heavy stress, who cannot provide the essential stability and care required by infants for healthy development.

Preschool

Most low-income and minority children have families able to provide the basic interpersonal environment for development, but not the rich educational environment necessary for school achievement. Fifty years of research has repeatedly shown that well-implemented preschool programs can help close the achievement gap (Heckman, 2007). Successful programs have been full-day and half-day, and lasted 1 to 5 years, but what distinguished the successful ones was the educational level and training of the teachers, the intentional and developmentally appropriate curriculum, and attention to families and their needs.

Recommendation: Fund educational preschool programs for all children at risk of school failure at a high enough level to engage teachers with a bachelor's degree, tested materials and curricula, and opportunities for parent and family participation.

Parent Education and Involvement

Successful preschool intervention programs have had a parent education component, and parent programs that have shown the most effectiveness were combined with a concomitant program for their young child. Brooks-Gunn and Markman (2005) listed the following characteristics for effective parenting/parent involvement programs: target both parents and children; provide parents with knowledge and skills to better support their children's development and provide opportunities for parents to practice these skills with their children; be comprehensive and long-lasting; create a relationship of trust and respect between school and family; understand cultural differences between families and schools (including how families conceive of "parental involvement") and work to bridge that divide; and understand families' needs and work to remove obstacles to their involvement (e.g., by providing transportation or child care or offering home-based services). Parent involvement in schooling is important because it strengthens the family's connection to the school and improves the school's perceptions of the family.

Although there are numerous reports attesting to the effectiveness of various program models, there is little evidence of significant changes in child outcomes.

Recommendation: Fund evaluation of various parent program models to determine which work with whom at what level of effectiveness.

Pre-K to Grade 3 Policy

Early childhood programs are not an inoculation. Children need an aligned K–3 program so that what they learn in preschool prepares them to learn the primary curriculum. Schools have an obligation to collaborate with parents and early childhood programs about what children should know and be able to do in kindergarten, and to see that kindergarten is aligned with the primary grades. Parents should be assured of a welcome across grade levels and expectations for involvement consistent between preschool and K–3.

> **Recommendations:** Ensure that families are represented on state Early Childhood Advisory Councils. Appoint state-level staff to plan for and oversee family engagement in all state funded pre-K–3 programs.
>
> Include family engagement as a core competency in teacher and administrator education and certification.

Beyond School: Other Means for Changing Outcomes for Children

Poverty and neighborhood resources affect families and their relationship to their children and their children's success in school. For example, school finance reform has led to a narrowing of the spending gap between low-income and higher income districts, and research indicates that this equalization has been associated with a reduction in the test score gap between these schools (Card & Payne, 2002).

> **Recommendations:** Revise funding formula so that children who most need additional resources are given priority, namely, children with disabilities, English language learners, children from low-income families, and children from low-performing schools.
>
> Facilitate and coordinate health, housing, and other community improvement efforts with early childhood centers and schools so that programs relieve stress on families.

REFERENCES

Archibald, S. (2006). Narrowing in on educational resources that do affect student achievement. *Peabody Journal of Education, 81*(4), 23–42.

Bakermans-Kranenburg, M. J., van Ijzendoorn, M. H., & Juffer, F. (2003). Less is more: Meta-analyses of sensitivity and attachment interventions in early childhood. *Psychological Bulletin, 129*(2), 195–215.

Black, M. M., Dubowitz, H., & Starr, R. H., Jr. (1999). African American fathers in low income, urban families: Development, behavior, and home environment of their three-year-old children. *Child Development, 70*(4), 967–978. doi:10.1111/1467-8624.00070

Bradley, R. H., & Corwyn, R. F. (2002). Socioeconomic status and child development. *Annual Review of Psychology, 53*, 371–399.

Brody, G. H., & Flor, D. (1997). Maternal psychological functioning, family processes, and child adjustment in rural, single-parent, African-American families. *Developmental Psychology, 33*, 1000–1011.

Bronfenbrenner, U. (1995). Developmental ecology through space and time: A future perspective. In P. Moen, G. H. Elder, Jr., & K. Lüscher (Eds.), *Examining lives in context: Perspectives on the ecology of human development* (pp. 619–647). Washington, DC: American Psychological Association.

Brooks-Gunn, J., & Duncan, G. J. (1997). The effects of poverty on children and youth. *The Future of Children, 7*(2), 55–71.

Brooks-Gunn, J., & Markham, L. B. (2005). The contribution of parenting to ethnic and racial gaps in school readiness. *The Future of Children, 15*(1), 139–168. Retrieved from http://www.eric.ed.gov/PDFS/EJ795847.pdf

Burchinal, M. R., Peisner-Feinberg, E., Pianta, R. C., & Howes, C. (2002). Development of academic skills from preschool through second grade: Family and classroom predictors of developmental trajectories. *Journal of School Psychology, 40*, 415–436.

Campbell, F. A. (1996, June). *Family factors associated with high and low reading and mathematics scores in children from low-income families.* Paper presented at the Head Start National Research Conference, Washington, DC. Retrieved from http://ezproxy.erikson.edu/login?url=http://search.ebscohost.com/login.aspx?direct=true&db=eric&AN=ED400063&site=ehost-live&scope=site

Card, D., & Payne, A. A. (2002). School finance reform, the distribution of school spending, and the distribution of student test scores. *Journal of Public Economics, 83*, 49–82.

Carlson, M. J., & Corcoran, M. E. (2001). Family structure and children's behavioral and cognitive outcomes. *Journal of Marriage and Family, 63*(3), 779–792.

Carreon, G. P., Drake, C., & Barton, A. C. (2005). The importance of presence: Immigrant parents' school engagement experiences. *American Educational Research Journal, 42*(3), 465–498.

Carter, D. R., Chard, D. J., & Pool, J. L. (2009). A family strengths approach to early language and literacy development. *Early Childhood Education Journal, 36*(6), 519–526.

Caughy, M., Nettles, S., & O'Campo, P. (2007). Community influences on adjustment in first grade: An examination of an integrated process model. *Journal of Child and Family Studies, 16*(6), 819–836. doi:10.1007/s10826-006-9128-8

Chazan-Cohen, R., Raikes, H., Brooks-Gunn, J., Ayoub, C., Pan, B. A., Kisker, E. E., & Roggman, L. (2009). Low-income children's school readiness: Parent contributions over the first five years. *Early Education and Development, 20*(6), 958–977.

Clark, R. M. (1983). *Family life and school achievement: Why poor Black children succeed or fail.* Chicago: University of Chicago Press.

Clotfelter, C., Ladd, H. F., Vigdor, J., & Wheeler, J. (2006). High-poverty schools and the distribution of teachers and principals. *North Carolina Law Review, 85,* 1345.

Connell, C. M., & Prinz, R. J. (2002). The impact of childcare and parent-child interactions on school readiness and social skills development for low-income African American children. *Journal of School Psychology, 40*(2), 177–193. doi:10.1016/S0022-4405(02)00090-0

Cooper, C. E., & Crosnoe, R. (2007). The engagement in schooling of economically disadvantaged parents and children. *Youth & Society, 38*(3), 372–391.

Currie, J., & Thomas, D. (2000). School quality and the longer-term effects of Head Start. *Journal of Human Resources, 35*(4), 755–774.

Darling-Hammond, L. (2000). Teacher quality and student achievement: A review of state policy evidence. *Education Policy Analysis Archives, 8(1),* 1–50.

Davis-Kean, P. E. (2005). The influence of parent education and family income on child achievement: The indirect role of parental expectations and the home environment. *Journal of Family Psychology, 19*(2), 294–304.

Davis-Kean, P. E., & Sexton, H. R. (2009). Race differences in parental influences on child achievement: Multiple pathways to success. *Merrill-Palmer Quarterly, 55* (3), 285–318.

Duncan, G. J., Huston, A., & Weisner, T. (2009). *Higher ground: New hope for the working poor and their children.* New York: Russell Sage.

Duncan, G. J., Ludwig, J., & Magnuson, K. (2007). Reducing poverty through pre-school interventions. *The Future of Children, 17,* 143–160.

Emory, R., Caughy, M., Harris, T. R., & Franzini, L. (2008). Neighborhood social processes and academic achievement in elementary school. *Journal of Community Psychology, 36*(7), 885–898.

Entwisle, D. R., & Alexander, K. L. (1995). A parent's economic shadow: Family structure versus family resources as influences on early school achievement. *Journal of Marriage and Family, 57*(2), 399–409.

Espinosa, L. M. (1995). *Hispanic parent involvement in early childhood programs.* Urbana, IL: ERIC Clearinghouse on Elementary and Early Childhood Education. (EDO-PS-95-3) Retrieved from http://www.evenst artnetwork.net/pdf/Article08.pdf

Feliciano, C. (2006). Beyond the family: The influence of premigration group status on the educational expectations of immigrants' children. *Sociology of Education, 79*(4), 281–303.

Ferguson, R. (1991). Paying for public education: New evidence on how and why money matters. *Harvard Journal on Legislation, 28,* 547–561.

Flouri, E., & Buchanan, A. (2004). Early father's and mother's involvement and child's later educational outcomes. *British Journal of Educational Psychology, 74,* 141–153. doi:10.1348/000709904773839806

Garmezy, N. (1991). Resilience and vulnerability to adverse developmental outcomes associated with poverty. *American Behavioral Scientist, 34*(4), 416–430. doi: 10.1177/0002764291034004003.

Gershoff, E. T., Aber, J. L., Raver, C. C., & Lennon, M. C. (2007). Income is not enough: Incorporating material hardship into models of income associations with parenting and child development. *Child Development, 78*(1), 70–95. doi:10.1111/j.1467-8624.2007.00986.x

Haith, M. M., & Sameroff, A. J. (1996). *The five to seven year shift: The age of reason and responsibility.* Chicago: University of Chicago Press.

Halle, T. G., Kurtz-Costes, B., & Mahoney, J. L. (1997). Family influences on school achievement in low-income, African American children. *Journal of Educational Psychology, 89*(3), 527–537.

Halpern, R. (1990). Poverty and early childhood parenting: Toward a framework for intervention. *American Journal of Orthopsychiatry, 60,* 6–18. doi: 10.1037/h0079162

Hammer, C. S., Farkas, G., & Maczuga, S. (2010). The language and literacy development of Head Start children: A study using the Family and Child Experiences Survey Database. *Language, Speech, & Hearing Services in Schools, 41*(1), 70–83. doi:10.1044/0161-1461(2009/08-0050)

Hao, L., & Bonstead-Bruns, M. (1998). Parent-child differences in educational expectations and the academic achievement of immigrant and native students. *Sociology of Education, 71*(3), 175–198.

Haskins, R., & Rouse, C. (2005). Closing achievement gaps. *The Future of Children, 15,* 1–7. Retrieved from http://69.18.145.94/upload/PublicationFiles/Policy_Brief__SPRING_2005pdf.pdf

Heckman, J. (2007). The productivity argument for investing in young children. *Applied Economic Perspectives and Policy, 29*(3), 446–493.

Heyneman, S. P., & Loxley, W. A. (1983). The effect of primary-school quality on academic achievement across twenty-nine high- and low-income countries. *American Journal of Sociology, 88*(6), 1162–1194.

Hood, M., Conlon, E., & Andrews, G. (2008). Preschool home literacy practices and children's literacy development: A longitudinal analysis. *Journal of Educational Psychology, 100*(2), 252–271.

Jeynes, W. T. (2005). A meta-analysis of the relation of parental involvement to urban elementary school student academic achievement. *Urban Education, 40*(3), 237–269.

Kohen, D. E., Brooks-Gunn, J., Leventhal, T., & Hertzman, C. (2002). Neighborhood income and physical and social disorder in Canada: Associations with young children's competencies. *Child Development, 73*(6), 1844–1860.

Kohen, D. E., Leventhal, T., Dahinten, V. S., & McIntosh, C. N. (2008). Neighborhood disadvantage: Pathways of effects for young children. *Child Development, 79*(1), 156–169.

Kohl, G., Lengua, L. J., & McMahon, R. J. (2000). Parent involvement in school: Conceptualizing multiple dimensions and their relations with family and demographic risk factors. *Journal of School Psychology, 38*(6), 501–523. doi: 10.1016/S0022-4405(00)00050-9.

Kozol, J. (1991). *Savage inequalities.* New York: Harper Perennial.

Knudsen, E. I., Heckman, J. J., Cameron, J. L., & Shonkoff, J. P. (2006). Economic, neurological, and behavioral perspectives on building America's future workforce. *PNAS, 103*(27), 10155–10162.

Landry, S. H. (2008). The role of parents in early childhood learning. In R. E. Tremblay, R. G. Barr, R. D. Peters, & M. Bovin (Eds.), *Encyclopedia on Early Childhood Development* [Online]. Montreal, Canada: Centre of Excellence for Early Childhood Development. Retrieved from http://www.child-encyclopedia.com/documents/LandryANGxp.pdf

Lee, V. E., & Burkam, D. T. (2002). *Inequality at the starting gate: Social background differences in achievement as children begin school.* Washington, DC: Economic Policy Institute.

Lee, V. E, & Loeb, S. (1995). Where do Head Start attendees end up? One reason why preschool effects fade out. *Educational Evaluation and Policy Analysis, 17*(1), 62–82.

Leventhal, T., & Brooks-Gunn, J. (2000). The neighborhoods they live in: The effects of neighborhood residence upon child and adolescent outcomes. *Psychological Bulletin, 126,* 309–337.

Lonigan, C. J., & Whitehurst, G. J. (1998). Relative efficacy of parent and teacher involvement in a shared-reading intervention for preschool children from low-income backgrounds. *Early Childhood Research Quarterly, 13*(2), 263–290. doi:10.1016/S0885-2006(99)80038-6

Lott, B. (2001). Low-income parents and the public schools. *Journal of Social Sciences, 57*(2), 247–259.

Masten, A. S., Best, K. M., & Garmezy, N. (1990). Resilence and development: Contributions from the study of children who overcome adversity. *Development and Psychopathology, 2*(04), 425–444. doi: 10.1017/S0954579400005812

Mather, M., & Foxen, P. (2010). *America's future: Latino chilld well-being in numbers and trends.* Washington, DC: National Council of LaRaza.

McLoyd, V. C. (1990). The impact of economic hardship on Black families and children: Psychological distress, parenting, and socioemotional development.*Child Development, 61,* 311–346.

McWayne, C., Hampton, V., Fantuzzo, J., Cohen, H. L., & Sekino, Y. (2004). A multivariate examination of parent involvement and the social and academic competencies of Uuban kindergarten children. *Psychology in the Schools, 41*(3), 363–377.

Melhuish, E. C., Sylva, K., Sammons, P., Siraj-Blatchford, I., Taggart, B., Phan, M. B., & Malin, A. (2008). The early years: Preschool influences on mathematics achievement. *Science, 321*(5893), 1161–1162. doi: 12.1126/science.1158808.

Miedel, W. T., & Reynolds, A. J. (1999). Parent involvement in early intervention for disadvantaged children: Does it matter? *Journal of School Psychology, 37*(4), 379–402.

Morris, P., Duncan, G., & Clark-Kauffman, E. (2005). Child well-being in an era of welfare reform: The sensitivity of transitions in development to policy change. *Developmental Psychology, 41*(6), 919–932. doi: 10.1037/0012-1649.41.6.919

Neitzel, C. (2009). Child characteristics, home social-contextual factors, and children's academic peer interaction behaviors in kindergarten. *Elementary School Journal, 110*(1), 40–62.

Orfield, G., & Lee, C. (2005). *Why segregation matters: Poverty and educational inequality.* The Civil Rights Project, Harvard University. Retrieved from http://www.civilrightsproject.harvard.edu

Payne, A. C., Whitehurst, G. J., & Angell, A. L. (1994). The role of home literacy environment in the development of language ability in preschool children from low-income families. *Early Childhood Research Quarterly, 9*(3–4), 427–440. doi:10.1016/0885-2006(94)90018-3

Peske, H. G., & Haycock, K. (2006, June). *Teaching inequality: How poor and minority students are shortchanged on teacher quality: A report and recommendations by The Education Trust.* Retrieved from http://www.edtrust.org/sites/edtrust.org/files/publications/files/TQReportJune2006.pdf

Phillips, B. M., & Lonigan, C. J. (2009). Variations in the home literacy environment of preschool children: A cluster analytic approach. *Scientific Studies of Reading, 13*(2), 146–174. doi:10.1080/10888430902769533

Piotrowski, C. S., Collins, R. C., Knitzer, J., & Robinson, R. (1994). Strengthening mental health services in Head Start: A challenge for the 1990s. *American Psychologist, 49*, 133–139.

Plybon, L. E., & Kliewer, W. (2001). Neighborhood types and externalizing behavior in urban school-age children: Tests of direct, mediated, and moderated effects. *Journal of Child & Family Studies, 10*(4), 419–437.

Powell, D. R. (1991). Parents and programs: Early childhood as a pioneer in parent involvement and support. In S. L. Kagen (Ed.), *Yearbook of the National Society for the Study of Education: Vol. 90. The care and education of America's young children: Obstacles and opportunities* (pp. 91–109). Chicago: National Society for the Study of Education.

Ramey, C. T., & Ramey, S. L. (1999). *Right from birth: Building your child's foundation for life, birth to 18 months.* New York: Goddard Press.

Reissland, N., Shepard, J., & Stephenson, T. (1999). Maternal verbal interaction in different situations with infants born prematurely or at term. *Infant and Child Development, 8*, 39–48.

Reynolds, A. J. (1992). Comparing measures of parental involvement and their effects on academic achievement. *Early Childhood Research Quarterly, 7*(3), 441–462. doi:10.1016/0885-2006(92)90031-S

Rodriguez, E. T., Tamis-LeMonda, C. S., Spellmann, M. E., Pan, B. A., Raikes, H., Lugo-Gil, J., & Luze, G. (2009). The formative role of home literacy experiences across the first three years of life in children from low-income families. *Journal of Applied Developmental Psychology, 30*(6), 677–694.

Romero, M., & Lee, Y.-S. (2008, January). *The influence of maternal and family risk on chronic absenteeism in early schooling.* New York: National Center for Children in Poverty, Columbia University. Retrieved from http://www.nccp.org/publications/pdf/text_792.pdf

Rowe, D. C., Jacobson, K. C., & Van den Oord, E. J. C. G. (1999). Genetic and environmental influences on vocabulary IQ: Parental education level as moderator. *Child Development, 70*(5), 1151–1162. doi:10.1111/1467-8624.00084

Rush, K. L. (1998). Preschool language experiences and early literacy skill development for families from low-income environments. *Dissertation Abstracts International: Section A. Humanities and Social Sciences, 58*(7–A). Retrieved from http://ezproxy.erikson.edu/login?url=http://search.ebscohost.com/login.aspx?direct=true&db=psyh&AN=1998-95001-025&site=ehost-live&scope=site

Rush, K. L. (1999). Caregiver-child interactions and early literacy development of preschool children from low-income environments. *Topics in Early Childhood Special Education, 19*(1), 3–14. doi:10.1177/027112149901900101

Sampson, R. W., Raudenbush, S. W., & Earls, F. (1997). Neighborhoods and violent crime: A multilevel study of collective efficacy. *Science, 277*, 918–924.

Seccombe, K. (2002). "Beating the odds" versus "changing the odds": Poverty, resilience, and family policy. *Journal of Marriage and Family, 64*(2), 384–394.

Seefeldt, C., Denton, K., Galper, A., & Younoszai, T. (1999). The relation between Head Start parents' participation in a transition demonstration, education, efficacy and their children's academic abilities. *Early Childhood Research Quarterly, 14*(1), 99–109. doi:10.1016/S0885-2006(99)80008-8

Sheldon, S. B. (2003). Linking school-family-community partnerships in urban elementary schools to student achievement on state tests. *The Urban Review, 35*(2), 149–165. doi:10.1023/A:1023713829693

Shonkoff, J., & Phillips, D. (2000). *From neurons to neighborhoods: The science of early childhood development.* Washington, DC: National Academy Press.

Starkey, P., & Klein, A. (2000). Fostering parental support for children's mathematical development: An intervention with Head Start families. *Early Education and Development, 11*, 659–680.

Sui-Chu, E. S., & Willms, J. D. (1996). Effects of parental involvement on eighth-grade achievement. *Sociology of Education, 69*, 126–141.

Sukhdeep, G., & Reynolds, A. J. (1996, August). *Role of parent expectations in the school success of at-risk children.* Paper presented at the biennial meeting of the International Society for the Study of Behavioural Development, Quebec City, Quebec, Canada. Retrieved from http://www.eric.ed.gov/PDFS/ED401019.pdf

Wang, M. C., Haertel, G. D., & Walberg, H. J. (1993). Toward a knowledge base for school learning. *Review of Educational Research, 63*(3), 249–294. doi:10.3102/00346543063003249

Wasik, B. A., & Hindman, A. H. (2010). Understanding the home language and literacy environments of Head Start families: Testing the family literacy survey and interpreting its findings. *NHSA Dialog: A Research-to-Practice Journal for the Early Intervention Field, 13*(2), 71–91.

Werner, E. E. (1990). Protective factors and individual resilience. In J. P. Shonkoff & S. Meisels (Eds.), *Handbook of early intervention* (pp. 115–134). Cambridge, UK: Cambridge University Press.

Yeung, W. J., Linver, M. R., & Brooks-Gunn, J. (2002). How money matters for young children's development: Parental investment and family processes. *Child Development, 73*(6), 1861–1879.

Zajicek-Farber, M. (2010). The contributions of parenting and postnatal depression on emergent language of children in low-income families. *Journal of Child & Family Studies, 19*(3), 257–269. doi:10.1007/s10826-009-9293-7

Zellman, G. L., & Waterman, J. M. (1998). Understanding the impact of parent school involvement on children's educational outcomes. *Journal of Educational Research, 91*(6), 370–380.

Part II

DANGERS TO CHILDHOOD
POSED BY OUR CULTURE

CHAPTER 5

Foreclosed Childhoods

Poverty, Inequality, and Discarding the Young

Valerie Polakow

> *It is a melancholy object to those who walk through this great town or travel in the country, when they see the streets, the roads, and cabin doors, crowded with beggars of the female sex, followed by three, four, or six children, all in rags and importuning every passenger for an alms. . . . I think it is agreed by all parties that this prodigious number of children in the arms, or on the backs, or at the heels of their mothers, and frequently of their fathers, is in the present deplorable state of the kingdom a very great additional grievance; and, therefore, whoever could find out a fair, cheap, and easy method of making these children sound, useful members of the commonwealth, would deserve so well of the public as to have his statue set up for a preserver of the nation. . . . I have been assured by a very knowing American of my acquaintance in London, that a young healthy child well nursed is at a year old a most delicious, nourishing, and wholesome food, whether stewed, roasted, baked, or boiled.*
>
> —Jonathan Swift, *A Modest Proposal* (1729)

Swift's "Modest Proposal" to rid the country of destitute Irish children in the 18th century is a grim commentary on Irish family poverty and England's harsh and exploitative economic policies; yet, in the first decade of the 21st century, neoliberalism has wrought its own distinctive, postmodern brand of eating its young, who have all but disappeared from the discourse of poverty and inequality in the United States. Invisible amid the startling statistics of rising unemployment and home foreclosures, devastated neighborhoods, school closures, eviscerated early childhood intervention programs, welfare defunding, social service cuts, and a myriad other contractions of the public space, children have become the "collateral damage" of free market fundamentalism and its silent wars on the most vulnerable, as the drumbeat for leaner and meaner "small government" reverberates across the corporate trinity of media-legislative-lobbyist air waves.

INEQUALITY AND ITS COSTS

As Tony Judt (2010) has pointed out, "It is one thing to dwell amongst inequality and its pathologies; [but] it is quite another to revel in them" and the evidence of "collective impoverishment" that surrounds us while public infrastructures crumble is everywhere (pp. 22, 12), juxtaposed against the staggering wealth that is concentrated among the top 1% who now control 23.5% of the total national income (Reich, 2010). During the past decades the welfare state in the United States has unraveled as economic deregulation has led to vast disparities in wealth, opportunities, and access to education and, argues Judt (2010), the corruption of our moral sensibilities is so endemic that we have become inured "to the human costs of apparently rational social policies, especially when we are advised that they will contribute to overall prosperity and thus—implicitly—to our separate interests" (p. 23).

The downward distribution of human costs disproportionately affects children, and, paradoxically, the youngest among us endure the worst of the damage. For single mothers and their children, the damage has been particularly corrosive—15.5 million women live in poverty and almost 5.5 million single mothers (87.8%) who have dependent children do not receive any TANF (welfare) cash assistance, and these numbers are highest in the swath of Southern states: Florida, Georgia, Alabama, Mississippi, Louisiana, and Texas (Henrici, Helmuth, Zlotnick, & Hayes, 2010). Standing silently in the shadows behind every mother lacking cash assistance are young children, who experience the developmentally damaging impacts of poverty with long-lasting and often irreversible scars. Paul Krugman (2008), writing in the *New York Times*, reports recent research from the American Association for the Advancement of Science that documents the toxic effects of poverty on young children's physical, neurological, and emotional development, leading Krugman to conclude that "to be poor in America is to be an outcast in your own country."

The United States is now an outlier among other wealthy, industrialized countries in failing to create a viable social safety net for children and their parents. The latest international UNICEF report on inequality and child well-being ranks the United States last among all 24 OECD countries in overall equality; 23rd in material well-being of children, 19th in educational well-being, and 22nd in health well-being—a shameful record, indeed, for one of the wealthiest and most powerful democracies. The Innocenti Report Card also highlights "bottom-end inequality" arguing that "protecting children during their vital, vulnerable years of growth is both the mark of a civilized society and the means of building a better future" (UNICEF, 2010, p. 1).

Clearly, by international standards the United States has failed to meet the criteria of a "civilized" democracy and violates children's rights to a viable future. In addition, the United States has still not ratified the central human rights treaty affirming children's rights—the United Nations Convention on the Rights of the Child (CRC)—and violates many of the fundamental provisions of the CRC: children's economic, social, and cultural rights (Article 4); the establishment of institutions, facilities, and social programs for the support of children, and the right to child care (Article 18); rights and access to services for *all* children with special needs (Article 23); access to and quality of health care (Article 24); rights to social insurance and social security (Article 26); and equality of opportunity in education (Article 28) (United Nations General Assembly, 1989).

As we begin the second decade of the 21st century, the "prerogatives of capital" and a "cultural trope" of personal responsibility dominate the inexorable machinery of neoliberalism, which is characterized by economic deregulation, welfare devolution, and an erosion of benefits juxtaposed against an ever-expanding penal state (Wacquant, 2009, pp. 306–307), with escalating harm to U.S. children and youth. Always the first targets of the full onslaught of conservative attacks on the "social state," it is clear that children's vulnerability increases as the public space contracts in the interests of privatization and "small government," with a consequent deficit of protective social policies. Perhaps the most disturbing outcome of the personal responsibility trope is the virtual eclipse of poverty from public discourse. Bob Herbert (2011), writing about the extremes of wealth and poverty in a *New York Times* op-ed column, rhetorically asks: "How do you imagine a family of four would live if its annual income was $11,000 or less?" pointing out that over 17 million people in the United States now live below half of the poverty line; yet, he comments, "no one talks about these families and individuals living in extreme poverty."

The social citizenship rights that exist in the European Union— particularly Scandinavia— guaranteeing universal rights of access to welfare, child care, health care, paid parental leave, social security, and education from infancy through the postsecondary years—create far more family stability and hence act as effective poverty remediation measures, influenced by the international obligations of the CRC which shape child policies and practices. Wherever greater degrees of *decommodification* are in place,[1] child poverty rates are lower, particularly in the top OECD countries—Denmark, Finland, The Netherlands, and Switzerland—and women and children tend to fare better during economic downturns. Such social citizenship rights are also critical gendered rights, for such rights guarantee "a positive state" for women and their children (Hobson & Lister, 2002) through the creation of policies that sustain families such as universal child care and paid family leave policies, making possible the combining of work and family life. Yet, in contrast to most countries in Northern and Western Europe and Canada, there is no commitment in the United States to the establishment of social citizenship rights, nor to the affirmative obligations engendered by the CRC. The European Union's emphasis on social inclusion, equality, and expanded access to child care services for infants and children in alignment with the CRC are absent, as is any public discourse about social citizenship rights, which have never found a ready foothold in the United States with the concomitant ideals of social solidarity and universal policies that promote economic and social rights to a minimally decent life. Fraser and Gordon (1992) point out that the United States has a rich discourse about "'civil citizenship' but a near total silence about 'social citizenship'" (p. 47). Even when such rights are diluted and promoted as a public good (witness the right-wing attack on health care reform), such policy proposals are transmuted into a threat discourse of "socialism" à la Glenn Beck, Fox News, Rush Limbaugh, and the frenzied Tea Party rhetoric, such that the pervasive hegemony of individual rights and privatization of interests is normalized, and the very notion of public responsibility becomes suspect.

Unfettered free market fundamentalism run amuck now characterizes the U. S. policy landscape in the 21st century. Escalating cuts to the remaining vestiges of the social state have further eroded benefits and services to vulnerable families and exacerbated the vast inequalities that characterize the daily lives of poor and ethnic-minority children. Child poverty is now the crisis of our times, demanding redress; yet it has hardly emerged as a critical issue amid the discourse of recession, unemployment, deficit reduction, social spending cuts, and, at the time of this writing, extension of the tax cuts for the wealthiest among us. Currently urban school reform, assessment, accountability, and student achievement—all of which do constitute critical educational issues—dominate the educational arena. However, scant attention has been paid to poverty and its jagged imprints; for on the shoulders of every vulnerable schoolchild there is a backpack weighted with poverty's burdens—chronic housing instability and homelessness, food insecurity, dislocated families, interrupted learning, and the childhood terrors that emerge from a resource-less daily world. It is essential that such material and social conditions are understood in the daily context of young lives, for poverty relentlessly maps the pathways of childhood, shaping the terrain of diminished possibilities and eroding human capabilities.

While children account for 25% of the U.S. population, they represent 36% of all poor people, and the poorest and youngest children live in single-female-headed households. There are 25 million young children under the age of 6—11.7 million live in low-income families[2] and 6.1 million live under the federal poverty level (FPL). In the years between 2000 and 2009, child poverty increased dramatically; and for very young children (under age 6) the numbers in poverty increased by almost 2 million—from 4.2 million in 2000 to 6.1 million in 2009, pointing to a 46% increase! Children of color (African American, Latino, and American Indian) are also disproportionately poor, with 41% of African American children under 6 living in poor families in contrast to 15% of young White children (Chau, Thampi, & Wight, 2010a). Food insecurity (defined as a lack of consistent access to sufficient food) has also increased dramatically, with almost 30% of poor households reporting food insecurity among children (Wight, Thampi, & Briggs, 2010). With 15.3 million of the nation's children living below the poverty threshold and 31.3 million living in low-income households (Chau, Thampi, & Wight, 2010b), child poverty is a pervasive and socially toxic threat to children's well-being.

The Katrina disaster of 2005 is an instructive case to examine in order to understand the callous public indifference toward impoverished communities—communities that frequently comprise disproportionate numbers of single mothers and their children. The confluence of poverty, race, and gender intersected dramatically in 2006 in New Orleans, illustrating the shameful disregard of the state toward its most vulnerable children and families. When a poor community gets hit by disaster in a society eviscerated by free market policies, children once again become the first victims of immense suffering.

POVERTY AND DISASTER IN A "DE-WELFARED" STATE

An examination of the 2006 Katrina tragedy is iconic of the indifference to social suffering in a "de-welfared" state and, too, is illustrative of what Klein (2007) has termed "disaster capitalism." With 1,500 deaths, a million residents displaced, and over $100 billion in damaged and destroyed infrastructures (Jones-DeWeever, 2008), profiteering, mass class/ethnic "cleansing," and the dismantling of the public school system—already in disarray pre-Katrina—became the order of the day. The impact of neoliberal policies takes particular form during and after a disaster, and such policies are inextricably entwined with the contracting of the public space. The human rights of women and children, particularly those who are vulnerable—poor, homeless, of color, and "other"—become expendable and their lives are disproportionately impacted (Henrici, Helmuth, & Braun, 2010; Jones-DeWeever, 2008; World Health Organization, 2002). For the impoverished women of New Orleans, Katrina was both a gendered and racialized disaster. Before the devastation wrought by Hurricane Katrina, the poverty rate for single mothers (40%) was one of the highest in the nation (Ransby, 2006). Most public housing was destroyed and there was a mass exodus of single mothers of color as all basic infrastructures were destroyed. In the years following, as New Orleans has rebuilt, poverty rates among low-income women and girls of color have plummeted, as many original residents have been unable to return because of the acute absence of housing in the public sector (Institute for Women's Policy Research, 2010).

In 2005, pre-Katrina New Orleans had one of the highest child poverty rates in the country, as families on the Gulf coast were trapped by poverty, lack of resources, scarring educational inequalities, and a school system in disarray. Poor children in Louisiana, Mississippi, and Alabama were among the poorest in the nation, with almost 25% of children in Mississippi living in poverty and 12% in extreme poverty (less than half of the federal poverty level). When the disaster struck, their families were trapped, lacking both resources and transportation to leave. The contrast in poverty rates among Black and White children in 2005 was strikingly emblematic of broader racial and economic discrimination: In those three Gulf coast states, for example, 44% of Black children lived in poverty in contrast to 9% of White children (Fass & Cauthen, 2005).

Children who experienced extreme poverty and chronic instability before the storm were also the children most traumatized when the hurricane hit, impacting their emotional development, their cognitive readiness, and their educational access. There were repeated disrupted attachments in time spent away from their mothers, relocations from schools and neighborhoods, and for many, terrors during the storm and its aftermath. Reports indicate that 20,000 children under age 6 were in shelters for prolonged periods of time, experiencing not only their own stress and anxiety, but that of their parents as well. Frequently, no parent was present to act as a buffer against traumatizing experiences of loss and desperation. Many young children who were evacuated and arrived in shelters were extremely withdrawn, could not eat, and were afraid of strangers. Estimates point to 56,000 pregnant women and 75,000 infants as physically harmed by Hurricane Katrina's aftermath. Lack of clean water, environmental toxins, no access to health care, unsanitary and crowded shelters—all contributed to the toxic environments for infants and their mothers (Callagan et al., 2007).

Early intervention services provided by Head Start centers ceased to exist (240 centers were damaged, 62 in Louisiana alone), and those services, even when functioning pre-Katrina, provided inadequate access to serve the needs of poor young children (Golden, 2006). For older children, many of them living without parents on their own, increases in the levels of school aggression and violence have been reported (Nossiter, 2006). Over 38% of children have been diagnosed with anxiety, depression, or a behavior disorder. The Gulf Coast Child and Family Health Study reports that, based on school enrollment and census data, more than 160,000 children under 18 were displaced and tens of thousands of children continue to be displaced from families, schools, and communities and were still unhoused 5 years after the storm.

Disasters exact a far more pernicious toll on children. There are multiple stressors, security and trust are crushed at critical stages of development, losses compound—home, friends, pets, artifacts, ties to school—and the poorer a child is, the more vulnerable to disasters with concomitant lack of resources and services (Abramson, Park, Stehling-Ariza, & Redlener, 2010). Physical violence, rape, compromised safety and security—all hit women and children hardest, particularly in public shelters; caregiving responsibilities are disrupted, pregnant women and young children are at increased risk for an array of infections and illnesses, and the stress affecting women compounds as many begin to suffer from symptoms of posttraumatic stress disorder (Jones-De Weever, 2008; Enarson & Morrow, 1998). In addition, as Enarson (2006) points out, the task of rebuilding communities without women's labor and engagement is extremely difficult, for households cannot function without the necessary social infrastructures, which include child care, schools, transportation, and public health clinics.

While the Katrina tragedy illuminates both the feminization and racialization of poverty in all its stark contours, women and children are living on the edges in vast numbers all across the United States, with African American and Latina women experiencing disproportionately high rates of poverty. Over a quarter of women living in poverty are single mothers with dependent children, and they are twice as likely to be poor compared to single fathers. The gender wage gap (women earn 77% of what men make in comparable occupations), occupational segregation in unstable, low-wage jobs, the dual responsibilities of being both provider and caregiver for dependent children (Cawthorne, 2008)—all coalesce to create fragile households with few exits out of poverty. In the absence of social care infrastructures, lack of access to child care is another edge issue frequently catapulting women and children into destitution and homelessness (Polakow, 2007).

To give life to the facts just presented, the following section portrays a snapshot of the daily struggles of a single mother coping with a traumatized child and a deficit of care.

TRAUMATIZED CHILDREN AND THE STRUGGLE FOR FAMILY SURVIVAL

June is a single mother of five children living in poverty in Iowa, a victim and survivor of domestic violence and now in recovery from a period of substance abuse, during which time her children were temporarily placed in foster care. She has recently regained custody of the children, and 5-year-old Joseph who has endured multiple foster care placements bears the most visible scars. Joseph is described by several adult caregivers and teachers as "unmanageable," and he has been expelled and bounced around from one child care setting to another, "demoted" from kindergarten, and recently placed on medication. June, whose custody of the children is dependent on her remaining "clean" and employed, faces the daunting prospect of searching for a low-wage job and finding good-quality child care. However, she cannot get any financial assistance from the Iowa welfare-to-work program for temporary child care, and now finds herself caught in the classic welfare paradox—no job without child care but no child care without a job—as she struggles to balance all the other competing demands of her fragile and destabilized family.

With assistance from a local advocacy coalition, June finds a job working in the kitchen of a local high school from 9 to 3 every day and, with child care subsidies in place, enrolls her baby and Joseph in a family day care setting. However, Joseph's disruptive behavior— hitting, spitting, screaming, biting—creates an ongoing problem for June as the child care provider isolates and punishes Joseph, causing the behavior to escalate, and will not keep him in the program nor attempt to work with June in helping to support him. Over the next months, Joseph is bounced around from placement to placement because of his misbehavior. Demoted from kindergarten, expelled from his public prekindergarten and several private child care settings, Joseph is a marginalized and unwanted young child. Because he has special needs, it is not easy to find a center that will accept him, as many centers use quotas to limit the number of children on state subsidies.

With the notable exception of an earlier and brief but successful Head Start placement in another city, the norm has been exclusion and an unwillingness to deal with his special needs. June remarks:

> They just aren't equipped to handle kids that have behavior issues. . . . They deal with it for a short time, but they get to the point where they can't handle it. And so, you know, the place that my child's currently in now, he [the provider] says he does crisis care, but he's getting to the point where he can't handle it either.

Joseph has been assessed by a psychologist at the mental health clinic; after a cursory and inadequate assessment, the psychologist prescribes Ritalin for Joseph and recommends sending Joseph away to a residential facility over 200 miles away. While Joseph is clearly an emotionally destabilized and demanding child, some of his "problem" behaviors—described as "aggressive" (hitting, scratching, biting), not paying attention, and not following directions—are not atypical and fall within the outer boundaries of challenging preschool behaviors. Joseph appears to be exhibiting some symptoms of posttraumatic stress disorder (PTSD), which no doubt arise from his early exposure to family violence as well as abandonment, when he was placed in several foster care placements during his critical early years, as his mother struggled to overcome a history of substance abuse. However, because June is a single mother in poverty, overwhelmed by multiple responsibilities—Joseph's "unmanageable" behaviors, her older children's problems, the demands of a new baby, a constant deficit of economic resources and time, dread of another child care expulsion, and the fear of losing her job—5-year-old Joseph has become a threat to his fragile family's existence, as June states:

> I can't keep going on like this. The day care guy's getting to the point where he can't do it anymore, and I have to go to work to pay the bills, and so if I don't have no day care, then I can't work, you know.

Sending a little boy away from his mother for up to a year indeed appears to be a drastic intervention born of a mother's desperate need to maintain a low-wage job, while feeling stretched to a breaking point by the competing demands on her time and emotional energy. Neither the mental health system, nor the welfare system, nor the public kindergarten or prekindergarten has invested adequate time and resources in providing ongoing and intensive therapeutic interventions for Joseph, a child coping with a traumatic early childhood. In addition, the glaring absence of affordable high-quality child care that could offer developmentally supportive interventions only increases the mounting pressure on June, who remarks that Joseph "has been through a lot of stuff . . . and it's not all his fault you know—he was in an environment where it wasn't good for the first 4 years of his life."

Clearly for poor children like Joseph who have "been through a lot of stuff," there is minimal public support available, certainly no high-quality professional child care settings where crisis interventions and appropriate developmental supports are provided. The absence of such supportive interventions in Joseph's life created a situation of forced abandonment because his desperate mother could see no other way out. The psychologist, in evaluating Joseph's failure to adapt and adjust to the inflexible routines of cheap, inferior-quality child care settings, failed to consider how negative and harsh child care environments may have actually contributed to Joseph's experience of rejection and exacerbated his fears of abandonment. It is significant that only a year earlier Joseph had shown considerable progress in a high-quality Head Start center in June's former community, where his special needs were acknowledged and he was given individualized attention and developmentally supportive interventions. However, having aged out of Head Start and in the absence of available and affordable high-quality child care programs, Joseph has been marked for expulsion and exile—where no doubt his earlier trauma of abandonment will only be compounded by the removal from his home. Rejection, as Garbarino (1995) points out "corrodes and damages the sense of self-worth in much the same way that cancer damages the body; it twists a child's outlook and makes every action painful" (p. 195).

In June's situation, poverty, family violence, and the accumulation of other risk factors overwhelmed her capacity to cope. Poverty, stressed parenting, emotionally destabilized childhoods, inadequate and inferior child care settings all increase psychosocial risks, where powerlessness is a key factor. Joseph at 5 years old is the visible casualty of a deficit of family policies that leads to a set of tragic outcomes. Investments in Joseph's early life and extensive family supports are not present in a society where the discourse of personal responsibility has eclipsed any form of public responsibility for the consequences of deep family poverty and inequality. Joseph's early childhood, like those of millions of other poor children, is highly commodified, and his rights to healthy development have been severely compromised. In another country perhaps June could dream of a different future for her family, but not here, not now, in the United States, where difficult poor children are easily discarded.

ACCESS AND QUALITY: A CRISIS OF CARE

In the absence of a national child care system, uniform licensing and credentialing requirements, or federal quality controls, the likelihood of poor children accessing high-quality child care is low; hence poor children are cheap children, populating the unlicensed sector (two of Joseph's placements) or cheap centers where staff salaries are lower and many lack any child care training. Standards are nonexistent in many states—only 21 require licenses for all child care centers and 40 have no postsecondary requirements for "teachers." In these states, only a high school education or GED is the minimal qualification, with no training in early education and child development required (Helburn & Bergmann, 2002; National Institute for Early Education Research [NIEER], 2003). While affluent parents can purchase high-quality child care (close to $16,000 a year for infant care and almost $12,000 a year for full-time preschool care), low-income parents, and specifically single mothers, also must purchase care on the private market. Nationally, only one seventh of low-income parents receive child care subsidies with long waiting lists across the states; and child care subsidies, pegged at 75% of market rates, do not pay the full cost of care, frequently leaving parents with high co-pays of several hundred dollars per month (Children's Defense Fund 2008; Polakow, 2007). Moreover, as states ax human services and education budgets, child care subsidies are rapidly eroded. Hence affordable care means the cheapest of care: inferior quality, unsafe locations, and unstable makeshift multiple care arrangements, with one third of poor children in the unlicensed and unregulated sector (Chaudry, 2004; Ebb, 1994; Helburn & Bergmann, 2002; Polakow, 2007). Many families spend more per month on infant care than on food, and in 2009 child care costs for two children exceeded median rent costs in all of the states (National Association of Child Care Resource & Referral Agencies, 2009).

The problem of substandard and often developmentally dangerous care for low-income children, particularly infants and toddlers, has been widely documented (Helburn, 1995; National Scientific Council on the Developing Child, 2007); at the same time, numerous research studies point to the positive benefits and increased cognitive and social competence of poor children enrolled in good-quality child care settings. High-quality child care for low-income children appears to function as a protective factor, with clearly beneficial outcomes for children with special education needs (Barnett, 1998; Peisner-Feinberg, Burchinal, & Clifford, 1999; Schweinhart, 2004).

While the research on the benefits of high-quality child care and early intervention is dramatic, both for children who have special needs and for those living in low-income families, it is precisely such children who lack access to high-quality child care services and early interventions. Children with multiple needs and challenging behaviors do not fare well in harsh and punitive child care programs that provide inferior-quality care and developmentally inappropriate interventions. Furthermore, in such settings many young children are constructed as "trouble" if they are not compliant and fail to adhere to rigid routines and management agendas that stifle curiosity and erode play. When bad child care leads to multiple, disrupted placements, marginalized children must endure yet another developmental assault, increasing the "social toxicity" of their small and vulnerable worlds.

While K–12 public education is free and accessible to all children despite eroding access and unequal opportunities, the same is not true for early childhood education, arguably the most critical and formative period of development. As Kozol (1992) points out in his damning indictment of the savage inequalities of education, "the immense resources which the nation does in fact possess go not to the child in greatest need but to the child of the highest bidder" (p.79). In the case of Joseph, a child with special needs compounded by family poverty, another widespread and disturbing phenomenon emerges: High-quality special needs child care is neither accessible nor affordable for the majority of low-income children. Publicly funded early interventions for troubled and traumatized young children do exist in select preprimary special education programs, but those programs require referrals and assessments, and many poor parents are simply unable to access them. Some states pay higher subsidy rates for special needs care, but there is a great variation among the states in terms of the criteria and additional costs, and the documentation required is often onerous so there is not much incentive for providers to accept poor children who are "problems." Early intervention programs like Head Start serve only half of eligible preschool children, and existing state-funded public prekindergarten initiatives lack quality standards and many provide only half-day programs (Children's Defense Fund, 2008; NIEER, 2003; Shonkoff & Phillips, 2000).

The increasing trend toward expulsion and disenrollment of toddlers and preschoolers from their child care programs for "out-of-control" behaviors appears to follow on the heels of broader "zero-tolerance" policies enacted within the K–12 public education system. Young children perceived by teachers and child care providers in early childhood settings to be disruptive and unmanageable are now being expelled and are in jeopardy of experiencing failure even before starting kindergarten. For poor children the consequences are particularly damaging, exacerbating existing inequalities that begin before children ever set foot in public school. For vulnerable young children like Joseph, who has already experienced multiple stressors in his early years—domestic violence, parental abandonment, poverty, unstable housing, poor-quality child care—an expulsion may be the tipping point in terms of family viability. Once expelled, a young child risks exclusion from other early childhood settings, and developmental risks compound. Poor children and children of color, traditionally ill-served by public education, are likely to suffer the most adverse consequences, as they are launched on a trajectory of academic and social failure. For single-parent families in particular, we can see how expulsion may also induce a downward spiral of events that threaten a family's survival: Lack of child care may lead to loss of a job, which in turn leads to eviction, homelessness, and destitution. It was precisely that threat that shaped June's decision regarding her son.

ZERO TOLERANCE AND THE SCHOOL-TO-PRISON-PIPELINE

Since the passage of the Gun-Free Schools Act (GFSA) of 1994, signed into law during the Clinton administration, states are required to implement a 1-year mandatory expulsion of students found in possession of a firearm on school property. However, school districts across the nation have expanded zero-tolerance policies to include drug offenses as well as minor behavioral infractions, such as insubordination, fighting, and failure to complete homework assignments. Every year more than 3 million children are suspended and 100,000 more are permanently expelled from school from kindergarten through 12th grade (Fuentes, 2003). The concept of zero tolerance has now infused educational policies and practices so that harsh punishment, rather than remediation and rehabilitation, has become the norm. Students of color are disproportionately impacted, vulnerable and needy children and youth are pushed out and/or are permanently barred from educational access; legal protections are rarely enforced; and many children are funneled into the juvenile justice or adult prison system. The Advancement Project and the Civil Rights Project (2000) joint report presents disturbing findings of racial bias and lack of due process for public school students, where nationally African American students are suspended at 2.3 times the rate of White students, effectively disrupting, or in many cases, terminating their education. Robbins (2008) argues that zero-tolerance policies exacerbate "racial injustice through exclusion and restriction of life opportunities" and that the consequences of such policies "threaten(s) the fabric and possibility of democracy" (p. 115).

The GFSA was ostensibly aimed at preventing weapons in schools; yet gun ownership was, and is, recklessly promoted in all other public spaces. Guns have long constituted the smallest category of school offenses, but zero-tolerance policies under GFSA have been expanded to include drug and alcohol offenses as well as minor student infractions of school discipline codes. Zero-tolerance policies further perpetuate existing school inequities, ignore children's developmental needs, and by criminalizing so-called problem behaviors, exacerbate the growing trend of a "school-to-prison pipeline" (Advancement Project, 2000; Zweifler & DeBeers, 2002). The criminalizing of children, the embedding of armed police in fortress-like schools, characterized by school lockdowns, locker searches, student interrogations, and surveillance cameras, has led to a dramatic increase in the number of school-based arrests (Dohrn, 2000). Student behaviors that in earlier decades might have been considered defiant or out-of-control, requiring school-based discipline, detention, or other sanctions, have now transmuted into school-based "crimes"—so that troublesome and troubled children are seen not as students in need of guidance and developmentally appropriate discipline, but rather as felons to be incarcerated. Extreme and harsh responses to "bad" behavior have resulted in innumerable publicized incidents of students, some in their primary years, being arrested and marched out of their schools in handcuffs (Hurst, 2005).

As increasing numbers of children are shut out of the education system, it is also clear that zero tolerance has extended downwards, so that even preschool children who exhibit "challenging" behaviors are no longer immune from the damaging consequences of exclusion, as we saw earlier in the case of 5-year-old Joseph. Recent trends indicate that it is actually very young children who are most at risk for expulsion; they are expelled from child care settings (which include all public and private prekindergarten and child care programs) at a rate that is 3.2 times higher than the rate for K–12 students; and a disproportionate number are low-income children with behavioral problems or special needs. Prekindergarten expulsion rates are higher in private, for-profit, and faith-affiliated child care programs than in classrooms located in public schools and Head Start centers, where regulation and accountability measures are more likely to be in place (Gilliam, 2005).

Once expelled, children may actually be deprived of their fundamental right to an education. By the year 2000, only 26 states required alternative education assignments for students suspended or expelled. After an expulsion takes place, no school is required to readmit the student, thus casting thousands of youths out onto the streets, often for minor nonviolent infractions: aspirin, paper clips, nail files, scissors, a grandfather's Swiss army knife used for "show and tell"— all apparent cause for expulsion for "drug and weapons possession" from kindergarten on up. A news clip from Mississippi is illustrative of this trend: Five African American boys were throwing peanuts on the school bus and one accidentally hit the driver. She called the police and the 16-year-olds were arrested for felonious assault, which carries a maximum penalty of 5 years in prison. The sheriff was quoted in the local newspaper, *The Clarion Ledger*, saying "this time it was peanuts, but if we don't get a handle on it, the next time it could be bodies!" (Advancement Project, 2000).

YOUTH INCARCERATION

The school-to-prison pipeline and the social shifts in sensibility and practice from rehabilitation to punishment, to "adult time for adult crime," have resulted in an unprecedented industry of child incarceration, increases in prison budgets, and decreases in education and mental health budgets as growing numbers of youth (particularly those with special needs) are placed in the adult and juvenile criminal systems. A recent editorial in the *New York Times* pointed out that "many of America's juvenile jails would be empty if schools obeyed federal law and provided disabled children with the special instruction that they need" ("Writing off Disabled Children," 2008, p. A19). This shift from rehabilitation to retribution constructs children and youth as "other"— they have lost their rights to childhood as a space for development and self-formation. Instead their early identities are fixed and framed as ex-children, and they are consigned to the liminal edges of the social order.

Where once the United States was a beacon of progressive juvenile reform with the first juvenile court established in Chicago in 1899, little more than a century later it has become an "incarceration nation." The 1998 Juvenile Justice Reform Act replaced the commitment to "the best interests of the child" with a far more menacing intent to hold children "accountable" for their misdeeds (Dohrn, 2000). This personal accountability and personal responsibility rhetoric mirrored the language of other legislation passed during the 1990s, most notably welfare "reform," and in the case of the 1998 Juvenile Justice Reform Act resulted in an erosion of public responsibility for children and youth. Large numbers of adolescents now spend their formative years in juvenile lockup facilities or, worse, in adult prisons.

Once incarcerated, children experience fundamental violations of their human rights. James Bell, founder and director of the W.

Haywood Burns Institute for Juvenile Justice, has documented the disproportional number of young people of color in the juvenile justice system. His work, monitoring conditions of confinement for youth and litigating on their behalf, points to alarming numbers of youth being incarcerated in overcrowded facilities and the growing number of states that have lowered the age at which juveniles can be charged in adult courts. Bell (2000) cites the case of an 11-year-old in Michigan who was prosecuted as an adult for second-degree murder. The report on human rights abuses of juveniles by Amnesty International (1998) documents appalling conditions of confinement and treatment of children in custody who have been "subjected to brutal physical force and cruel punishments" (p. 1) and, once they enter the prison pipeline, "they experience violations of their fundamental human rights" (p.1).

A recent national study by Human Rights Watch and Amnesty International (2005) that investigated the practice of trying children as adults and sentencing them to life without parole, reveals that there are at least 2,225 children in adult prison sentenced to life without parole. All were for crimes committed before the youths were 18 years old and 16% of the youth offenders were 13–15 years old, with almost 60% first-time offenders. In addition, 26% of youth serving life without parole were not convicted of murder, but instead were convicted of "felony murder" (where anyone involved in the commission of a crime when someone is killed, irrespective of intent, is also judged guilty of murder). African American youth are disproportionately sentenced to life without parole (6.5 per 10,000 in comparison to White teens at 0.6 per 10,000). William Schulz, Executive Director of Amnesty International, is quoted in the report as decrying the actions of courts that function as "assembly lines that mass produce mandatory life without parole sentences for children that ignore their enormous potential for change and rob them of all hopes for redemption" (Human Rights Watch, 2005, p. 2). Legislation in 42 states now permits youth to receive life-without-parole sentences.

While the scope of this chapter does not include an analysis of the $60 billion incarceration industry, and the outsourcing of confinement to privatized "Blackwater" sites, it is noteworthy that the United States, with 5% of the world's population, holds 25% of the world's inmates in U.S. prisons (Talvi, 2007), incarcerating more people than any other country, including China and Russia. The Pew Center (2008) reports that 2.3 million adults (1 in 100) are now incarcerated. While one in 54 men, 18 years and older, is incarcerated, for African American men in that same age group, the figure jumps to 1 in 15 (and for African American men 20–34, to 1 in 9). Although men are 10 times more likely to be incarcerated than women, the female incarceration rate is rapidly increasing, particularly for African American young women, and 80% of the women behind bars are mothers. In addition, the costs that individual states spend on corrections have skyrocketed in the past decade, and the collective increases that states across the nation committed in expenditures for prisons stand in sharp contrast to expenditures for higher education—127% versus 21%—indicative of grossly misplaced priorities where states that house sparkling new prisons simultaneously scramble to find scarce preschool funding dollars. Ironically, the prison industry has become the largest public housing program, with construction budgets for prisons exceeding those for higher education (Wacquant, 2009).

When we consider the alarming growth of the prison state, and the toxic consequences for children and youth, it is clear that the United States violates the human rights of children and youth in a myriad of ways—damaging their human capabilities, crushing their educational opportunities, and in the most dire cases, discarding them for life. Having failed to ratify the Convention on the Rights of the Child, or to implement the provisions of the International Covenant on Civil and Political Rights, the United States now occupies the position of a pariah state on the world stage; U.S. "exceptionalism" has led to one of the worst records among wealthy industrialized countries in terms of the treatment, care, protection, and affirmation of the rights of children.

POVERTY AND CHILDREN'S RIGHTS

It is the growing inequality in and between societies that generates so many social pathologies. Grotesquely unequal societies are also unstable societies. They generate internal division and, sooner or later, internal strife—usually with undemocratic outcomes.

—Tony Judt (2010, p. 235)

Despite the promise of the Obama presidency, poverty and inequality have been eclipsed from the public discourse where it seems any policy proposals that speak to the public good form the basis for frenzied right-wing attacks against any vestiges of social citizenship rights. At the time of writing, a Democratic congresswoman from Arizona has been critically wounded, the victim of an attempted assassination, for vocally opposing Arizona's draconian immigration practices and for supporting the health care reform bill (Lacey & Herszenhorn, 2011). And as our society becomes even more "grotesquely unequal," the anger, bigotry, and racism unleashed against President Obama, as well as the unrelenting onslaught against any social spending that targets poverty, the vitriol against undocumented immigrants and the so-called anchor babies, and the unremitting hostility targeted against those who are "other," all create fertile ground for the development of neofascist policies (such as Arizona's anti-immigrant policies), fueling the growth of the "penalization of poverty" and the construction of "social insecurity" (Wacquant, 2009, p. 295). Democratic policies that speak to redistribution of wealth and resources and the articulation of the public good become highly suspect and are branded as "Socialist" or "Communist" not only by fringe groups but by sitting legislators.

WHAT LIES AHEAD?

The contemporary discourse about poverty has been effectively transmuted into a discourse of private responsibility; however, until systemic poverty is analyzed as both a constructed consequence of economic and social policies that flourish under deregulation and upward distribution of wealth, with a concomitant absence of social citizenship rights, it is very difficult to advance progressive agendas for children. The role of government in ensuring that strong measures are taken to ensure children's healthy development and well-being means changing the discourse from one of instrumentalism to one about rights. A rights-based approach views poverty as a violation of rights and is based on the assumption that poverty can and should be eliminated in a wealthy industrialized society. Affirming children as rights bearers under the United Nations Convention on the Rights of the Child (CRC) would obligate the United States to move toward a progressive realization of the key articles of the CRC—thereby ensuring a commitment to eradicate poverty and ensure economic and social rights and eliminate hunger and homelessness (Article 4); implement universal child care for working parents (Article 18); implement universal health care (Article 24); ensure rights to youth justice, banning life imprisonment for children (Article 37); and explicitly affirm children's participation and voice in decision making about their lives (Article 12) (United Nations, 1989).

It is clear that poverty forecloses on children's human capabilities and embeds them in stratified trajectories of diminished social and educational capital. And the younger they are, the more diminished their life chances. Until we deal with child poverty and its spiraling circles of injustice, we cannot frame a progressive, democratic policy agenda that promotes the healthy development, well-being, and equality of life chances for children.

There is neither a dearth of policy models nor an absence of innovative programs and expertise to redress child poverty, both nationally and internationally. It a question of national commitment and redirection of resources. The Scandinavian countries have been most successful and emerge in international studies of child well-being, educational achievement, and poverty remediation as the most successful among wealthy countries. In countries where universalism is strong and children's well-being is premised on rights, child poverty remediation measures have been effective, and generous cash transfers, parental and maternity leave policies, and high investments in child care spending per child are critical. There are dramatic differences in spending on child care when the Scandinavian expenditures are contrasted with those in the United States: Sweden, $6,409 per child; Norway, $6,425 per child; and Denmark, $8,126 per child; whereas in the United States, with no national child care system in place and no federal paid parental leave, expenditures per child are a paltry $794 (Economic Policy Institute, 2010).

Britain's spending on child care has also increased dramatically in the past decade, to $3,563 per child, due to radical policy changes as a consequence of the 2003 Green Paper, *Every Child Matters*, and the Children's Act of 2004 (HM Government, 2003, 2004). With high rates of child poverty, Britain has achieved impressive reductions in little over a decade. Under former Prime Minister Blair, who pledged to reduce child poverty in half by 2010 and to end child poverty by 2020, Britain's New Labour government made considerable progress; and poverty remediation policies were continued under Prime Minister Gordon Brown. Waldfogel's (2010) recent comprehensive analysis points to the success of extensive family supports, combined with a large expansion of child care facilities and child care slots, which, together with an increase in the minimum wage, resulted in a dramatic 50% reduction of child poverty rates from 3.4 million to 1.8 million children in the decade between 1999 and 2009. Investments in Sure Start for low-income families with infants and toddlers and the expansion of child care placements despite the economic recession have resulted in dramatic improvements in child and family well-being as investments in child care led to expanded facilities, training, and access. Describing the British record on poverty remediation as "extraordinary," Waldfogel lays out several policy lessons for the United States, proposals that echo those of the Center for American Progress (CAP), and the Economic Policy Institute, and other liberal think tanks. These proposals include: heavy investments in early education and child care from birth to school-age; guarantees of child care subsidies to all low-income families with universal preschool for all children age 3 and up; paid parental leave, raising the minimum wage, and universal health care; expanding child tax credits; and introducing antipoverty initiatives such as "Half in Ten," which CAP initiated based on the British policy initiatives. In 2007, CAP estimated that the poverty reduction strategies would cost about $90 billion a year. This contrasts dramatically with the recent Republican opposition to allowing the Bush tax cuts to expire for those with incomes over $200,000—which might have yielded $100 billion a year (Herszenhorn, 2010). That alone could have financed CAP's poverty reduction agenda. Yet, the Obama White House and the Democrats yielded in the face of intransigent opposition and reached a bipartisan compromise that resulted in an $801 billion tax cut with $57 billion in extended unemployment benefits. Hence the first decade of the 21st century ended with a shower of perks for the wealthiest and deepening gulfs of poverty for increasing numbers of Americans.

As child poverty inexorably rises, we may well ask, What are the moral boundaries of a modern and powerful democracy? How much loss and constructed harm (by policy fiat) will be tolerated? Hungry children when food supplies run out midmonth? Children sick and untended from lack of health care? Infants left alone in cribs because their destitute single mothers are working in minimum wage jobs, at shifts that run from 3 pm to midnight? Children expelled from school at 15 years old due to zero-tolerance policies, with nowhere to go? Children begging in the streets as postmodern street urchins? Children dying from dangers on the streets, caught up in drug and gang warfare as portrayed so starkly on HBO's series *The Wire*? Children whose childhoods have been foreclosed? At what point are the foundations of a democratic "civilized" society severely undermined by the existential and material consequences of deep inequality? Nussbaum (2000) argues that there is a set of universal norms of human capability that should form the foundation for a set of rights that citizens should receive from their governments. The principle of human capabilities means that all human beings, including children, should be treated as ends not means, "each with a life to live, deserving of both respect and resources" (p. 65). Surely, then, millions of children living in hunger, destitution, and public squalor are also our public responsibility and our future.

NOTES

1. Esping-Andersen (1990) uses the term *decommodification* to refer to the degree of independence from the harmful effects of the free market due to the protective nature of stable and universal entitlements that exist within the society. Women are particularly vulnerable to economic downturns in advanced capitalist societies and to the extent that child care, health care, parental leave, and so on are decommodified, they and their children are protected from the ravages of the free market.

2. The Federal Poverty Level (FPL) in 2010 was $22,050 for a four-person family and $18,310 for a three-person family. Families living between 100 and 200% of the FPL are classified as low-income.

3. This case narrative is drawn from Chapter 6 of *Who Cares for Our Children? The Child Care Crisis in the Other America* (Polakow, 2007).

REFERENCES

Abramson, D. M., Park, Y. S., Stehling-Ariza, T., & Redlener, I. (2010, August 23). Children as bellwethers of recovery: Dysfunctional systems and the effects of parents, households, and neighborhoods on serious emotional disturbance in children after Hurricane Katrina. *Disaster Medicine and Public Health Preparedness, 4.* doi: 10.1001/dmp.2010.7

Advancement Project and Civil Rights Project. (2000, June). Opportunities suspended: The devastating consequences of zero tolerance and school discipline policies. Cambridge, MA: Civil Rights Project, Harvard University. Retrieved from http://civilrightsproject.ucla.edu/research/k-12-education/school-discipline/opportunities-suspended-the-devastating-consequences-of-zero-tolerance-and-school-discipline-policies/crp-opportunities-suspended-zero-tolerance-2000.pdf

Amnesty International. (1998, November). *Betraying the young: Children in the U.S. justice system.* Washington, DC: Author.

Barnett, W. S. (1998). Long-term cognitive and academic effects of early childhood education on children in poverty. *Preventive Medicine, 272*(2), 204–207.

Bell, J. (2000). Throwaway children: Conditions of confinement and incarceration. In V. Polakow (Ed.), *The public assault on America's children: Poverty, violence and juvenile injustice* (pp. 188–210). New York: Teachers College Press.

Callaghan, W. M., Rasmussen, S. A., Jamieson, D. J., Ventura, S. J., Farr, S. L., Sutton, P. D., Mathews, T. J., & Posner, S. F. (2007). Health concerns of women and infants in times of natural disasters: Lessons learned from Hurricane Katrina. *Maternal and Child Health Journal, 11*(4), 307–311.

Cawthorne, A. (2008, October). *The straight facts on women in poverty.* Washington, DC: Center for American Progress. Retrieved from http://www.americanprogress.org/issues/2008/10/women_poverty.html

Center for American Progress (CAP). (2007, April). *From poverty to prosperity: A national strategy to cut poverty in half.* Retrieved from http://www. americanprogress.org/issues/2007/04/pdf/poverty_report.pdf

Chau, M., Thampi, K., & Wight, R. V. (2010a, October). *Basic facts about low-income children, 2009: Children under age 6.* New York: National Center for Children in Poverty. Retrieved from http://www.nccp.org/publications/ pub_972.html

Chau, M., Thampi, K., & Wight, R. V. (2010b, October). *Basic facts about low-income children, 2009: Children under age 18.* New York: National Center for Children in Poverty. Retrieved from http://www.nccp.org/publications/ pdf/download_368.pdf

Chaudry, A. (2004). *Putting children first: How low-wage working mothers manage child care.* New York: Russell Sage Foundation.

Children's Defense Fund. (2008). *The state of America's children.* Retrieved from http://www.childrensdefense.org/child-research-data-publications/data/ state-of-americas-children-2008-report.html

Dohrn, B. (2000). Look out kid, it's something you did: The criminalization of children. In V. Polakow (Ed.), *The public assault on America's children: Poverty, violence, and juvenile injustice* (pp. 157–187). New York: Teachers College Press.

Ebb, N. (1994, January). *Child care tradeoffs: States make painful choices.* Washington, DC: Children's Defense Fund.

Economic Policy Institute. (2010, November). *State of working America preview: A world of difference in child care funding.* Washington, DC: Author. Retrieved from http://www.epi.org/economic_snapshots/entry/state_of_ working_america_preview_a_world_of_difference_in_child_care_f/

Enarson, E. (2006, June 11). Women and girls last?: Averting the second post-Katrina disaster. *Understanding Katrina: Perspectives from the Social Sciences.* Brooklyn, NY: Social Science Research Council. Retrieved from http:// understandingkatrina.ssrc.org/Enarson/

Enarson, E., & Morrow, B. H. (Eds.). (1998). *The gendered terrain of disaster: Through women's eyes.* Westport, CT: Praeger.

Esping-Andersen, G. (1990). *The three worlds of welfare capitalism.* Cambridge, UK: Polity Press.

Fass, S., & Cauthen, N. K. (2005, September). *Child poverty in states hit by Hurricane Katrina* (Fact Sheet No. 1). New York: National Center for Children in Poverty. Retrieved from http://www.nccp.org/publications/ pdf/text_622.pdf

Fraser, N., & Gordon, L. (1992). Contract versus charity: Why is there no social citizenship in the United States? *Socialist Review, 22,* 45–68.

Fuentes, A. (2003). Discipline and punish: Zero tolerance policies have created a "lockdown" environment in schools. *The Nation, 277*(20), 17–19.

Garbarino, J. (1995). *Raising children in a socially toxic environment.* San Francisco, CA: Jossey-Bass.

Gilliam, W. (2005, May). *Prekindergarteners left behind: Expulsion rates in state prekindergarten programs.* New York: Foundation for Child Development.

Golden, O. (2006, February 11). *Young children after Katrina: A proposal to heal the damage and create opportunity in New Orleans*. Washington, DC: Urban Institute. Retrieved from http://www.urban.org/publications/900920.html

Helburn, S. W. (Ed.). (1995, June). *Cost, quality and child outcomes in child care centers. Technical Report*. (ED 386297). Denver: Center for Research in Economic and Social Policy, University of Colorado.

Helburn, S. W., & Bergmann, B. R. (2002). *America's child care problem: The way out*. New York: Palgrave.

Henrici, J. M., Helmuth, A. S., & Braun, J. (2010, August). *Women, disasters and Hurricane Katrina*. (IWPR No. D492). Washington, DC: Institute for Women's Policy Research. Retrieved from http://www.iwpr.org/publications/pubs/women-disasters-and-hurricane-katrina

Henrici, J. M., Helmuth, A. S., Zlotnick, F., & Hayes, J. (2010, September). *Women in poverty during the great recession* (IWPR No. D493). Washington, DC: Institute for Women's Policy Research. Retrieved from http://www.iwpr.org/pdf/D493.pdf

Herbert, B. (2011, January 8). Misery with plenty of company. *The New York Times*. Retrieved from http://www.nytimes.com/2011/01/08/opinion/08herbert.html

Herszenhorn, D. (2010, December 16). Congress sends $801 billion tax cut bill to Obama. *The New York Times*. Retrieved from http://www.nytimes.com/2010/12/17/us/politics/17cong.html

HM Government. (2003). *Every child matters*. Retrieved from http://www.education.gov.uk/consultations/downloadableDocs/EveryChildMatters.pdf

HM Government. (2004). *Every child matters: Change for children*. Retrieved from http://www.infed.org/archives/gov_uk/every_child_matters.htm

Hobson, B., & Lister, R. (2002). Citizenship. In B. Hobson, J. Lewis, & B. Siim (Eds.), *Contested concepts in gender and social politics* (pp. 23–54). Cheltenham, UK: Edward Elgar.

Human Rights Watch & Amnesty International. (2005, October). *The rest of their lives: Life without parole for child offenders in the United States*. New York: Human Rights Watch. Retrieved from http://hrw.org/reports/2005/us1005/

Hurst, M. (2005, May 17). Handcuffing of children raises questions. *Education Week*. Retrieved from http://www.edweek.org

Institute for Women's Policy Research (IWPR). (2010, August). *Women in New Orleans: Race, poverty, and Hurricane Katrina* (IWPR No. D490). Washington, DC: Author. Retrieved from http://iwpr.org/pdf/D490.pdf

Jones-DeWeever, A. (2007, October). Women and Katrina two years after the storm. *Vital Speeches of the Day*. Washington, DC: Institute for Women's Policy Research. Retrieved from http://www.iwpr.org/pdf/vitalspeeches.pdf

Jones-DeWeever, A. (2008). *Women in the wake of the storm: Examining the post-Katrina realities of the women of New Orleans and the Gulf Coast*. Washington, DC: Institute for Women's Policy Research. Retrieved from http://www.iwpr.org/pdf/D481.pdf

Judt, T. (2010). *Ill fares the land*. New York: Penguin Press.

Klein, N. (2007). *The shock doctrine: The rise of disaster capitalism*. New York: Metropolitan Books.

Kozol. J. (1992). *Savage inequalities: Children in America's schools*. New York: Harper Perennial.

Krugman, P. (2008, February 18). Poverty is poison. *The New York Times*. Retrieved from http://www.nytimes.com/2008/02/18/opinion/18krugman.htmlhind

Lacey, M., & Herszenhorn, D. (2011, January 8). In attack's wake, political repercussions. *The New York Times*. Retrieved from http://www.nytimes.com/2011/01/09/us/politics/09giffords.html?_r=1

National Association of Child Care Resource & Referral Agencies (NACCRA). (2009). *Parents and the high cost of child care: 2009 update*. Arlington, VA: Author. Retrieved from http://www.naccrra.org/publications/naccrra-publications/parents-and-the-high-price-of-child-care-2009

National Institute for Early Education Research (NIEER). (2003, August/September). America shortchanges its preschoolers: Few states require teacher training. *Preschool Matters, 1*(1). Retrieved from http://nieer.org/psm/index.php?article=5

National Scientific Council on the Developing Child. (2007). *The science of early childhood development: Closing the gap between what we know and what we do*. Retrieved from http://www.developingchild.net/

Nossiter, A. (2006, November 1). After the storm, students left alone and angry. *The New York Times*. Retrieved from http://www.nytimes.com/2006/11/01/education/01orleans.html

Nussbaum, M. C. (2000). *Women and human development: The capabilities approach*. Cambridge, UK: Cambridge University Press.

Peisner-Feinberg, E. S., Burchinal, M. R., & Clifford, R. M. (1999, June). *The children of the cost, quality, and outcomes study go to school: Executive summary*. Chapel Hill: University of North Carolina at Chapel Hill, Frank Porter Graham Child Development Center.

Pew Center on the States. (2008, February 28). *One in 100: Behind bars in America 2000*. Washington, DC: Pew Public Safety Performance Project. Retrieved from http://www.pewcenteronthestates.org/uploadedFiles/One%20in%20100.pdf

Polakow, V. (2007). *Who cares for our children: The child care crisis in the other America*. New York: Teachers College Press.

Ransby, B. (2006). Katrina, Black women, and the deadly discourse on Black poverty in America. *Du Bois Review, 3*(1), 215–222.

Reich, R. (2010). *Aftershock: The next economy and America's future*. New York: Knopf.

Robbins, C. (2008). *Expelling hope: The assault on youth and the militarization of schooling*. Albany, NY: State University of New York Press.

Schweinhart, L. J. (2004). *The High/Scope Perry Preschool study through age 40: Summary, conclusions, and frequently asked questions*. Ypsilanti, MI: HighScope Press.

Shonkoff, J. P., & Phillips, D. A. (Eds.). (2000). *From neurons to neighborhoods: The science of early childhood development*. Washington, DC: National Academy Press.

Swift, J. (1729). *A modest proposal.* Retrieved from http://art-bin.com/art/omodest.html#hit

Talvi, S. (2007, January 5). Incarceration nation. *The Nation.* Retrieved from http://www.thenation.com/doc/20070122/incarceration_nation

UNICEF Innocenti Research Centre. (2010, November). *The children left behind: A league table of inequality in child well-being in the world's rich countries* (Report Card 9). Retrieved from http://www.unicef-irc.org/files/documents/d-3796-The-Children-Left-Behind-.pdf

United Nations General Assembly. (1989). *Convention on the Rights of the Child.* Retrieved from http://www2.ohchr.org/english/law/crc.htm

Wacquant, L. (2009). *Punishing the poor: The neoliberal government of insecurity.* Durham, NC: Duke University Press.

Waldfogel, J. (2010, December 7). *Tackling poverty and improving child well-being: Lessons from Britain.* Retrieved from http://www.firstfocus.net/library/reports/tackling-child-poverty-and-improving-child-well-being-lessons-from-britain

Wight, V. R., Thampi, K., & Briggs, J. (2010, August). *Who are America's poor children? Examining food insecurity among children in the United States.* New York: National Center for Children in Poverty. Retrieved from http://www.nccp.org/publications/pdf/text_958.pdf

World Health Organization. (2002, July). *Gender and health in disasters.* Geneva, Switzerland: Author. Retrieved from http://www.who.int/gender/other_health/en/genderdisasters.pdf

Writing off disabled children. [Editorial]. (2008, August 8). *The New York Times,* p. A19.

Zweifler, R., & DeBeers, J. (2002, Fall). How zero tolerance impacts our most vulnerable youth. *Michigan Journal of Race and Law, 8*(1), 191–220.

CHAPTER 6

Working with Latino Preschoolers

The Literacy and Language Goals of Teachers and Mothers

Delis Cuéllar and Eugene E. García

In order to better serve young Latino children from immigrant families, early childhood programs need to incorporate linguistically and culturally responsive teaching techniques in their everyday practices (Espinosa, 2010; National Task Force on Early Childhood Education for Hispanics, 2007). However, educational policies that have banned language accommodations for emergent bilinguals (also referred to as English language learners), the shortage of in-service professional development opportunities that focus on the special needs of students learning English as a second language, and the general lack of bilingual professionals in the early education system are serious roadblocks to providing young Latino English language learners (ELLs) with the education that they need (Buysse, Castro, West, & Skinner, 2005; García & Wiese, 2009; Lucas & Grinberg, 2008). In fact, these conditions have negatively affected the language and literacy education that they receive in the early years (García, Wiese, & Cuéllar, in press).

In recognition of the role of language in the changing demographics that U.S. schools are experiencing, we start this chapter by describing the exceptional growth in the numbers of Spanish-speaking English learners. We then briefly summarize antibilingual educational measures that have affected a large number of Latino ELLs. Next, we highlight the language issues that teachers who work with children who are learning English as a second language face by discussing the findings of a study that explored teachers' and Mexican immigrant mothers' language and literacy goals for a group of Head Start ELL children. Finally, we provide practical, research-based recommendations for addressing the needs of young Latino ELLs.

SPANISH-SPEAKING ENGLISH LANGUAGE LEARNERS

Presently a total of 55 million people age 5 and older speak a language other than English at home, an increase of 19% since 2000 (García & Cuéllar, 2006; U.S. Census Bureau, 2011). This numerical increase implies that the United States is becoming a more linguistically diverse nation. In fact the growth in the number of emergent bilingual children is a countrywide trend, for which Spanish/English is the most common combination (García & Cuéllar, 2006; National Center for Education Statistics [NCES], 2008). This is unsurprising since the United States is the fifth-largest Spanish-speaking country (Gonzalez, 2005) and children in Latino immigrant families are the fastest growing segment of the U.S. population. Moreover, of all Latin American countries represented in the United States, Mexico is the country of origin for the largest proportion of children living in immigrant families (Hernandez, Denton, & McCartney, 2007).

Latino children grow up in a variety of language environments, including English monolingual, Spanish monolingual, and multilingual homes. Using a national representative sample of children born between December 2001 and January 2002, Lopez, Barrueco, and Miles (2006) found that the great majority (75%) of 9-month-old Latino infants live in homes where at least some Spanish is spoken, with 34% growing up in homes where Spanish is the primary language, 22% where English is the primary language, and 19% where Spanish is the only language spoken. An analysis of 2000 Census data showed that a high proportion (71%) of Latino children in immigrant families live with at least one parent whose English skills are limited or who does not speak English exclusively or very well, and about half (49%) of them live with two such parents (Hernandez, 2006). Additional research shows that almost 3 of every 10 (28%) Latino toddlers (ages 0–2) reside in linguistically isolated homes, where no person over the age of 13 speaks only English or speaks English very well. This proportion increases substantially, totaling 43%, for Latino children living in immigrant households (Calderón, 2007). Notably, Latino youth show differences in language proficiency among their various generational immigration statuses. This variability suggests a strong intergenerational trend toward English monolingualism (Hernandez, 2006).

The U.S. educational system has been significantly challenged by the rapid and steady increase in the number of children who are learning English as a second language. The ELL population in public schools more than doubled, increasing from 5.1% to 10.5% between the academic years of 1993–94 (2.1 million) and 2004–05 (5.1 million) (NCES, 2004; Pearson, 2006). Most children who are learning English as a second language in the country's public schools are of Latino background, and a large proportion of Latino students are ELLs. In fact, the 45% of Latino students who are ELLs constitute 80% of all ELLs in U.S schools (Beltran & Goldwasser, 2008; Capps et al., 2005). Additionally, an impressive 86% of all Head Start programs serve children who are learning English as a second language (Beltran & Goldwasser, 2008).

ANTIBILINGUAL EDUCATIONAL INITIATIVES

At the same time that schools have experienced a significant growth in the population of Spanish-speaking students who are learning English as a second language, some states have enacted laws that have made it increasingly difficult to provide ELLs instruction in their native language. California (in 1998), Arizona (in 2000), and Massachusetts (in 2002) have all passed very similar initiatives to ban bilingual education in their respective K–12 public school systems (García & Wiese, 2009). All three laws require that English learners be transferred to mainstream, English-only classrooms after their completion of a 1-year Structured English Immersion (SEI) program. Arizona law defines SEI as:

> an English language acquisition process for young children in which nearly all classroom instruction is in English but with the curriculum and presentation designed for children who are learning the language. Books and instructional materials are in English and all reading, writing, and subject matter are taught in English. (A.R.S. §§ 7-15)

Teachers in SEI classrooms may use the native languages of students learning English as a second language only to assist them with completing a task or to answer a question, but not when formally instructing them. Additionally, while all three initiatives allow parents of English learners to request that their children receive bilingual education, the waiver procedures are very stringent and difficult for parents to follow (García et al., in press).

HOME AND SCHOOL LANGUAGE GOALS FOR PRESCHOOL LATINO ENGLISH LANGUAGE LEARNERS

The English, Spanish, and bilingual proficiency of Latino children is associated with their generational status, state laws mandating public schools' language of instruction, schools' and teachers' implementation of such laws, and family preferences and practices. The discussion below of a qualitative study illustrates how some of these variables affect the literacy and language teaching that Latino preschool children receive. We share findings that are part of a larger study that explored the literacy development of Mexican American, Spanish-dominant children at home and school. Here we focus on what we learned about the literacy pedagogical methods and concomitant ideology of the center's lead teacher, Diana (pseudonym), from observations and interviews with her and five Mexican immigrant Head Start mothers.

Both the conversations with Diana regarding literacy in the preschool years and the observational data gathered in her classroom were heavily infused with issues of language, culture, and politics. This seems unsurprising in hindsight, given the recent Arizona passage of Propositions 203 and 103 and Senate Bill 1070. Specifically, the passage of Proposition 203 in 2000 requires the great majority of ELLs to be placed in English-only immersion classes during a temporary transition period. Proposition 103 passed in 2006 makes English the official language of the state. Finally, in 2010 Arizona's governor signed Senate Bill 1070. This bill attempts to identify, prosecute, and deport undocumented immigrants. Many argue that it makes racial profiling legal. The following vignette introduces the reader to the way that Diana conceptualized language development in her classroom.

English as the Official Language

It's breakfast time. You can hear the crunch, crunch from children eating their Rice Krispies. Suddenly, Diana pokes me [Cuéllar, the first author of this chapter] in the arm and asks, "Remember you asked me about major changes that I have lived through in terms of teaching?" Before I could answer yes and with a sense of urgency in her voice as if time was going to run out and she would not be able to share with me her thoughts, she mentions, "The language! You know, here in Arizona I do not know the logistics, but now the children will only get English schooling. You know we have to prepare them here because there will only be English in kindergarten." Francisca [teacher assistant] asked in disbelief, "Really?" as Diana answered an emphatic, "Oh, yes! Not here in Kidtown [a pseudonym for the center], but once they hit kindergarten." She continues by stating, "In the past I used to give them a little more time, but now by the middle of the year, I really have to push them to talk to me in English. I want to hear that English. I want them to try to talk to me in English. It's for their good."

From Diana's comments above, it became apparent that it was out of concern that she began to diminish the use of the home language with her students. Doing this, however, clashed with the parents' desire. When the mothers were interviewed, they demonstrated a clear desire that their children develop Spanish-speaking skills. The following interaction depicts what mothers reported about what occurs in their homes, based on a conversation Cuéllar had with one of the mothers during a home visit regarding emergent literacy.

¡Nuestras Raíces y Cultura! (Our Roots and Culture)

Marcela opens the door of her trailer home and welcomes me by saying, "Buenas noches" (Good evening). She seems a bit nervous. She clears her throat, signaling me to start the conversation and says, "Sabes, estoy un poco nerviosa pero contenta de que vamos hablar de la educación de las niñas. Ellas son lo más importante en este mundo." (You know, I am a little nervous but happy that we are going to talk about my girls' education. They are what is most important in this world.) After chatting for a while about her work and family, I asked her to share with me typical activities that occur in her home related to literacy. She looked at me quietly and intently for a minute and said, "Nos la pasamos platicando. Es como dice el dicho, 'hablando se entiende la gente.' Para niñas chiquitas como ella es el aprender a comunicarse y decir sus necesidades lo que es de más importancia. . . . Aquí en la casa nosotras hablamos en español, escuchamos la radio en español y vemos la tele en español y todo. Para mí, sería muy triste si a ella se le olvidara su idioma. No me puedo imaginar eso. Sería muy feo. Hablándoles en español es como yo les enseño sobre nuestra cultura y raíces." (We talk to each other. It is like the saying goes, 'People understand one another by talking.' For little ones like her, just learning how to communicate to say what she needs is the most important. . . . Here in the house we talk in Spanish, we listen to Spanish radio, watch Spanish TV and everything. For me it would be very sad if she forgot her language. I cannot imagine that. It would be awful. Talking to them in Spanish is how I teach them about our culture and our roots.)

THE CULTURAL MODELS APPROACH TO UNDERSTANDING LITERACY GOALS: A PRESCHOOL EXAMPLE

To better understand the contrasting and somewhat contradictory language and literacy goals of Diana and the preschool children's mothers, we use a "cultural models" approach (Gee, 1992, 1999, 2005). Gee categorizes cultural models as a type of taken-for-granted mental script that helps people engage in meaning-making activities. He suggests that cultural models consist of the cultural and social resources that color a person's perception as to what constitutes "normal," "natural," or "appropriate." In other words, people take these models and scripts and uncritically use them as accepted wisdom, which is then used to filter their everyday experiences.

For someone's speech or actions to be considered a cultural model, D'Andrade (1992) suggests that their actions or speech need to imply a frequent interpretation of a given phenomenon. Once we ascertained the cultural models used by the mothers and Diana, we examined them using Vygotsky's (1978) sociocultural framework as our lens. This framework proposes that children's past knowledge, including language and culture, must be incorporated in any teaching/learning process.

The Preschool: Kidtown

Our case study took place in Kidtown, a half-time Head Start preschool center in an urban, predominantly Latino immigrant community in Arizona. Kidtown is part of one of several communities in an area planned by Habitat for Humanity. The community was built in 6 years (from 1995 to 2002) with a total of 195 homes, 2 of which are used as community resources. One houses Kidtown and the other adjacent structure houses youth/adult programs including mentoring, college preparation classes, free English-as-a-Second-Language (ESL) courses, and courses in financial literacy. The parents at Kidtown are encouraged to use these services.

The Teacher and Mothers

Diana, the teacher, identifies as a full-blooded Native American, preschool teacher, wife, and mother of three. She was born in Arizona to a Comanche father and Navajo mother. She holds an associate's degree in early childhood education. Diana got involved with Head Start as a parent volunteer when her second child attended preschool. As the years went by, she became a teacher assistant and then a lead teacher. At the time of the study we discuss here, she had been working in the early childhood education sector for more than 16 years and with Latino families for 12 of those years. Over the course of her career she has learned to understand and speak some Spanish.

The five mothers who participated in the study were all Mexican-born women with a child attending Kidtown. All of them had at least one child older than the Kidtown-participating student. All mothers spoke Spanish, were in their 20s and 30s, and differed in legal status from undocumented to permanent resident to U.S. citizen.

Differences in the Language Goals of the Teacher and Mothers

To explore the perspectives of the teacher and the mothers, we collected classroom observations and interviews with the teachers and mother over an entire academic year.

We found that there were important language discontinuities between the mothers in the study and Diana, the teacher. All of the mothers were deeply concerned with making sure their children became fluent Spanish speakers. They expressed a strong desire to instill a strong sense of Mexican identity in their children, which they believed to be indelibly linked to fluency in Spanish. However, in the classroom, students were only encouraged to develop their English-speaking skills in response to the English-only legislation that has been passed as a result of the widespread hostility toward Mexican immigrants in the state of Arizona. Notably, Diana demonstrated a limited understanding of the development of early literacy skills in general and for ELLs in particular.

Spanish and Mexican Identity Development: The Mothers' Point of View. All the mothers in the study created an environment in their homes where the dominant language was Spanish. Although in one home both English and Spanish were spoken, and in another Spanish and Nahuatl (an Aztec language, mainly spoken in Mexico) were often used, Spanish was the principal language for lingual and cultural development because the families wanted to maintain its use. The following are examples of how the mothers conceptualized Spanish as a cultural anchor:

Carla: The culture at home is the Mexican culture. We talk to them in Spanish. Well, it is just that I would not like my children to forget their Spanish.

Esther: I value for her and her brother to be bilingual, but that does not mean that I do not care about Spanish. For me, it is important that she speaks Spanish. Well, we are from Mexico, and, well, we cannot forget that . . .

Antonieta: It is my responsibility and I think the responsibility of all Mexican parents living here [meaning in the United States] to assure themselves that their children learn Spanish. It's the language of our family.

Spanish and a sense of origin are taken very seriously by these mothers, who expressed a strong belief that losing these is tantamount to losing a sense of self-identity, to know who they are. Additionally, three of the five mothers used metaphors when talking about the importance of developing their children's Spanish-speaking skills:

Antonieta: What we wanted to do was give them a *base* and to have them learn their language at an early age. We do not want them to forget their Spanish.
Carla: I need them to have their little feet *planted* on this earth and know who they are. In here I take care of the Spanish, and at school he can learn English.
Marcela: Talking to them in Spanish teaches them about our culture and our *roots.*

The words *base, planted,* and *roots* carry powerful meanings in Spanish. As pointed out by García (2001, p. 5), the two Spanish proverbs "El árbol fuerte tiene raíces maduras" (A strong tree has mature/strong roots) and "Del árbol caído, todos hacen leña" (From a fallen tree, anyone/everyone makes firewood) can be distilled into an important life lesson: "If you have no raíces (roots), how can you withstand the test of the environment that surely will come and prey on your vulnerabilities?" These mothers may be expressing a fear that without a strong sense of their Mexican identity, including Spanish fluency, their children may forget essential elements that would allow them to resist wayward influences and stand up to the challenges of living in a hostile environment.

The Importance of English Development: Diana's Point of View. Diana's conceptualization of literacy emphasized the children's ability to identify letters, to know their English corresponding sounds, as well as to develop English-speaking skills. She justified her strong focus on English acquisition by explaining that once her students left preschool they "[would] only get English schooling." Although at times Diana would comment on her wishes that her students would become bilingual, she often stressed the importance of speaking English by stating her opinion that without English skills, her students would have difficulty attaining academic success. Notably, by the end of the academic year, two of the children would refuse to speak Spanish with their families and their classmates, a practice that caused significant anxiety at home.

Literacy as English Phonics Skills

English phonics instruction was the main technique utilized by Diana to teach literacy development in her classroom. Throughout the school year her focus was to teach the children the alphabet and to associate letters with their corresponding English sounds. In fact, at the end of the school year the children were expected to begin to read and write simple words such as *cat* and *star*. A standard literacy lesson, documented in our field notes, follows:

> During Circle Time Diana plays the phonics song in the background as she shows the children a brightly colored piece of construction paper. On this paper, two letters are written and they take most of the space of the paper. She describes them as "big *K* and little *k*." She also reminds them that *K* comes after yesterday's letter *J*. Diana asks the children, "Do you know what sound this letter makes?" The children look at her wide-eyed with no answer. Diana asks again, "Come on friends, does anyone know the sound that letter *K* makes? It sounds like the name of the letter. It's the letter *K* and its sound is /kc/-/kc/, like in kitty." Diana then goes around the carpet and asks every child to pronounce the sound that the letter *K* produces. Once the children produce the sound, they go back to the breakfast tables (where the assistant has set up the tables with magazines, newspapers, construction paper, scissors, and glue). There they write a large letter *K* with a crayon on an 8 x 10 inch sheet of construction paper, cut out as many letter *K*s as they can find in the magazines and newspapers, and paste them on the contour of their larger letter *K*.

English as Literacy

When asked to talk about literacy development in her preschool classroom, Diana described a metric that allows her to decide how to teach literacy at the beginning of the year:

> First, I want to know how much English they have from home. I want to see how much they are getting from home. I get a good idea at the home visits, what we do in the summer. [That is] when we meet all the children and whoever lives with them,

you know, mom, dad, grandma, brothers. With these kids I knew I had my work cut out when I visited and no one spoke English.

When probed about her literacy goals for her students, she answered,

By midyear it is really going to be, come on, I am really going to want to pull the words out. I think to myself, "Come on, can you use English? How many English words?" Diana would often, especially in the second half of the year, ask students to translate into English what they wanted to convey by asking them, "Can you say it in English?" or "Okay, now say it in English." or "And how can we say that in English?"

In the following example, Diana clearly defines her job as a teacher of English. She made the following comment as a part of a conversation about the parents' reactions to English-only legislations. Diana knew that the laws "offend" and "anger" parents and reported that her response to the parents' indignation is to tell them,

Yes, we know your child should not lose their language. As long as you continue it at home, your child is never going to lose it. . . . Give them some more. Here in the school we can teach them in English how to read and stuff in English all of these things like pronunciation and spelling. You can do that in Spanish.

English and Being an American

Diana's attitudes concerning her students' English development were focused on helping them assimilate to the English-speaking culture. In the following excerpt she discusses why at times she uses both English and Spanish in the classroom:

I talk kind of both [English and Spanish] in the classroom at the beginning because I know it is going to be real hard and that would really intimidate them [the children] if I only talked English. . . . I want them to feel comfortable, you know? I mean, for a lot of these kids, they have no experience with English or American culture. Here I introduce a lot of them to American culture. They have to learn the American ways to succeed.

On a different occasion, when speaking of different methods used to teach English as a second language in the K–12 system in the United States she talked about the anger that "Americans" feel toward those who need extra help learning English:

> I know this gets Americans really mad. Like, the schools will spend millions for special ESL classes for them, you know? And while our American children are getting their classes taken away, like drama and music. I know Americans get real mad about that.

Throughout the year Diana called several of the children in her classroom by anglicized forms of their names. This was a practice that one of her students did not welcome: He was very attentive to the pronunciation of his and his friends' names, often correcting the teacher by saying, "No, that is not his name." For example, if a student's name is Jorge and the teacher called that student George, he would say, "Teacher, his name is not George. It's Jorge."

School and Home Discontinuities in Language Socialization

The findings of this study bring to light large discontinuities in the language socialization practices and cultural expectations that young Mexican American ELLs experience between their school and their homes. At school, the students were exposed to an environment that did not recognize the literacy learning that occurred in their Spanish-speaking homes, and focused instead on teaching them exclusively in English. At home, however, the children's interactions with their families reinforced their Spanish-speaking skills and Mexican culture.

From a sociocultural standpoint, it is understood that children's development—including literacy development—is connected to their social milieu (Vygotsky, 1978). For instance, research shows that "interlocutors [people who have discussions with each other] are among the most significant influences that support and determine children's emergent literacy" (Reyes, 2006, p. 286). For the children in the study, their main source of discussion and other social interaction before entering preschool was their Spanish-speaking families. Thus, by actively participating with their families, the children unquestionably gained literacy knowledge in their first 4 years of life. Diana, however, did not take into account the literacy practices occurring in her students' Spanish-speaking homes. Her early literacy development cultural model—one that emphasizes English skills above and beyond any other ability—clearly influenced her instructional practices.

By believing that her job as a literacy teacher was made more difficult by the fact that in many of her students' homes adults did not speak English or by her perception that parents and children did not have much experience with American culture, Diana demonstrates that she regards the differences between the home and school according to a deficit model. When teachers understand their students via such a deficit model, the students' home life is considered educationally lacking in relation to the school (Banks, 1994). Diana's conceptual unification of English development, Americanization, and success exemplifies an assimilationist agenda. Assimilation theory argues that individuals attain higher levels of education and success as time goes by and as immigrants become more like the mainstream (Alba & Nee, 2003). However, studies show that Mexican assimilation is actually much more complex (Massey, Durand, & Malone, 2002; Telles & Ortiz, 2008) and that immigrant children are often negatively affected by assimilationist teaching techniques (García, 2001; Rodríguez-Brown, 2001; Telles & Ortiz, 2008; Valdés, 1996). Importantly, recent research shows that the language and cultural practices in the homes of ELLs are "fragile and susceptible to dominance by the English language and mainstream culture" (Espinosa, 2010, p. 90).

Although throughout the year Diana expressed wishes that her students would become bilingual, her methods of teaching were not conducive to such a goal. When bilingualism is the objective for students, researchers recommend teaching strategies that differ significantly from what she did—encouraging both the home language and English as legitimate modes of communication and giving them each comparable status in the classroom (Dworin, 2003). In Diana's classroom, Spanish and English did not have the same value, and children were keenly aware of it. The strong emphasis on English acquisition, the anglicization of names, and the fact that the children would be expected to translate what they would say from Spanish to English (causing them extra work) is likely to have mediated the dislike that two children had toward the end of the year for speaking Spanish at home and school.

Teachers are the primary enforcers of educational policies (Roskos & Vukelich, 2006) and must make decisions on how to best implement them. Diana acknowledged that before Proposition 203 was enacted, which requires that ELLs be placed in English-only classes in the K–12 system, she would "give them more time" to learn English, and would speak more Spanish to her students throughout the school year. She mentioned that the chief reason why she felt she needed to increase the amount of English to which the children were exposed was fear that they would not be academically successful given the new legal requirements of English-only schooling. Diana's pedagogical decision to diminish use of Spanish to accommodate Proposition 203 demonstrates not only her lack of knowledge about second-language acquisition, but also the subtractive effect that English-only laws have on the education of Latino ELLs.

RECOMMENDATIONS ABOUT LANGUAGE ACQUISITION

A common theme in the academic literature on how to improve education for ELLs is the ever-increasing need for well-prepared teachers (Ballantyne, Sanderman, & Levy, 2008; García, Arias, Harris-Murri, & Serna, 2010). Below we share some promising classroom practices, which contrast sharply with those practiced by Diana. We also suggest educational experiences that can be offered to educators to improve their abilities and confidence when working with English learners.

Promising Classroom Practices

Espinosa (2005) encourages teachers working with Latino ELLs to "systematically integrate the students' values, beliefs, histories, and experiences and build curriculum around mutual respect" (p. 840). More recently in a comprehensive review of the literature she provides teachers with a list of classroom practices that have been found to accelerate young ELL children's literacy development and to support the home language (Espinosa, 2010, pp. 96–99):

- Recruit bilingual paraprofessionals, assistants, family members, community volunteers, and/or older, more competent students to interact with, read to, and assist ELL children, individually or in small groups.
- Incorporate the home language in the classroom via song, poetry, dances, rhymes, and/or counting.
- Incorporate the use of "identity texts" where children with the help of their families create books where they are the main character.
- Use picture books and photo albums to make up stories with students.
- Use books with predictable texts, rhymes, and alliterations that promote phonological awareness.
- Review key concepts and vocabulary before reading a book.
- Make connections between the content of the story and the students' daily lives.
- Use dialogic reading techniques when reading books in both large- and small-group formats. (Dialogic reading is a form of

active reading, where children talk about the story or book, and are involved in making sense of it by asking and/or answering questions about it.)

- After reading a book, allow students to use the new vocabulary and extend the early literacy skills to other areas of the curriculum, such as math or science.

Bilingual development expert Claude Goldenberg (2006) made the following suggestions for teachers so that their ELL students are better engaged:

- The home language should be used strategically (i.e., for the introduction of new activities and or concepts).
- Students should have a daily schedule and well-structured instructional routines.
- Teachers should use physical gestures and visual cues.
- Teachers should focus on the similarities/differences between English and Spanish words (i.e., cognates).
- Teachers should plan for additional time when reading stories.

Classroom practices that positively affect the literacy development of Spanish-speaking youngsters include the following set of roles undertaken by successful teachers (Saracho, 2003):

- *Discussion leader:* Using culturally relevant artifacts, the teacher frequently asks questions in the home language that require the students to think about what they are presently doing and draw out elaborate answers.
- *Demonstrator:* Using props, the teacher models/demonstrates how particular skills are used and/or activities completed, gives students opportunities to try out new skills, and reinforces correct use of knowledge or skill.
- *Story Teller:* Teacher reads or tells children stories and actively engages them by having them predict what will happen next, encouraging them to retell the story to the class or a partner, asking them to put the story's events in sequential order, and/or by having the students describe the characters and settings.
- *Decision Maker:* Teachers must be flexible and aware that in a given day or week they will make a variety of decisions to improve learning, such as providing extra time for an assignment or repeating the instructions to an activity for those

students who do not understand. Teachers are encouraged to make long-term, planned decisions such as weekly thematic units that can expose children to deeper vocabulary and content knowledge.

Research specifically related to the development of vocabulary suggests that instruction should be explicit and systematic (August & Shanahan, 2006). Echeverria (1998) suggests how this might be utilized for ELLs:

> One form of vocabulary development includes short, explicit segments of class time in which the teacher directly teaches key vocabulary. These minute segments would consist of the teacher saying the vocabulary word, writing it on the board, asking students to say it and write it and defining the term with pictures, demonstrations, and examples familiar to the students. (p. 220)

Academic Experiences for Prospective Teachers

Studies show that the best qualified teachers for working with ELLs are those who are ESL certified or hold bilingual certification (Karabenick & Clemens Noda, 2004; Reeves, 2006). The fact is, however, that a great majority of teachers working with ELLs do not have such academic experiences, and colleges and universities lack capacity to train the number of teachers that are needed (Ballantyne et al., 2008). Nevertheless, educational researchers have made recommendations about the types of preservice experiences that are likely to benefit both ELL students and their teachers. Experts suggest that given the growing number of ELLs, teacher preparation programs should be grounded within language-minority communities, and that student teachers should have a strong presence in school districts with high proportions of English language learners (García et al., 2010). Studies show that preservice teachers (those in teacher preparation programs) attain a better understanding of the challenges that Latino ELLs experience as well as higher confidence in their ability to teach ELL students when their coursework includes a service-learning component or other organized field-based experiences in schools with a high percentage of immigrant students (Bollin, 2007; Hollins & Guzman, 2005).

Others argue that in addition to working with ELLs in their schools, preservice teachers should have academic requirements that include foreign language courses (Lucas & Grinberg, 2008; National Task Force on Early Childhood Education for Hispanics, 2007) and strong theoretical and practical understanding of teaching a diverse student body (Gallavan, Porter, Troutman, & Jones, 2001). Goe, Bell, and Little(2008) suggests that preservice teachers should take coursework that familiarizes them with the following educational competencies:

- Sociocultural and political foundations for teaching ELL students
- Foundations of second-language acquisition
- Knowledge for teaching academic content to ELL students
- Effective instructional practices for teaching academic content to ELL students
- Assessment practices and accommodations for ELL students

Training All Teachers (TAT), a federally funded program focusing on the educational experiences of preservice teachers that aims to improve the education of children learning English as a second language, successfully infuses ELL issues throughout a teacher preparation core curriculum via organized discussions (45–60 minutes) on language, culture, and the administration of educational services for ELLs. Research about this program has shown that both preservice and in-service teachers alike who participated have a more developed knowledge base about ELLs and plan to incorporate this knowledge in their teaching practice (Meskill, 2005). Lastly, in recognition of the logistical complications involved in training large numbers of teachers who are well prepared to teach ELLs, researchers also suggest that a cadre of second-language-learning specialists be developed. These professionals would provide ongoing training, coaching, and guidance to teachers on issues of culture, second-language acquisition, and academic development of ELLs (National Task Force on Early Childhood Education for Hispanics, 2007).

CONCLUSION

In this chapter we described a multifaceted set of issues (political, linguistic, cultural, and pedagogical) related to the language and literacy education of young Spanish-speaking children who are learning English as a second language in U.S. schools. It is clear that schoolteachers (such as Diana) are often misinformed and ill-equipped to work with linguistically diverse children, particularly on issues of language and literacy. There is an urgent need to prepare teachers to better meet the challenges of teaching a linguistically and culturally diverse student body. Fortunately, in the literature there exists a set of guidelines that, if implemented, could both improve the education of future teachers and also enhance the learning of English language learners in the classroom.

REFERENCES

Alba, R., & Nee, V. (2003). *Remaking the American mainstream: Assimilation and contemporary immigration.* Cambridge, MA: Harvard University.

August, D., & Shanahan, T. (Eds.). (2006). *Developing literacy in second-language learners: Report of the National Literacy Panel on language-minority children and youth.* Mahwah, NJ: Erlbaum.

Ballantyne, K. G., Sanderman, A. R., & Levy, J. (2008). *Educating English language learners: Building teacher capacity.* Washington, DC: National Clearinghouse for English Language Acquisition. Retrieved from http://www.ncela.gwu.edu/files/uploads/3/EducatingELLsBuildingTeacherCapacityVol2.pdf

Banks, J. (1994). Ethnicity, class, cognitive, and motivational styles: Research and teaching implications. In J. Kretovics & E. J. Nussel (Eds.), *Transforming urban education.* Needham Heights, MA: Allyn & Bacon.

Beltran, E., & Goldwasser, A. (2008). *A renewed Head Start: New opportunities for Latino children.* Washington, DC: National Council of La Raza.

Bollin, G. G. (2007). Preparing teachers for Hispanic immigrant children: A service learning approach. *Journal of Latinos and Education, 6*(2), 177–189.

Buysse, V., Castro, D. C., West, T., & Skinner, M. L. (2005). Addressing the needs of Latino children: A national survey of state administrators of early childhood programs. *Early Childhood Research Quarterly, 20,* 146–163.

Calderón, M. (2007). *Buenos principios: Latino children in the earliest years of life.* Washington, DC: National Council of La Raza.

Capps, R., Fix, M., Murray, J., Ost, J., Passel, J., & Hewrantoro-Hernandez, S. (2005). *The new demography of America's schools; Immigration and the No Child Left Behind Act.* Washington, DC: Urban Institute.

D'Andrade, R. (1992). Schemas and motivation. In R. D'Andrade & C. Strauss (Eds.), *Human motives and cultural models* (pp. 23–44). Cambridge, UK: Cambridge University Press.

Dworin, J. (2003). Examining children's biliteracy in the classroom. In A. I. Willis, G. E. García, R. Barrera, & V. J. Harris (Eds.), *Multicultural issues in literacy research and practice* (pp. 29–48). Mahwah, NJ: Erlbaum.

Echevarria, J. (1998). Preparing text and classroom materials for English language learners: Curriculum adaptations in secondary school settings. In R. Gersten & R. Jimenez (Eds.), *Promoting learning for culturally and linguistically diverse students: Classroom applications from contemporary research* (pp. 210–229). Pacific Grove, CA: Brooks/Cole.

English Language Education for children in public schools. (2000). Ariz. Stat. Ann. §§ 7–15.

Espinosa, L. M. (2005). Curriculum and assessment considerations for young children from culturally, linguistically and economically diverse backgrounds. *Psychology in the Schools, 42,* 837–853.

Espinosa, L. M. (2010). *Getting it right for young children from diverse backgrounds: Applying research to improve practice.* Upper Saddle River, NJ: Pearson.

Gallavan, N. P., Porter, L., Troutman, W., & Jones, P. (2001). Cultural diversity and the NCATE standards: A story in process. *Multicultural Perspectives, 3*(2), 13–18.

García, E. E. (2001). *Hispanic education in the United States: Raíces y Alas.* New

York: Rowman & Littlefield.

García, E. E., Arias, B., Harris-Murri, N. J., & Serna, C. (2010). Developing responsive teachers: A challenge for a demographic reality. *Journal of Teacher Education, 61*, 132–142.

García, E. E., & Cuéllar, D. (2006). Who are these linguistically and culturally diverse students? *Teachers College Record, 108*(11), 2220–2246.

García, E. E., & Wiese, A. M. (2009). Policy related to issues of diversity and literacy: Implications for English learners. In L. M. Morrow, D. Lapp, & R. Rueda (Eds.), *Handbook of research on literacy and diversity* (pp. 32–54). New York: Guilford Press.

García, E. E., Wiese, A. M., & Cuéllar, D. (in press). Language, public policy and schooling: A focus on Chicano English learners. In R. Valencia (Ed.), *Chicano school failure and success, past, present and future* (3rd ed.). New York: Routledge.

Gee, J. P. (1992). *The social mind: Language, ideology and social practice.* New York: Falmer.

Gee, J. P. (1999). *An introduction to discourse analysis: Theory and method.* New York: Routledge.

Gee, J. P. (2005). *An introduction to discourse analysis: Theory and method* (2nd ed.). New York: Routledge.

Goe, L., Bell, C., & Little, O. (2008). *Approaches to evaluating teacher effectiveness: A research synthesis.* Washington, DC: National Comprehensive Center for Teacher Quality.

Goldenberg, C. (2006, July 26). Improving achievement for English learners. *Education Week, 25*(43), 34–36.

Gonzalez, J. (2005). *Speculations on the future of the Spanish language in the United States of America.* Paper presented at the 5th International Symposium on Bilingualism. Barcelona, Spain.

Hernandez, D. (2006). *Young Hispanic children in the U.S.: A demographic portrait based on Census 2000.* Report to the National Task Force on Early Childhood Education for Hispanics. Tempe: Arizona State University.

Hernandez, D. J., Denton, N. A., & Macartney, S. E. (2007). *Children in immigrant families—The U.S. and 50 states: National origins, language, and early education* (Research Brief Series Publication No. 2007–11). Albany: State University of New York, Child Trends and the Center for Social and Demographic Analysis.

Hollins, E., & Guzman, M. T. (2005). Research on preparing teachers for diverse populations. In M. Cochran-Smith & K. M. Zeichner (Eds.), *Studying teacher education: The report of the AERA Panel on Research and Teacher Education* (pp. 477–548). Mahwah, NJ: Erlbaum.

Karabenick, S. A., & Clemens Noda, P. A. (2004). Professional development implications of teachers' beliefs and attitudes toward English language learners. *Bilingual Research Journal, 28*(1), 55–75.

Lopez, M. L., Barrueco, S., & Miles, J. (2006). *Latino infants and their families: A national perspective of protective and risk factors for development.* A report to the National Task Force on Early Childhood Education for Hispanics. Tempe: Arizona State University.

Lucas, T., & Grinberg, J. (2008). Responding to the linguistic reality of mainstream classrooms: Preparing all teachers to teach English language learners. In M. Cochran-Smith, S. Feiman-Nemser, & D. J. McIntyre (Eds.), *Handbook of research on teacher education* (3rd ed., pp. 606–636). New York: Routledge.

Massey, D. S., Durand, J., & Malone, N. J. (2002*). Beyond smoke and mirrors: Mexican immigration in an era of economic integration.* New York: Russell Sage Foundation.

Meskill, C. (2005). Infusing English language learner issues throughout professional educator curricula: The training all teachers project. *Teachers College Record, 107*(4), 739–756.

National Center for Education Statistics (NCES). (2004). *English language learner students in U.S. public schools: 1994 and 2000.* Washington, DC: U.S. Department of Education.

National Center for Education Statistics (NCES). (2008). *The condition of education 2008,* Washington, DC: U.S. Department of Education.

National Task Force on Early Childhood Education for Hispanics. (2007). *Expanding and improving early education for Hispanics: Executive report.* Tempe: Arizona State University.

Pearson, G. (2006). *How many school-aged English-language learners (ELLs) are there in the U.S.?* Washington, DC: National Clearing House for English Language Acquisition and Language Instruction Education Programs.

Reeves, J. R. (2006). Secondary teacher attitudes toward including English-language learners in mainstream classrooms. *Journal of Educational Research, 99*(3), 131–142.

Reyes, I. (2006). Exploring connections between emergent biliteracy and bilingualism. *Journal of Early Childhood Literacy, 6,* 267–292.

Rodríguez-Brown, F. V. (2001). Home-school collaboration: Successful models in the Hispanic community. In P. Mosenthal & P. Schmitt (Eds.), Reconceptualizing literacy in the new age of pluralism and multiculturalism, advances in reading & language research(pp. 273–288). Charlotte, NC: Information Age Publishing.

Roskos, K., & Vukelich, C. (2006). Early literacy policy and pedagogy. In D. K. Dickinson & S. B. Neuman (Eds.), *Handbook of early literacy research, Vol. 2* (pp. 295–308). New York: Guilford.

Saracho, O. (2003). Teachers' roles: Literacy-related play of kindergarten Spanish-speaking students. *Journal of Hispanic Higher Education, 2*(4) 358–376.

Telles, E., & Ortiz, V. (2008). *Generations of exclusion: Mexican Americans, assimilation and race.* New York: Russell Sage Foundation.

U.S. Census Bureau. (2011). Language spoken at home by state: 2008. Statistical Abstract of the United States: 2011. Washington, DC: Author. Retrieved from http://www.census.gov/compendia/statab/2011/tables/11s0054.pdf

Valdés, G. (1996). *Con respeto: Bridging the distances between culturally diverse families and schools.* New York: Free Press.

Vygotsky, L. S. (1978). *Mind in society: The development of higher psychological processes* (M. Cole, V. John-Steiner, S. Scribner, & E. Souberman, Eds. & Trans.). Cambridge, MA: Harvard University Press. (Original work published 1934)

CHAPTER 7

Media, Technology, and Commercialism

Countering the Threats to Young Children

Nancy Carlsson-Paige

Children today are growing up in a world vastly different from the one their parents grew up in just a generation ago. Media, marketing, and technology have become pivotal influences in children's lives and they are profoundly altering the basic foundation on which healthy childhoods depend. American children ages 2 to 5 now spend more than 32 hours a week on average engaged with screen media (Mc-Donough, 2009), a figure that rises sharply with age as children become more involved with video games, handheld devices, and the Internet (Rideout, Foehr, & Roberts, 2010). Much of the entertainment media that children see depicts a world of violence where relationships are based on hurt, coercion, and disrespect. Corporations market to children without restrictions through television, movies, the Internet, video and computer games, fast-food chains, retail stores, and even schools. Taken together, these influences have become a dominant and harmful force in children's lives at a time when the potential of schools and parents to counteract them is diminishing. In the nation's schools, with their overemphasis on testing and academic standards, little room remains for attending to the needs and interests of the whole child. And many parents are too preoccupied with the struggle to survive in an increasingly harsh economic climate to find the time and energy to try to counteract these social forces.

Media, technology, and commercialism are undermining some of the basic building blocks of children's healthy development: creative

133

play, a secure sense of self, and authentic relationships rooted in compassion and caring. These building blocks are already weakened for
an increasing number of the nation's children whose basic needs are
not well met. The United States ranks far below other advanced nations when comparing the well-being of children along lines of poverty, health, and education (United Nations Children's Fund, 2007).
So while it is the children already at risk who are the most vulnerable
to harm from media and marketing forces, virtually all of the nation's
children, regardless of their circumstances, are affected by these influences pervading childhood today.

A HEALTHY FOUNDATION THROUGH PLAY

Researchers who have tracked children's creativity for 50 years are seeing a significant decrease in creativity among children for the first
time, especially younger children from kindergarten through sixth
grade (Bronson & Merryman, 2010). This is not surprising given the
number of hours children spend consuming media and the disappearance of creative play from their lives. Play is a remarkably creative
process that fosters original thinking, problem solving, learning, and
imagination. As children actively invent their own scenarios in play,
they work their way though the challenges life presents and gain confidence and a sense of mastery.

In a kindergarten classroom I visited, I watched Sarah who came to
school many mornings distraught, holding tight to her mom who was
often hurrying to get to her high-pressure job as a retail executive. The
teacher in this classroom set up a "business office" in the play area,
and this was where Sarah frequently headed upon arrival at school.
Typically she would choose a doll, stick the doll in a chair or on a
bed, and then bid her goodbye. Sarah would then enter the "business
office" where she'd sit busily writing on papers at the desk and talking on the phone. Periodically Sarah would walk back to the doll and
speak to her, sometimes with concern such as "Oh my darling, how
are you?" and other times with harsh admonishments such as "Stop
crying, I have to go to work."

Sarah's frequent play episodes were vital for helping her cope with
the complex feelings she had about separating from her mom and
going to school. Healthy play summons each child's imagination and
ability to create original scenes and scripts. When children have the
opportunity to become thoroughly engaged in play, they can experience deep, inner satisfaction that strengthens their sense of self and

their inner resilience. These are the qualities children need today to withstand societal forces that threaten to destabilize their security and well-being.

Play is also vital to learning and inseparable from it. We know from decades of research and child development theory, now backed up by findings from neuroscience, that young children learn through play. When children play with materials, they are building a foundation of understanding for concepts and skills that form the basis for later academic learning. For example, a young child understands the concept of "four"—that it represents a quantity that is separate from objects—through manipulating objects in various ways, not by copying down the numeral "4" on paper. Open-ended materials such as blocks, play dough, and building materials encourage children to construct an understanding of concepts through their play. Neuroscience tells us that as children do this, connections and pathways in the brain become activated and solidified.

By moving through their environment—exploring, touching, and investigating through play—not only are children learning concepts, they are learning how to learn: to take initiative, to ask questions, to create and solve their own problems. Good teachers know how to build on what children do in play by providing follow-up activities to extend learning. There is a growing body of research to show that play is essential for children's academic success; and when teachers intervene to scaffold new learning, the benefits of play are especially potent (Isenberg & Quisenberry, 2002; Singer, Singer, Plaskon, & Schweder, 2003).

ENDANGERED PLAY

Children today are spending less time playing at home, outdoors, and at school. The more time young children clock in front of screens, the less time they spend engaged in creative play. In our nation's schools, the focus on academic skills and scripted teaching, alarmingly, has pushed down even to preschools and kindergartens where play experiences are disappearing (Miller & Almon, 2009). Our poorest children who are in the most overcrowded classrooms with the least qualified teachers receive the most drill-based instruction and the fewest opportunities for play.

Not only are children today playing less, their capacity to play creatively has diminished. The very play process itself has been eroding ever since the Federal Communications Commission (FCC) deregulated the broadcasting industry in the mid-1980s and the floodgates opened for big business to market shows, products, and toys linked together around single themes (Levin & Carlsson-Paige, 2006). Once this happened, teachers began saying that children's play was looking more like imitations of TV scripts than original scenarios invented by children. Teachers' concerns about the loss of creative play have intensified over the years as marketing campaigns have extended their reach to include Hollywood movies, video and computer games, the Internet, fast-food chains, and even schools.

We see the disappearance of play in childhood beginning with infants and toddlers. A Kaiser Family Foundation report found that in a typical day, 61% of children under the age of 2 watch screen media for more than an hour (Rideout & Hamel, 2006). At the same time, the American Academy of Pediatrics recommends no screen time for children under the age of 2 because of concerns that TV affects early brain growth and the development of social, emotional, and cognitive skills (American Academy of Pediatrics, 2001). The authors of the Kaiser report write that baby videos, computer games, and TV shows for infants and toddlers are becoming commonplace, and that an increasing number of TV shows, videos, websites, software programs, video games, and interactive TV toys are designed specifically for babies, toddlers, and preschoolers.

I visited a home recently where two boys, 2 and 4 years of age, were both playing with electronic toys. Four-year-old Ronin had a plastic multicolored radio and he was pushing the buttons one after the other. Each time he pushed a button, a different song played, but Ronin was pushing the buttons as fast as he could without listening to the songs. His 2-year-old brother Jake had a talking alphabet toy, and he was also pushing buttons that would activate a voice saying letter names that matched pictures of objects starting with those letters.

Electronic toys have become extremely popular with many parents who think they are educational. But these toys have real limitations. They don't allow for the level of exploration and learning that open-ended materials invite. Instead, they encourage more superficial interactions. The voices, actions, and lights that are built into electronic toys teach children to be entertained by the toy, to look to the toy to do something rather than to invent a question to explore through their own initiative. A friend told me recently that she babysat for a 3-year-old who picked up the ball she'd brought to play with and asked, "How do you turn it on?"

Anne, a former graduate student who returned to teaching after raising three children, wrote recently to tell me how the children today seemed different:

> I've noticed a change for the worse in a time span of about 10 years. Play is missing from children's lives today. They do not know how to pretend and it's a tragedy. I'm noticing that they don't know how to create either. I have open-ended art materials in my art area and very few children know how to experiment, explore, or create with them. They seem happier with the product than the process and that scares me. The block corner is not half as popular as it used to be. We sit at circle and the little faces look at me as if to say, "Okay, entertain me."

Hearing comments like this from teachers both informally and through my research, as well as observing these trends firsthand, has convinced me that as the forces of screen technology and commercialism have loomed larger in children's lives, the creative aspects of their play truly have been slipping away. No one knows what the long-term consequences will be for children who cannot use this natural resource we call *play* to its fullest. But I believe that the risks to children and to society of losing healthy, creative play are far-reaching and even dangerous, and that we should do everything we can to counteract the influences that threaten play, and reclaim this vital resource for children.

RECLAIMING HEALTHY PLAY

Even in the face of societal trends that are threatening children's healthy play, there are a great many things we can do to help children's play lives to thrive. In our local schools and communities, we can advocate for early childhood classrooms that foster play and hands-on learning. We can help administrators and policy makers understand that through play children develop the foundation for success in school later on (Coolahan, Fantuzzo, Mendez, & McDermott, 2000). We can cite the research showing that through play children develop critical thinking (Vygotsky, 1976), self-regulation (Whitebread, Coltman, Jameson, & Lander, 2009), constructive problem solving (Wyver & Spence, 1999), creativity (Moore & Russ, 2008), and the ability to wrestle with life's challenges (Winnicott, 1971).

We can support children's creative play at home and in other settings in our communities such as parks and after-school programs. Children need uninterrupted playtime every day. In all of the settings where children play, we can provide access to open-ended materials—blocks, sand, water, play dough, building and collage materials, generic dolls, and animals. As we watch children play, we can make comments, ask

questions, and suggest materials—based on what we see children doing in their play—that will help their play deepen and expand.

We can avoid buying media-linked and electronic toys that place
limits on what children can do and imagine. If a child is using a media-
linked toy such as a Princess Ariel doll, we can try to introduce a more
open-ended material such as blocks to use along with it, and gently
suggest ideas for a story that break from the Ariel "script." When we
are choosing toys and materials for children to use in any context, we
can ask ourselves, "What is the potential of this toy for fostering imaginative play and creative problem solving?" and choose those that can
optimally foster imagination and learning.

THE CONSUMER CHILD AND THE WHOLE CHILD

There has been a staggering increase in marketing to children in the
last 2 decades. Corporations pour about $17 billion annually into
huge marketing campaigns that are increasingly fueled by rapid and
continuing technological advances and innovations in marketing tac-
tics (Horovitz, 2006). Most young children in the United States today
are immersed in a world saturated with commercial images. Parents
tell me they can't find toys, lunchboxes, and pajamas that aren't tied
to some corporate logo or Hollywood movie. When the last *Star Wars*
film was released and marketed heavily to children through toys,
food, and a host of other products, a boy sitting at his math table in a
second-grade classroom turned to me and said, "*Star Wars!* I can't get
it out of my head!"

The commercial culture children grow up in today is largely the
result of a free pass handed to corporations in 1980 for unrestricted
marketing to children. Before that time, the Federal Trade Commission (FTC) had the authority to regulate advertising to children, and
there were a number of important restrictions in place to protect children from deceptive and unfair advertising (Linn, 2004). But in 1980,
when the FTC decided it was time to enact a ruling that would ban
all advertising to children under the age of 8, corporations reacted
by feverishly lobbying Congress. The end result was legislation that
stripped the FTC of all power to regulate advertising to children.

A federal regulation that prohibits advertising to young children
is in the absolute best interest of a nation's children. The nature of
advertising requires children to understand that someone with an
underlying motive of self-interest is trying to sell them something.
Because young children tend to see things at face value without com-
prehending the intention or motive beneath the surface, advertising

is inherently unfair or exploitive of their developmental capabilities. Many parents tell me that when their children see ads on TV, they shout, "I want that!" Of course this is the case, because the pull of the visual image is strongly persuasive to the mind of a young child.

Beneath all the products that marketers sell to children there is one central message: Happiness comes from consuming: "You will be happy if you have this toy, if you eat this cereal, if you have these clothes." Children get the message that satisfaction comes from outside of oneself, not from within, that self-worth is based on what you have and how you look rather than who you are as a person. One first-grade teacher I spoke with told me that the little girls in her class are preoccupied with fashion, clothes, makeup, and hair, that they compete with each other around these things and isolate little girls who are not dressed in popular fashions.

The consistent message children hear from consumer culture— there is something you need to acquire—undermines their ability to find peace and satisfaction where they are in any given moment. It's no wonder that research shows that the more children buy into consumer culture, the less happy they are, the more anxious, and the lower their self-esteem (Schor, 2004). Dora, a teacher and a parent, told me that she went to a birthday party for a 6-year-old boy who opened presents at lightning speed, and threw them aside one after the other saying, "I have that," or "I don't want that." Dora said she felt alarmed and sad. The boy seemed to have no connection to the item or the people who gave it to him.

COMBATING THE COMMERCIAL CULTURE

There is growing awareness of the dangers of marketing to children and mounting evidence that parents and professionals are concerned. I believe that the problem requires action at the federal level and that we should push for a return to the regulation of advertising to children by the FTC and for FCC regulations that will stop the marketing of media-linked toys and products to young children. Public health and medical organizations such as the American Psychological Association and the World Health Organization have called for restrictions on marketing to children (WHO Forum, 2006). Several advocacy groups, most notably The Campaign for a Commercial Free Childhood (CCFC; http://www.commercialexploitation.org), a national coalition of health care professionals, educators, advocacy groups, and concerned parents, have launched campaigns to push back against the commercialization of childhood. On the CCFC website you can see a variety of ways to take action and download the list of *10 Things You Can Do to Reclaim Childhood from Corporate Marketers* (http://www. commercialfreechildhood.org/events/screenings/actions.pdf).

In our schools and communities, we can help raise awareness about the hazards of marketing to children by organizing discussion events on the topic. There is an impressive list of new documentary films about commercialized childhood available from a variety of sources, one being the Media Education Foundation (http://www. mediaed.org) that has several valuable films, including the acclaimed *Consuming Kids*.

With the children in our own lives, we can limit exposure to screens and commercial influences. When we see ads—on television, cereal boxes, as logos, as product placement in films—we can point these out to children. We can ask them why they think these ads are there, and talk with them about this, keeping in mind that young children will have unique ideas of their own and only gradually come to understand marketing as we do.

THREATS TO RELATIONSHIPS AND SOCIAL AND EMOTIONAL LEARNING

The images children see in the media have a powerful influence in shaping the view of the world they develop. The antisocial messages they absorb have great impact because children spend so many hours with media and many fewer hours interacting with peers and parents than in the past. Many shows tell children a similar story—of a world that is dangerous, where there are "good guys" and "bad guys," where people need weapons and must fight to settle their differences. As hundreds of teachers reported in my research (Carlsson-Paige, 2008), children take the behaviors they've seen in the media and try them out in their own interactions with other children—kicking, fighting, using mean-spirited and hurtful words—setting their relationships with peers in a downward spiral.

In the summer of 2000, after reviewing all of the relevant research, six major medical groups issued a joint statement: Viewing entertainment violence can lead to emotional desensitization and increases in aggressive attitudes, values, and behavior in children (American Academy of Pediatrics, 2000). More recently, other public health professionals have issued a similar statement about playing violent video games that can increase the likelihood of aggressive behavior in children and youth (National Institute on Media and the Family, 2006). Yet even with all these expert voices raising red flags about the dangers of viewing entertainment violence, media that is fraught with violence—television shows, media-linked toys, movies, video games—continue to be routinely marketed to children. One common strategy that lures young children into violence is the promotion of highly enticing violent toys that are linked to movies for teens and adults—rated PG-13 or R. The big media companies have used this approach successfully with *Star Wars*, *Transformers*, *Lord of the Rings*, and *X-Men*, to name just a few. Young kids play with these toys, have the logos on their underpants and toothbrushes, and then beg their parents to take them to see the movie. Parents, often confused by this marketing, go to see these films with their kids and later receive criticism because they don't say "no" to violent entertainment.

The violence in children's entertainment media is designed to look exciting and fun. Young kids are drawn to the graphic action of what's on the screen and don't see the hurtful effects of the violence. Before they are even old enough to understand that hurtful acts cause pain, many kids have become desensitized to violence and have even begun to acquire an appetite for it. This is especially troubling because researchers have shown that children exposed to violent programming at a young age have a higher tendency for violent and aggressive behavior later in life than children not so exposed (American Academy of Pediatrics, 2000).

LEARNING EMPATHY AND HOW TO CARE FOR OTHERS

In recent years there has been a growing recognition that children's success in school and in life depends to a large extent upon their social and emotional skills: self-awareness, being able to handle difficult emotions, having a capacity for empathy with others and the ability to "put oneself in their shoes," and dealing effectively with relationships. Researchers have been able to show conclusively that social and emotional skills and competencies result in improved academic achievement and higher grades in school (Collaborative for Academic, Social, and Emotional Learning, 2007). And neuroscience has shown that how we interact with children can do a lot to influence and strengthen the neural connections in the brain that represent social and emotional skills.

At a time when children are exposed to so many antisocial models through media and commercial products, and given their more limited opportunity for play and social interaction both at home and at school, children today need more help learning relationship skills than they did in the past. But how do we teach these to children?

We can't just tell children they *should* care about other people or *be kind*. No, they have to learn these things the same way they learn everything: through firsthand experiences that encourage them to construct their own awareness and build their own skills.

As I think about how to encourage social and emotional learning in children, I find it helpful to keep two general goals in mind: giving children alternatives to models of violence and coercion and helping children learn social and emotional skills The possible ways these goals might be implemented by the creative adults in children's daily lives are truly endless. What any of us choose to do will be shaped by our situation—the developmental levels of the children we work with, their interests and needs, our cultural background and that of the children, and our own creative ideas.

GIVING CHILDREN AN ALTERNATIVE TO MODELS OF RELATIONSHIPS BASED ON COERCION AND VIOLENCE

Children need to see and, more importantly, experience alternatives to the models of violence and disrespect that surround them. In our interactions with children, we can present these alternatives. We can accomplish our adult goals while using noncoercive, nonviolent approaches; we can present children with a way of being based on dialogue, negotiation, and joint problem solving. Let me give you a couple of examples of what this can look like.

I was at the park one day with a group of kids including 3-year-old Brian. As Brian ran exuberantly across the park, he bumped into a little girl and knocked her over. Brian saw the little girl fall, then spun around and ran off in the other direction. I ran after Brian calling his name, but he wouldn't stop. Finally I caught up with him, calling, "Brian, I want to talk to you!" He turned around as he kept running to say, "I don't want a time-out." I realized then that Brian thought I would make him sit out on a bench or have some kind of "consequence" for knocking over the little girl. Immediately I wanted Brian to understand that I was not going to use my adult power to punish him. "We're not going to have a time-out," I said. "But let's go over and find out how the little girl is who you knocked over." Hand in hand, we walked over to talk with the girl and her mother.

We adults have opportunities every day to decide how to get children to do what we want. Many of us do what our own parents and teachers did with us: We use time-outs, rewards, bribes, and punishments—all approaches that use our adult power *over* children. Every time we use such approaches, we are showing children that we too believe that coercion is necessary to get what we want from each other.

In the case of Brian, we walked over to talk to the little girl he'd hurt. I helped Brian ask how she was and to make amends. I *showed* Brian that I wanted to help him find a positive way to resolve this situation, not *force* him to behave by my standards. This approach helped Brian feel some concern for the little girl because he saw and talked with her, and could go beyond his first aim of avoiding punishment. As Piaget (1965) wrote, the more authority we adults use *over* children, the less likely they will learn to regulate their own behavior from within. Because we want children to learn to feel genuine kindness toward others, we have to use approaches that will help them build feelings of empathy and caring from the inside out.

Here's a second example of how we might show children alternatives to coercion, this time using a conflict situation. Because kids see so many examples of adversarial conflict resolution in the media—of "we" versus "them" and "might makes right"—they need to see how things could be done differently. I went to a street fair with several families, including Lara and her 5-year-old son Quentin. There was a vendor there selling small bird statues and Lara bought one. As we were riding home, Quentin began saying that he wanted to put the new statue in his room, but his mom had clearly bought the statue for herself. Lara has taught conflict resolution to parents for several years, and she wanted to work out this problem cooperatively with Quentin. Here is how their discussion went:

Quentin: I want the statue to be in my room.

Lara: You want it to be in your room?

Quentin: Yes. I want to wake up and look at it in the morning.

Lara: That would be nice, wouldn't it, to wake up in the morning and look at the statue?

Quentin: It's beautiful. I love birds.

Lara: You really love birds, don't you? Well, I bought this statue to put in our living room. So, you want it in your room and I want to put it in the living room. What do you think we can do about this?

Quentin: I want it in my room!

Lara: So—you want the statue in your room. Hmmm. And I would like to put the statue on the black table in the living room. What can we do? Do you have any ideas?

Quentin: We could put it in my room for a year.

Lara: You want to have the statue for a whole year? I would really miss it if it went into your room for a whole year! How about we try it in your room for a week and then put it in the living room?

Quentin: Okay, I'll put it in my room for a week.

Lara: And I will tell you when the week is over and it's time to put it in the living room. Do you think you can do that—put it in the living room after a week?

Quentin: Yes I can, Mommy.

Later, Lara and I talked about how she had worked out this conflict with Quentin. I noticed how she had begun the discussion by listening carefully to Quentin and reflecting back what she heard him saying, and I commented on this. Lara told me that she had learned that *listening*—and really giving it her full attention and her presence—is the most powerful skill she knows as a parent. As Lara listens to her son, he feels safe and secure; he trusts that he can express what he truly feels. It can be hard to listen as Lara does in conflict situations with our kids—often we don't want to hear what they are saying. But in order to resolve conflicts with children, they first have to feel they've been heard. Once this occurred with Quentin, he and Lara were able to look for a solution to their problem. It's important to see that Lara doesn't "give in" to Quentin's request. She states her own needs and asks him to help solve their shared problem. The solution they come up with is often called a *win-win solution* because both sides feel satisfied with it.

As Lara resolves this conflict with her son, she is showing Quentin an alternative to *power-over* ways to resolve conflicts. She shows him how even parents and children can work things out fairly without one person winning and another losing.

There are teachers who use this same problem-solving approach in their classrooms with individual children and with groups of children. Jim teaches kindergarten and he regularly asks questions of his class at meeting time: "We have a new aquarium in the room—how can we feed these fish so that every one gets a fair chance?" And, "I have noticed that there's been a lot of fighting in the block area lately. What do you think we can do about this?" Lengthy discussions usually follow Jim's questions, as children express their ideas and opinions about the problem and the group looks for a way to solve it that the whole class agrees to.

Jim has a Peace Corner in his classroom where children go to work out their conflicts. It has soft cushions, paper and markers for drawing, and stick puppets, each with a photo of a child in the class. Sometimes the children hold up their puppets and talk through them, especially when they are very angry. Jim has taken photos of children as they work out their conflicts and he's written down and posted their solutions on one wall of the Peace Corner. These solutions give ideas to other children who come to the Peace Corner with problems. They say things like:

> Roseanne asked James, "How can I help you feel better?"
> Jasmine and Tony are going to share blocks next time.
> Melissa asked Danisha to say, "I'm sorry," and she did.
> Robert and Jacob shook hands. We are friends now.

HELPING CHILDREN LEARN SOCIAL AND EMOTIONAL SKILLS

Social and emotional skills develop throughout childhood and are still developing for many of us long after. These skills can present challenges to young children, who tend to think in egocentric ways, making it hard for them to understand how their behavior affects others or how someone else might feel. In addition, media models that glorify violence present additional challenges to children's social and emotional learning.

We can begin working on social and emotional skills when children are very young, but we have to do it in ways that match how young children think and learn, that is, through active learning experiences embedded in real social situations. The social and emotional skills that we can begin working on in the early years include: self-awareness, learning about our feelings and the feelings of others, developing empathy for how others feel, understanding someone else's view, and dealing effectively with relationships. Creative teachers and parents can generate an infinite number of learning moments to help young children develop these skills.

There are teachers around the country who are exploring ways to help young children develop the skill of *self-awareness* through various activities that focus children's attention on how their bodies and emotions feel. Jane teaches kindergarten in New York City. She has had a Peace Corner in her classroom for many years, but recently Jane has begun integrating moments of quiet reflection throughout the day. When it's time to transition to a new activity, for example, Jane turns out the lights, which tells the children it's time for a moment of quiet—to take some deep breaths, focus on their belly breathing, and the feeling of calm they may notice inside.

Jane and other teachers often start the day with passing the "Hug a Planet" ball—a big, soft planet Earth—from child to child. Before she passes the ball, Jane asks the children in the circle for a moment of silence—to close their eyes and check inside on how they are feeling.

When a child gets the ball, she can say how she is feeling that day. Jane said that recently, when one young child got the ball, he paused, then said, "I realize I'm very sleepy. Things are very bad at home and I can't sleep." Jane followed up later with the child's family, but was glad the boy felt safe enough to share his feelings.

Giving children moments like this at home and school on a regular basis can help them gradually become more self-aware and develop a growing capacity for reflection (Lantieri, 2008). These skills, sometimes termed *inner life skills*, can build children's resilience and give them a deep sense of calm that can help them cope with the pressures from commercial culture.

Here is a second example of how we might teach social and emotional skills to young children, this one from some very ingenious teachers in a day care center in Boston. These teachers devised an interactive storytelling activity called Problem Puppets. They used puppets to tell lively stories based on, but not identical to, the social dynamics they were observing among the children. One day when I was visiting this center, two girls who were playing under the tire swing at outside time told a third child that she could not join them. When it came time for the Problem Puppets that day, the teachers introduced the puppets by their fictitious names and began telling a story to the class. They told about two girls who were playing in the block area when a third girl asked to join in. But the two girls said, "You can't play with us—we don't like you!" As soon as the puppets said this, the preschoolers began calling out, "Problem! Problem!" The teacher stopped and asked, "What is the problem?" And then many hands flew up, excited to describe what had happened. The teachers went on to ask many questions: "How does the girl feel who can't play?" "What could she say to the other girls?" "How can the two girls help her feel better?" "What could they do next time?" After a while of collecting the children's ideas, the teachers completed the story using some of the ideas they'd heard.

Because the puppet stories grow out of interactions the teachers have observed among the children, they are always meaningful to the children and well matched to their developmental level. The children listen intently to these stories, waiting to shout out "Problem!" and then contribute their ideas. As teachers pose open-ended questions about the story, it challenges the children to think more deeply about how we get along and affect each other in our relationships. Through this active and engaging activity, children are helped to gradually construct social and emotional awareness and skill.

TAKING BACK CHILDHOOD

To reverse the trends undermining healthy childhoods today will require social action and systemic change that may be a long time in coming. But as we continue to press for public policies that will bring greater equality and well-being to all children and protect them from media and marketplace exploitation, we can also take many steps with the children in our own homes, schools, and communities to reclaim for them some of the vital childhood experiences they are losing out on today. I can never hear the words of Margaret Mead enough: "Never doubt that a small group of thoughtful people can change the world. Indeed, it's the only thing that ever has." I believe that you and I, with our commitment to children and recognition of the impediments they face today, can act on their behalf wherever we are and in our own ways, to bring a better society into being that truly will support all children as they grow up to reach their full potential as human beings.

REFERENCES

American Academy of Pediatrics. (2000). *Joint statement on the impact of entertainment violence on children*. Presented at the Congressional Public Health Summit, Washington, DC.

American Academy of Pediatrics, Committee on Public Education. (2001). Children, adolescents, and television. *Pediatrics, 107*(2). 423–426.

Bronson, P., & Merryman, A. (2010, July 10). The creativity crisis. *Newsweek*. Retrieved from http://www.newsweek.com/2010/07/10/the-creativity-crisis.print.html

Carlsson-Paige, N. (2008). *Taking back childhood: Helping your kids thrive in a fast-paced, media-saturated, violence-filled world*. New York: Hudson Street Press.

Collaborative for Academic, Social, and Emotional Learning. (2007). The benefits of school-based social and emotional programs: Highlights from a forthcoming CASEL report. *CASEL Update*. Retrieved from http://www.melissainstitute.org/documents/weissberg-3.pdf

Coolahan, K., Fantuzzo, J., Mendez, J., & McDermott, P. (2000). Preschool peer interactions and readiness to learn: Relationships between classroom peer play and learning behaviors and conduct. *Journal of Education Psychology, 92*(3), 458–465.

Horovitz, B. (2006, November 22). Six strategies marketers use to make kids want things bad. *USA Today*, p. 18. Retrieved from http://www.usatoday.com/money/advertising/2006-11-21-toy-strategies-usat_x.htm

Isenberg, J., & Quisenberry, N. (2002). *Play: Essential for all children*. A position paper of the Association for Childhood Education International. Retrieved from http://365waystounplugyourkids.com/play_Essential_for_kidsl.htm

Lantieri, L. (2008). *Building emotional intelligence.* Boulder, CO: Sounds True.

Levin, D. E., & Carlsson-Paige, N. (2006). *The war play dilemma: What every parent and teacher needs to know.* New York: Teachers College Press.

Linn, S. (2004). *Consuming kids: The hostile takeover of childhood.* New York: The New Press.

McDonough, P. (2009, October 26). TV viewing among kids at an eight-year high. *NielsenWire.* Retrieved from http://blog.nielsen.com/nielsenwire/media_entertainment/tv-viewing-among-kids-at-an-eight-year-high/

Miller, E., & Almon, J. (2009). *Crisis in the kindergarten: Why children need to play in school.* College Park, MD: Alliance for Childhood.

Moore, M., & Russ, S. W. (2008). Follow-up of a pretend play intervention: Effects on play, creativity, and emotional processes in children. *Creativity Research Journal, 20*(4), 427–436.

National Institute on Media and the Family (NIMF). (2006, October). *Consensus statement.* Paper presented at the National Summit on Video Games, Youth, and Public Policy, University of Minnesota Continuing Education and Conference Center, Falcon Heights, MN.

Piaget, J. (1965). *The moral judgment of the child.* New York: Free Press.

Rideout, V., Foehr, U. G., & Roberts, D. (2010). *Generation M2: Media in the lives of 8 to 18 year olds.* Menlo Park, CA: Kaiser Family Foundation.

Rideout, V., & Hamel, E. (2006). *The media family: Electronic media in the lives of infants, toddlers, preschoolers, and their parents.* Menlo Park, CA: Kaiser Family Foundation.

Schor, J. (2004). *Born to buy.* New York: Scribner.

Singer, D., Singer, J., Plaskon, S. L., & Schweder, A. (2003). A role for play in the preschool curriculum. In S. Olfman (Ed.), *All work and no play: How educational reforms are harming our preschoolers* (pp. 43–70). Westport, CT: Praeger.

United Nations Children's Fund (UNICEF). (2007). *Child poverty in perspective: An overview of child well-being in rich countries.* Florence, Italy: United Nations Children's Fund.

Vygotsky, L. S. (1976). Play and its role in the mental development of the children. In J. S. Bruner, A. Jolly, & K. Sylva (Eds.), *Play: Its role in development and evolution* (pp. 536–552). New York: Basic Books.

Whitebread, D., Coltman, P., Jameson, H., & Lander, R., (2009). Play, cognition and self-regulation: What exactly are children learning when they learn through play? *Educational and Child Psychology, 26*(2), 40–52.

WHO Forum. (2006, May 5). *Marketing of food and non-alcoholic beverages to children: Report of a WHO forum and technical meeting, Oslo, Norway, 2–5 May 2006.* Geneva, Switzerland: World Health Organization.

Winnicott, D. W. (1971). *Playing and reality.* New York: Basic Books.

Wyver, S. R., & Spence, S. H. (1999). Play and divergent problem solving: Evidence supporting a reciprocal relationship. *Early Education and Development, 10*(4), 419–444.

CHAPTER 8

Standardized Testing

Unheeded Issues That Impact Children's Learning

George Madaus and Terrence Lee-St. John

In the United States, standardized tests, which emerged after World War I, were not at first seen as a threat to most teachers and children. As one observer put it, "[they] knew virtually nothing was ever done with the results. When the teacher spent the morning giving a [standardized] test, it was an easy morning for him or her, and a not unpleasant one for most of the pupils. Such tests were much less threatening to the children than a test prepared by the teacher on which a grade might depend" (Travers, 1983, p. 142). Soon after World War II, however, the impact of testing on teachers and students began to change substantially. Each succeeding decade, starting in the 1950s and culminating in this century, witnessed a relentless shift, at first subtle, then dramatic, in the significance of standardized tests in education, culminating in the passage of the No Child Left Behind Act (NCLB) of 2001.

Today's tests are more important in the lives of children, their parents, and teachers, than at any time in our country's history. Over the last 6 decades, testing America's children has become an increasingly contentious issue with conflicting educational, political, cultural, business, media, and monetary dimensions. For many politicians at the federal, state, and local levels, and for many in the business and testing communities, testing has morphed from a means of obtaining information about the education system to a key strategy for improving educational quality. Proponents of test-driven reform assume that test scores can serve as objective, accurate sources of information about student ability, as well as teacher and school quality.

This way of thinking is certainly not new. The Prime Minister of Ireland, Eamon DeValera, arguing in Parliament for a system of certification examinations at the end of primary school, said in 1941:

> But if we want to see that a certain standard is reached and we are paying the money, we have the right to see that something is secured for that money. The ordinary way to test it and try to help the whole educational system is by arranging our tests in such a way that they will work in a direction we want. (Dáil Éireann, 1941, col.119)

Given the assumed infallibility of test scores for these accountability purposes, high-stakes testing is thought by proponents to be a vehicle of positive change, driving what is taught, how it is taught, what is learned, and how it is learned; a technology that can increase our nation's productivity, restore the country's global competitiveness, and provide the basis for paying teachers for their students' performance.

How did testing become so important and so ubiquitous in American society? We begin with a snapshot of how testing has affected different sectors of our society. Next, we present an abbreviated history of testing young children. We then point out the nonacademic factors that affect the test performance of children. Finally, we describe how these high-stakes tests affect our children, parents, and schools.

THE PRESENCE OF TESTING IN TODAY'S AMERICAN SOCIETY

Testing our children is an issue of concern for diverse organizations, from the Business Roundtable to the National Council of Churches, from the National Governors Association to the Children's Defense Fund. It is a topic for talk show hosts, the media, and entertainment industries (Madaus, Russell, & Higgins, 2009). The growth in testing is a boon for the publishing, test preparation, and tutoring industries, generating more than a billion dollars in revenue each year (Eduventures, 2006; Miner, 2004; Saulny, 2006). On top of this windfall, the indirect costs of testing programs incurred by our teachers, school administrators, and students range from 4 to more than 50 times the direct costs (Haney, Madaus, & Lyons, 1993). While these estimates are from 1993, they probably underestimate indirect costs because of the increase in mandated testing under the 2001 federal education act, No Child Left Behind (NCLB).

Hardly a day passes without a newspaper or television news report concerning testing. One such story was about a principal ordering

3,600 peppermint candies to help improve performance on the day of the statewide test (Aratani, 2007). Another was about a town's school that received an "unacceptable" rating on the state test, prompting homeowners to call real estate companies to talk about selling their homes because they feared that housing values would plunge. There was news coverage of one affluent suburban town that wanted to "catch up" with its neighbors by getting more students to the advanced level on the state test—the proficient level just wasn't good enough anymore (Sacchetti, 2006). One local newspaper reported that just a single third-grade boy in an inner-city school reached the state goal on the reading mastery test, while 4 miles away in an affluent school, five out of six third graders reached the goal (Green, 2006).

Of course, it is the children who must sit for a state-mandated test who are directly affected by the testing craze. Children talk about state-mandated tests at the dinner table, while waiting at the bus stop, and during play dates. Children even start thinking about state tests years before they actually take them. In some schools, 10-year-olds now take two to four tests per week focusing on the skills and knowledge their teachers expect will appear on the state test (Madaus et al., 2009). While some look forward to taking these tests, others have trouble sleeping, become sick to their stomachs, and ask to stay home from school (Clarke et al., 2003).

Parents play a major part in the present sociology of testing. Given the perceived importance of high-stakes tests, many parents attempt to advantage their young in ways that have questionable short- and long-term effects. Some parents with enough capital turn to gadgets in hopes of giving their offspring a competitive edge. Cell phones present children with practice questions while they wait for the bus. Websites give students instant feedback on sample tests. Parents also buy toys purporting to improve test performance several years down the road; for example, Time Tracker, a $34.95 toy on the market for Christmas 2004, purported to help children as young as age 4 better manage their time when taking a high-stakes standardized test years later (Bick, 2006).

To increase the chances that their children will pass their first high-stakes state test in the third grade, some parents enroll their children in tutoring and test preparation courses. In Texas, prekindergarten voluntary program certification is linked to how well the program predicts their pupils' subsequent kindergarten scores on reading and social skills tests (Hupp, 2007). More recently, *The New York Times* reported that picture book sales are down, due in no small measure to parents who are looking forward to their children taking the all-important state test. Parents press their kindergartners and first graders to move instead to "text-heavy chapter books" (Bosman, 2010).This shift away from picture books is yet another indicator of parental anxiety about helping their offspring meet future challenges not only in school, but elsewhere—for example, Baby Mozart and soccer classes for children 18 to 24 months old (Hyman, 2010).

Finally, while many parents recoil at schools using "intelligence" test scores for admission to kindergarten or promotion to the first grade, it is unobjectionable to them when a test with the same kinds of questions is named a "readiness test" (Sheppard & Smith, 1986). Nonetheless, indicative of the anxiety parents feel, those with enough capital in New York City are willing to subject their young to an "intelligence test" entrance exam called the E.R.B. when trying to get their preschool children into top private schools (Maslin, 2010).

TESTING CHILDREN: A BRIEF HISTORY

The importance of testing is not a new phenomenon. Seen as a mechanism for addressing society's political, social, educational, and economic concerns, testing has been embraced by diverse cultures across the centuries (Madaus et al., 2009). However, during much of this history, testing of young children was limited to a relatively small number of privileged children fortunate enough to receive an education.

The Protestant Reformation produced the first widespread formal testing technique—the catechism—to evaluate a child's attainment of a fixed body of knowledge. Luther and his fellow reformers, Catholic counterreformers, as well as rabbis (Lewy, 1996), used the catechism to ensure the transmission of religious orthodoxy (Graves, 1920).

In 1444 a contract between the town fathers of Treviso and its schoolmaster was, arguably, the earliest coupling of teacher accountability to children's performance on tests. Based on student performance, the schoolmaster received four levels of reward, ranging from a half ducat for proficiency in the alphabet to two ducats for success in stylistic exercises or rhetoric (Madaus & Kellaghan, 1993).

This idea of holding teachers accountable for student attainment by coupling their pupils' examination results with monetary rewards became known as "payment by results"; it was used in the 18th century in Ireland; in the 19th in Australia, Great Britain, Ireland, and Jamaica; and in the 20th and 21st centuries in the United States (Madaus et al., 2009). The high stakes attached to payment-by-results tests historically have affected not only children and parents in the ways we have mentioned above, but have also affected teaching methods and student learning. For example, in 1868 during the payment-by-results era in England, Mathew Arnold rendered the classic indictment of payment-by-results schemes in whatever form:

> a game of mechanical contrivance in which teachers will and must learn how to beat us. It is found possible by ingenious preparation, to get children through the . . . examination in reading, writing and ciphering, without their really knowing how to read, write and cipher. (1867–1868, p. 52)

The shift in testing from a means of obtaining information to a key strategy for improving educational quality is a continuing problem in education. This is wonderfully illustrated in the following observation from an early-20th-century British school inspector who observed firsthand the negative effects of high-stakes payment-by-results programs operating in England and Ireland.

> Whenever the outward standard of reality (examination results) has established itself at the expense of the inward, the ease with which worth (or what passes for such) can be measured is ever tending to become in itself the chief, if not sole, measure of worth. And in proportion as we tend to value the results of education for their immeasurableness, so we tend to undervalue and at last to ignore those results which are too intrinsically valuable to be measured. (Holmes, 1911, p. 128)

The paradoxical costs associated with the spread of multiple-choice tests—to improve efficiency and ease scoring as the numbers of students swelled—were substantial. By 1922 the boast was made that "most of the tests [on] the market, unless measuring handwriting, do not call for written answers" (Pressey & Pressey, 1992, p. 186). The multiple-choice test has come to be an end in itself, as described by Tom Wolfe (1987) in *The Bonfire of the Vanities*:

> "Let me ask you this. How does he do on his written work?" Mr. Rifkind let out a whoop. "Written work? There hasn't been any written work at Rupert High for fifteen years! Maybe twenty! They take tests. Reading comprehension, that's the big thing. That's all the Board of Education cares about." (pp. 130–131)

Arnold's observations and Wolfe's satire illustrate how high-stakes tests influence both teacher and pupil behavior. The exams come to exercise prescriptive authority and delimit and eventually define what and how things are taught and learned.

All payment-by-results schemes made two assumptions. First, if teachers taught correctly, pupils would surely learn; and second, examinations would insure that students received proper instruction (Hearn, 1872). For example, in an 1845 letter to Samuel Gridley Howe, Horace Mann embraced both assumptions when he offered advice on how to use results for political leverage using the newly introduced printed, written examination in the Boston public schools:

> Some pieces should be immediately written for the papers, containing so much of an analysis of the answers, as will show that the pupils answered common and memoriter questions far better than they did questions involving a principle; *and it should be set forth most pointedly, that in the former case, the merit belongs to the scholars, in the latter the demerit belongs to the master. . . . Children will not learn such things by instinct. They will not fail to learn them, under proper instruction* [emphasis added]. (Mann, 1845–46, Box 8)

The belief that all students could learn if properly taught seriously began to erode in the latter part of the 19th century, when compulsory attendance, immigration, and the abolition of child labor forced educators to deal with diverse populations that never before had been of concern.

Two developments in testing provided a basis and rationalization for a change in the belief that all students could learn if teachers taught correctly. First, there was an implicit assumption of an absolute standard of proficiency—students should be able to master *all* of the content measured by a test. This assumption began to be replaced by normative standards of attainment—the median score of students across a district became the standard. Walker Percy (1991) highlights why using an absolute standard of proficiency must eventually give way to normative standards:

> The scientist, in practicing the scientific method, cannot utter a single word about an individual thing or creature insofar as it is an individual but only insofar as it resembles other individuals. This limitation holds true whether the individual is a molecule of NaCl or an amoeba or a human being. (pp. 211–212)

Second, toward the end of the first decade of the 20th century, the "IQ" test was used to "explain" why many children could not be expected to do well. Educators shifted the explanation for poor attainment away from teaching and to a lack of a student's "ability" to learn, or to the student's home background (Judd, 1918).

Policy wise, these developments in testing have brought us full circle: from the belief that pupils will surely learn if teachers teach correctly, to attributing poor attainment to a lack of student's abilities or other contextual factors, and back to pupils will surely learn if teachers teach correctly. Interestingly, despite the current policy focus on in-school factors, a majority of adults now blame low educational achievement on children's parents (Blankinship, 2010). However, both nonacademic variables and teacher influences affect student attainment.

OUT-OF-SCHOOL FACTORS AFFECTING CHILDREN'S TEST PERFORMANCE

Research is clear: Class, culture, and the properties of the test itself interact to influence a student's test score.

Socioeconomic Issues

Research has demonstrated that socioeconomics has a powerful impact on children's development. Parents whose jobs requires them to collaborate are more likely to have their children think through problems in order to figure out answers; thus children whose parents are professionals tend to take a more inquisitive and active approach to learning than children whose parents are from the working class (Rothstein, 2004). Some studies have found that even the amount of words exchanged between parents and children affected by parents' past educational experience: Parents who are college educated have been noted to speak more than 2,000 words an hour to their children compared with 1,300 words for working-class parents and only 600 for mothers who are on public assistance. Relevant here is the fact that the quantity of words spoken to infants has been linked to the infants' subsequent rates of language development (National Public Radio, 2011). Similarly, other studies have documented that for every one reprimand, toddlers of college-educated parents receive six utterances of encouragement, while children from working-class parents receive only two per reprimand; and children whose parents are on public assistance receive one encouragement for every two reprimands (Diuguid, 2005), resulting in differential levels of self-esteem, which has been shown to relate to motivation.

At about 20%, the rate of children living in poverty in 2010 was the highest in several decades (Isaacs, 2010). Rates are even higher in urban settings. To put this in context, the United States ranks last of all OECD countries in the overall indices for equality in child well-being (UNICEF, 2010). This inequality impacts children's achievement and growth in three major ways.

- *Constraints on Investments.* Poverty can limit a family's ability to invest money, time, and energy in fostering children's growth (e.g., less money for books, puzzles, and a comfortable place to study; less time to read and talk with their children; fewer opportunities to ensure that children follow their interests in sports, music, and art).
- *Stress.* Economic scarcity can create pervasive stress within families and their neighborhoods—stress that undermines children's sense of well-being and safety (e.g., economic stress increases the likelihood of exposure to community violence, undermining children's social-emotional stability and their ability to self-regulate).
- *Chaotic Circumstances.* In the context of economic scarcity, life can be chaotic: Transportation, municipal services, and businesses are often less reliable than in more affluent, resourced communities. Moreover, poorer communities often receive a disproportionate share of exposure to environmental contagions (e.g., lead and air pollution).

For children living in poverty, these out-of-school factors clearly impact their ability to succeed in school. Limited resources, stress, and the chaos of poverty all contribute to poor school attendance, high mobility, social-emotional dysfunction, lack of readiness for school, and limited cultural capital to understand schools as institutions (Dearing, 2008).

Research estimates that out-of-school factors account for 67% of the variance on tests, while in-school factors account for 33% (Rothstein, 2004). Thus this suggests that addressing social factors is at least as crucial as addressing in-school factors in order to increase student achievement.

Cultural Issues

Cultural influences on test performance begin at a very young age and affect how an individual child and groups of children are perceived and treated throughout their time in school. High-stakes testing incorporates two culturally held values: Achievement is an individual accomplishment, and individuals must display their accomplishment publicly.

Most middle-class children have been socialized to accept these two values. Early on, they assume the role of information givers (Deyhle, 1986). Prior to entering school, they are "tested" by their parents. For example, babies are repeatedly asked to point to their nose, bottle, shoes, and so on; toddlers are asked "Where is the truck?" or "Point to the horse" in a picture; preschoolers are asked about stories in books or about people and events in their lives.

However, children from some cultural backgrounds, prior to attending school, are not necessarily asked by adults to be information givers (Tyler, 1979). This is true, for example, for many American Indian children. Rather than emphasizing the development of verbal skills, Indian cultures socialize children through nonverbal communication and emphasize spatial skills, sequential visual memory, and motor skills. Tribal cultures also emphasize sharing and working together. In contrast, the tests they encounter in school focus primarily on verbal skills and require children to work alone (Locust, 1988).

American Indians are not the only people who have a culture clash with tests. Culture influences the test performance of other minorities, recent immigrants, bilingual students, and females (National Commission on Testing and Public Policy, 1990).

Students' Interpretation of Test Items

A crucial factor in test development is the quality of a test's items or questions. The presentation of an item or its accompanying directions can cause an examinee who has the necessary knowledge, skill, or ability for that problem to get the item wrong; or, conversely, it can be presented in such a way that a student who does *not* have the required knowledge, skill, or ability for that problem gets it right. Items on tests generally stand alone, without benefit of detailed context to further define the situation or the problem. The writers of these items do not always foresee how the items will be interpreted. Moreover, they do not always write the types of items that can get at what cognitive psychologist Jerome Bruner argued is most important: knowing not only what children can *do*, but also what they *think* they are doing and their reasons for doing it (Bruner, 1996; Haney & Scott, 1987).

Two studies shed light on the limitations and fallibility of test items for some children and adolescents. One is by Clifford Hill and Eric Larsen (2000), who describe the dilemma facing test item writers. When constrained by time and space for testing, item writers often produce brief and therefore decontextualized passages that can lead children astray. In their study, Hill and Larsen found that children faced with the item's condensed story tend to expand it to achieve meaning, often pulling from what is familiar rather than from the passage, which leads them to select the wrong answer.

Another example of this phenomenon is illustrated by a study conducted by Haney and Scott (1987) who asked young children to explain why they chose a particular answer to items on commonly used standardized achievement tests. One particular item is a good illustration of their findings: Students were asked which plant needs the least amount of water. They were shown a pot with flowers in it, a cabbage, and a pot with a cactus in it. When asked why they chose the "incorrect" option (cabbage) instead of the "right" answer (cactus), a number of students explained that the cabbage, which was not in a pot, had been picked and therefore no longer needed water. Despite this reasonable explanation, children who chose the cabbage distracter were marked wrong.

Such problematic items on a test can have an adverse impact on the classification and subsequent treatment of students who are within a few points of achieving a passing or important cut score on a test.

Test Error

Test scores themselves are subject to varying degrees of error. Even if we assume that a test is measuring the same ability for all students, the scores are only estimates of that underlying ability. Not only do different tests estimate ability with different amounts of error, but even within the same test, various levels of ability are estimated with various amounts of error.

High-stakes tests attach rewards and sanctions to cut scores (i.e., failing, needs improvement, proficient, advanced) on tests. Nonetheless, each cut score has its own error component. This error ensures that some students will always be misclassified (i.e., false positive or false negative). If the error at a cut score is small, it reduces the instances of misclassification. Nonetheless, for individuals who are misclassified as "failing," consequences can be dire.

Very slight, seemingly innocuous alterations in the design of the test can produce very different classifications of student performance. For example, the dramatic drop in the National Assessment of Educational Progress (NAEP) reading scores from 1984 to 1986 was so large that people thought it improbable. Beaton and Zwick (1990) showed that small changes—switching the order of the questions (item 3 becomes item 7), using stapled instead of saddle-stitched test booklets, having students fill in an oval rather than circle a letter to mark their answers, and using brown or black instead of blue print—explained the "Infamous Reading Anomaly." In other words, the changes in test scores, used to make inferences about changes in student achievement, were affected by subtle changes in the test format rather than changes in students' actual skills and knowledge.

Relying solely on test scores to make important decisions about students, teachers, and schools on the surface seems like an objective, cost effective strategy for implementing education reform. However, doing so ignores the complicated nature of measuring cognitive abilities.

HOW HIGH-STAKES TESTING AFFECTS CHILDREN

High-stakes testing has a number of unintended consequences associated with it. These include narrowing of the curriculum, increased retention and dropout rates, lessening of student motivation, and negative emotional effects on students and their families.

Narrowing of the Curriculum

The high stakes attached to test scores often determine what is taught and not taught at a particular grade. They lead to more emphasis being placed on academic skills at the expense of social, emotional, and physical goals for children. To better prepare students for the high-stakes tests that will be given in the upper grades, the curriculum in kindergarten and first grade is often altered (Madaus et al., 2009).

Pressure to improve scores on mandated tests can decrease the use of classroom time for intensive instructional strategies and more lengthy enrichment activities that help to produce critical thinkers and active learners. Instead, emphasis is placed on narrowly focused test preparation (Pedulla et al., 2003). This is particularly problematic when the test is multiple-choice. For example, as early as 1981 Deborah Meier reported that in New York City reading classes, students spent large portions of their school day preparing for the tests they would take in the spring by reading dozens of commercially prepared, testlike paragraphs about which they then answered multiple-choice questions (National Institute of Education, 1981).

Another serious problem with high-stakes tests that directly affects children is the effect they have on nontested subjects. One study found that 71% of school districts reduced time in at least one subject to expand time for reading and math instruction. More specifically, 33% of districts reduced time for social studies, 29% reduced time for science, and 22% reduced time for art and music. The study also found that in some districts the amount of time struggling students spent on tested subjects doubled, at times causing them to miss other subjects altogether (Center on Educational Policy, 2006).

And shortchanging time is not limited only to nontested subjects. It also extends to recess. Millions of American schoolchildren are missing out on unstructured play and exercise with their peers as schools eliminate recess to spend more time on test preparation (National PTA, 2006; Otterman, 2011). For young children, recess provides a learning space to acquire peer-level social skills, imagination, creativity, and physical fitness/coordination. Though this may initially seem irrelevant to reading and math attainment, recent studies have linked exercise to increases in math achievement (Corwin, 2011). Similarly, social skills development has also been linked to improved academic achievement (Sparks, 2011).

Additionally, recess provides children with a respite from academic subjects. Such respite is especially necessary for young children because they are still developing attention skills. Though a 2-hour block of intense reading instruction may seem like the best way to increase reading ability, for young children, two 50-minute blocks separated by a 10-minute recess may in fact go further toward increasing reading abilities (Ramstetter, 2010).

As academic subjects, measured by standardized tests, now dominate instruction, schools are moving away from emphasizing important aspects that contribute to learning, such as attendance and respectful classroom behavior. What matters is a student's performance on tests (Tyre, 2010). One can only wonder how productive and happy the life of an adult will be if he or she lacks the proper discipline and social skills required to survive in a professional workplace.

Retention and Dropping Out

Another consequence of high-stakes testing is that some school districts have started to "red shirt" kindergarten students. Red shirting originally was a practice of holding back a scholarship athlete from playing for a year to let him or her develop further in the given sport. Now, in elementary schools the practice of red shirting is used with children who either are not allowed to enter kindergarten despite meeting the age requirement or who are required to repeat kindergarten for a second year. By delaying the start of kindergarten or first grade, the hope is that test scores will be higher down the road if for no other reason than that red-shirted students are a year older when they take a high-stakes test (Bronson, 2003).

In addition, some schools and teachers have adopted the practice of "triaging"—focusing intensive test preparation on "Bubble Kids," those who are on the bubble of passing the test or of moving up to the next performance level. Researchers, here and in England, have found that teachers concentrate instruction on those most likely to succeed in moving up to the next performance level, to the detriment of those not expected to do well (Booher-Jennings, 2005; Kellaghan & Greaney, 1992). Both red shirting and triaging often result in students being retained in a grade. And retention in any grade (including elementary school) has been documented to result in higher probabilities of students dropping out in high school (Darling-Hammond & Falk, 1997).

Further, in addition to these informal red shirting and triaging practices, formal retention policies are increasingly being implemented as a result of high-stakes testing. In a national survey, 30% of U.S. teachers in states with high-stakes tests reported that state test results were used as the sole determinant in promoting or retaining students in grade (Pedulla et al., 2003). These formal retention practices can begin as early as third grade (the initial grade students are now being exposed to high-stakes tests under the 2001 No Child Left Behind Act). For example, Indiana has passed legislation requiring third graders to "pass" a statewide reading test in order to be promoted to the fourth grade. The bill, which would go into effect in 2013, has been sent to the governor for his expected approval (Elliot, 2011).

Such formal retention policies are being implemented despite a solid body of research that documents how grade retention does not generally help students improve academically. Instead, retention has been found to actually eat away at students' sense of academic worth, which is related to lower rates of both school attendance and intrinsic motivation to succeed academically (Anderson, Whipple, & Jimerson, 2002). Though no one advocates grade promotion without learning, grade retention is not particularly effective at increasing learning. Without changing the nature of the learning experience, it often puts students in situations where they must repeat what did not work for them the first time.

Motivation

Research supports the view that motivation, particularly crucial during adolescence, is an important determinant of learning and achievement (Anderman & Maehr, 1994; Lens, 1994). High-stakes testing, however, has not been found to motivate unmotivated students. What students are motivated to do as a result of high-stakes tests is often very different from what some assume will happen. While some students study harder and some develop intrinsic interest in subjects tested, others are only motivated to pass and focus primarily on strategies such as rote memorization or test gaming.

In order for high-stakes tests to increase motivation, students must believe that the rewards attached to test performance are both important and realistically within reach. But this is not the case for many. Some students who perceive their ability to be low tend to avoid challenge, behave helplessly, and demonstrate little persistence. Still others do not equate test performance with improved job or college prospects due to the scarcity of jobs or lack of relevance of college in their family and community settings. For them, the rewards for passing the test are illusory.

Students who are not motivated by high-stakes testing are more likely to become alienated, not only from the tests but from the entire educational process. These students may react by avoiding academic challenges, quitting school, or just not learning in order to protect their self-esteem.

Another important factor that limits the motivational effect of high-stakes testing is a student's age. When the importance of a test is communicated to young students, if it is remote in time—months and perhaps several grades away—the relevance is often beyond their capacity to understand (Kellaghan, Madaus, & Raczek, 1996).

The Emotional Toll

Although high-stakes tests are intended to motivate students, the pressure to perform well on them also exerts an unintended emotional toll on many students and their families. No one that we are aware of has attempted to systematically quantify this emotional toll. However, these effects are pervasive throughout literature and in the testimony of today's classroom teachers.

Rafferty (1985) has chronicled how authors across different literary genres in England and Ireland have depicted testing. He found that some have employed prayer, religious diction, allusion, and imagery to illuminate the importance of major tests in the lives of students and their families. Other literary works depict the testing system as a series of obstacles or an elaborate race that sifts out "successful" candidates and fails others. For example, John McGahern (1977) views the 3-hour test as having its parallel with 3 hours on the Cross. Maureen Duffy (1962) portrays tests as a *"long-distance run* I'd started on, with people *dropping out* all along the way at the higher and higher *examination hurdles"* (p. 186). V. S. Naipaul (1984) describes the potential impact of a scholarship exam: "[The winners] were the *elect,* the *anointed . . .* We all knew who among them were *the candidates for glory . . .* I too would be *immortalized* and become *an object of veneration* to succeeding generations" [emphasis added] (pp. 57–58). Conversely, A. A. Milne (1930) describes how his poor exam performance evoked the biblical gesture of doomed resignation from his father: "When he read [the results], father turned his face to the wall, and abandoned hope" (p. 112).

This practice of identifying high scorers (and complementarily, publicly embarrassing low scorers) still occurs today and is not limited to England and Ireland. For example, recently a school in Bakersfield, California, gave high-scoring children wristbands. The school also planned to throw a private, celebratory BBQ for those who received the wristbands. Feedback from concerned parents, however, resulted in all children from the school being allowed to attend the BBQ (Barrientos, 2010).

Rafferty (1985) concludes there is "little doubt that the metaphors and images reecho a prevailing sense of the examination as the unique testing time of youth, their parents, and teachers. Some few students may glory in the challenge, most feel demeaned and used by a system that casts a shadow over schooling and leaves the student as prey to forces he still resents" (p. 302).

Today's classroom teachers echo many of the emotional effects of high-stakes tests found throughout literature. Every teacher can recount the emotional stress high-stakes tests have on some students. As an example, a fourth-grade teacher in a large urban district reports: "I've seen kids break down: 'I'm not doing this.' Crying. Complete frustration. I've seen kids get sick to their stomach. What normally took children anywhere from two [to three] hours . . . took this poor child two days. And by . . . the second day, he wet his pants he was so nervous and so upset. . . . There were kids in tears over [the test], and there have been for the last two years. Kids who didn't want to come to school. Kids that had stomachaches they never had before, who would just put down their pencils in frustration" (Clarke et al., 2003, pp. 82–83).

These literary and teacher descriptions attest to the fact that many children, motivated or not, experience unintended negative effects when subjected to the pressures of a high-stakes test. One can only wonder how many children's development of a love of learning has been harmed by the negative, visceral reactions brought about by high-stakes tests, and what consequence this has had on later, higher, deeper levels of achievement.

CONCLUSION

In language applicable to the present debate about testing policy, Sir Geoffrey Elton (1991) argues that history teaches us to "think more deeply, more completely and on the basis of an enormously enlarged experience about what it may be possible or desirable to do now." He further concludes, "a knowledge of the past should arm [people] against surrendering to the panaceas peddled by too many myth makers" (p. 72).

One very clear historical lesson is that testing is a technology that people cannot do without; over centuries and many countries, there has been an enduring need to test. A second lesson is that human nature being what it is—since the introduction of weights and measures to tests of all kinds—attempts to beat or game the system have always been associated with important measurements.

The ways in which past testing programs have solved problems, been corrupted, and have helped some, but dealt a weaker hand to others, should be a cautionary tale in the contemporary debate about high-stakes testing programs for our children. While history may not exactly repeat itself, human nature and the motives and actions that flow from it are timeless.

The term *iatrogenic* refers to a doctor-induced illness that is a negative, unanticipated effect on a patient of a well-intended treatment by a physician. The paradox of high-stakes testing might well be called *peiragenics,* that is, well-intended testing policies that ignore the consequences of testing can negatively affect not only young children, but their parents, teachers, and school. The history of testing over the past 200 years is testimony to peiragenics. On the one hand, the intent of policy makers in mandating testing programs has been corrective rather than malevolent or punitive. Policy makers have used examinations, coupled with rewards or sanctions, as a practical, efficient, and relatively inexpensive means of correcting what they consider to be defects in the educational system. Tests have been mandated for such laudatory purposes as eliminating patronage; opening access to groups hitherto excluded; assuring basic literacy and numeracy for all students; establishing and/or maintaining standards of excellence; holding teachers, students, or schools accountable for learning; and allocating scarce resources to the most able or deserving. On the other hand, in using tests to address these laudatory purposes, well-intentioned testing programs have often produced unintended negative consequences that have impacted heavily on schools and on certain children and their families. What is going on today is a classic example of peiragenics. This 1936 quote from an international conference on public examinations captures this paradox of peiragenics: "Gentlemen, the experience in our country in attempting to solve our difficulties has been that as soon as we think we have solved one problem we almost invariably find that by the solution we have created another" (Monroe, 1936, p. 10).

It is important to recognize, however, that it is not the tests alone that cause these peiragenic disorders. In addition to the problematic quality of some testing measures, it is the stakes associated with test scores, as well as the problem of relying on them exclusively to measure students' progress, that drive teachers, students, and other stakeholders into behavior that results in the many paradoxical unintended outcomes discussed in this chapter. The conundrum in this paradox is that high stakes are the driving force behind current reform policies.

So, which reform policy do we adopt? Do we accept research findings from cognitive developmental scientists and sociologists that tell us high academic achievement is reached through stimulation of multiple cognitive and physical pathways, then incorporate this knowledge into the design of the school day and into decisions on which instructional strategies/focus to utilize and what kind of tests we design? Or do we embrace a "tough love," one-size-fits-all approach relying heavily on tests that measure what is easiest to measure and drive teaching toward direct instruction of reading, math, and science at the expense of the development of more complex cognitive skills?

Of course, as we have seen in this chapter, fixation on reading, math, and science, among other negative consequences, denigrates the worth of those important subjects that are *not* tested (e.g., recess can disappear; less time is available for social studies, art, and music). Further, and most disturbing, high-stakes test results are being used as a requirement for promotion and graduation from high school.

But there is another elephant in the room—the current push by some "reformers" to come up with a 21st-century version of a 15th-century idea of using students' test performance as the indicator of good teaching. If they heed Elton's advice and examine carefully the long, sobering history, from the 15th century to the present, of linking financial rewards with students' performance on tests, they will find that this strategy does not increase numeracy and literacy or improve teacher efficiency and instruction.

The linking of financial rewards with students' performance raises yet another key issue. Poland's leading economic historian, Witold Kula (1986), reminds us that in the Hebrew Bible, the New Testament, and the Koran, pragmatic social conceptions of measures were transformed into the symbolic "just" measure—a symbol for the just person, for justice as such, and of just human relations. But attempts to standardize and make weights and measures equitable and just failed as long as other concomitant reforms, such as feudal rights, provincial particularism, and equity before the law, were neglected. Likewise, any testing system that today's policy makers put in place to make high-stakes decisions about individuals or schools will produce inherently unjust measures for some as long as we neglect nonacademic barriers to learning. As noted above, research estimates that out-of-school factors account for 67% of the variance on tests, while in-school factors account for 33% (Rothstein, 2004).

As Sizer put it in 1984, reforms like testing do not go "to the heart of the problem: the fundamental mis-design of schools and the instability of the families and communities from which students come" (p. xiii). In 2011, some 26 plus years later, Diane Ravitch has also pointed out that poor (student) performance is mostly due to poverty and racial isolation (Ravitch, 2010). We have to heed these calls for addressing the nonacademic barriers to learning and the effects of poverty, while taking into account the limitations of test results. There is a real danger that our love of the technical/testing solution to perceived educational issues will blind us to the reality. One thing is for certain, we cannot test our way out of our educational problems.

REFERENCES

Anderman, E., & Maehr, M. L. (1994). Motivation and schooling in the middle grades. *Review of Educational Research, 64,* 287–309.

Anderson, G., Whipple, A., & Jimerson, S. (2002). *Grade retention: Achievement and mental health outcomes.* Retrieved from Center for Development and Learning website: http://www.cdl.org/resource-library/articles/grade_retention.php

Aratani, L. (2007, March 20). The power of peppermint is put to the test. *The Washington Post.* Retrieved from http://www.washingtonpost.com/wp-dyn/content/article/2007/03/19/AR2007031901624.html

Arnold, M. (1867–1868). *Annual report of the Committee of Council of Education.* London: Her Majesty's Stationary Office.

Barrientos, J. (2010, November 29). School award stirs debate. *Bakersfield.com.* Retrieved from http://www.bakersfield.com/news/local/x716460859/School-award-idea-stirs-debate

Beaton, A., & Zwick, R. (1990). *The effects of changes in the national assessment: Disentangling the NAEP 1985–86 reading anomaly.* Princeton, NJ: Educational Testing Service.

Bick, J. (2006, May 28). Sunday money: Spending; the long (and sometimes expensive) road to the SAT. *The New York Times.* Retrieved from http://www.nytimes.com/2006/05/28/business/yourmoney/28test.html

Blankinship, D. (2010, December 12). *Adults blame parents for education programs.* Retrieved from Yahoo News website: http://news.yahoo.com/s/ap/20101211/ap_on_re_us/us_education_poll_blaming_parents

Booher-Jennings, J. (2005). Blow the bubble: "Educational triage" and the Texas accountability system. *American Educational Research Journal, 42* (2), 231–268.

Bosman, J. (2010, October 7). Picture books no longer a staple for children. *The New York Times*. Retrieved from http://www.nytimes.com/2010/10/08/us/08picture.html?_r=1&scp=1&sq=picture%20books,%20long%20a%20staple&st=cse

Bronson, P. (2003, September 3). Should children redshirt kindergarten? *Newsweek*. Retrieved from http://www.newsweek.com/blogs/nurture-shock/2009/09/03/should-children-redshirt-kindergarten.html

Bruner, J. (1996). *The culture of education*. Cambridge, MA: Harvard University Press.

Center on Educational Policy. (2006). *From the capital to the classroom: Year 4 of No Child Left Behind*. Washington, DC: Center on Educational Policy.

Clarke, M., Shore, A., Rhoades, K., Abrams, L., Miao, J., & Li, J. (2003). *Perceived effects of state-mandated testing programs on teaching and learning: Findings from interviews with educators in lo-, medium, and high-stakes states*. Chestnut Hill, MA: National Board on Educational Testing and Public Policy, Boston College.

Corwin, T. (2011, February 11). Exercise improves math skills, brain study suggests. *The Augusta Chronicle*. Retrieved from http://www.edweek.org/ew/articles/2011/02/10/21mct_gaexercise.h30.html?tkn=STZFX7j1Mjebhkzz8yOJLgb6hXYeVVIsys3Z&cmp=clp-edweek

Dail Eireann. (1941). Parliamentary Debates, Col 1119.

Darling-Hammond, L., & Falk, B. (1997). Using standards and assessment to support student learning. *Phi Delta Kappan, 79*(3), 1990–1999.

Dearing, E. (2008). Psychological costs of growing up poor. *Annals of the New York Academy of Sciences, 30*, 1–9.

Deyhle, D. (1986). Success and failure: A micro-ethnographic comparison of Navajo and Anglo students' perception of testing. *Curriculum Inquiry, 16*(4), 365–389.

Diuguid, L. (2005, December 28). Addressing classism will improve school performance. *Kansas City Star*. Retrieved from http://texasedequity.blogspot.com/2006/01/achievement-gap-addressing-classism.html

Duffy, M. (1962). *That's how it was*. New York: Doubleday.

Eduventures. (2006). *K–12 solutions: Learning markets & opportunities 2005*. Boston: Eduventures.

Elliot, S. (2011, February 9). Third-graders would have to pass reading test. *Indystar.com*. Retrieved from http://www.indystar.com/article/20110209/NEWS04/102090328/1013/news04/More-education-reform-Third-graders-would-pass-reading-test

Elton, G. (1991). *Return to essentials: Reflections on the present state of historical studies*. Cambridge, UK: Cambridge University Press.

Graves, F. P. (1920). *A history of education during the Middle Ages* (2nd ed.). Westport, CT: Greenwood Press.

Green, R. (2006, August 8). If kids can't read, what can they do later? *Hartford Courant*. Retrieved from http://articles.courant.com/2006-08-18/news/0608181100_1_board-of-education-member-third-graders-lack-basic-reading-skills

Haney, W., Madaus, G., & Lyons, R. (1993). *The fractured market place for standardized testing*. Boston: Kluwer.

Haney, W., & Scott, L. (1987). Talking with children about tests: An exploratory study on test item ambiguity. In R. Freedle & R. Duran (Eds.), *Cognitive and linguistic analyses of test performance* (pp. 69–87). Stamford, CT: Ablex.

Hearn, W. E. (1872). *Payment by the results in primary education.* Melbourne: Stellwell & Knight.

Hill, C., & Larsen, E. (2000). *Children and reading tests.* Stamford, CT: Ablex

Holmes, E. (1911). *What is and what might be: A study of education in general and elementary in particular.* London: Constable.

Hupp, S. (2007, August 24). Accountability and assessment in Texas. *Early stories: On journalism, children, and learning.* Retrieved http://earlystories. org/content/accountability-and-assessment-in-texas_193/

Hyman, M. (2010, November 30). Sports training has begun for babies and toddlers. *The New York Times.* Retrieved from http://www.nytimes. com/2010/12/01/sports/01babies.html?scp=1&sq=children%20 soccer&st=cse

Isaacs, J. (2010). *Child poverty during the Great Recession: Predicting state child poverty rates for 2010.* Washington, DC: First Focus.

Judd, C. (1918). A look forward. In G. Whipple (Ed.), *The measurement of educational products.* Bloomington, IL: Public School Publishing.

Kellaghan, T., & Greaney, V. (1992). *Using examinations to improve education. A study in fourteen African countries.* Washington, DC: World Bank.

Kellaghan, T., Madaus, G., & Raczek, A. (1996). *The use of external examinations to improve student motivation.* Washington, DC: American Educational Research Association.

Kula, W. (1986). *Measures in men* (R. Szreter, Trans.) Princeton, NJ: Princeton University Press.

Lens, W. (1994). Motivation and learning. In T. Husen & T. Postlethwaite (Eds.), *The international encyclopedia of education* (2nd ed., pp. 3936–3942). Oxford: Pergamon.

Lewy, A. (1996). Postmodernism in the field of achievement testing. *Studies in Educational Evaluations, 22*(3), 223–244.

Locust, C. (1988). Wounding the spirit: Discrimination and traditional American Indian belief systems. *Harvard Educational Review, 58*(3), 315–330.

Madaus, G., & Kellaghan, T. (1993). The British experience with "authentic" testing. *Phi Delta Kappan, 74*(6), 458–469.

Madaus, G., Russell, M., & Higgins, J. (2009). *The paradoxes of high stakes testing: How they affect students, their parents, teachers, principals, schools, and society.* Charlotte, NC: Information Age.

Mann, H. (1845–1846). Letter to Samuel G. Howe. *Horace Mann papers, Box 8 (1845–1846).* Boston: Massachusetts Historical Society.

Maslin, S. (2010, October 27). For some youngsters, a second chance at an exclusive xchool. *The New York Times.* Retrieved from http://www.nytimes. com/2010/10/28/nyregion/28private.html

McGahern, J. (1977). *The dark.* New York: Quartet.

Milne, A. A. (1930). *Autobiography.* New York: Dutton.

Miner, B. (2004). Keeping public schools public: Testing companies mine for gold. *Rethinking Schools.* Retrieved from http://webcache.googleusercontent. com/search?q=cache:eaT-B8T8KDYJ:www.rethinkingschools.org/special_ reports/bushplan/test192.shtml+gao+standardized+testing+billion&cd=1 &hl=en&ct=clnk&gl=us

Monroe, P. (1936). *Conference on examinations.* New York: Bureau of Publications, Teachers College, Columbia University.

Naipaul, V. S. (1984, September 17). A Trinidad childhood. *The New Yorker,* pp. 57–58.

National Commission on Testing and Public Policy. (1990). *From gatekeeper to gateway: Transforming testing in America.* Chestnut Hill, MA: National Commission on Testing and Public Policy, Boston College.

National Institute of Education. (1981). *Transcripts of the Minimum Competency Testing Certification Hearings.* Washington, DC: Alderson Reporting.

National PTA. (2006). *Recess is at risk, new campaign comes to the rescue.* Retrieved from http://www.peacefulplaygrounds.com/pdf/right-to-recess/ national-pta-recess-at-risk.pdf

National Public Radio. (2011, January 10). Closing the achievement gap with baby talk. Interview on Morning Edition. National Public Radio. Retrieved from http://www.huffingtonpost.com/2011/01/10/alan-mendelsohn-of- new-yo_n_806911.html

Otterman, S. (2011, January 11). More play, please, for kindergarteners, parents ask. *The New York Times.* Retrieved from http://cityroom.blogs.nytimes. com/2011/01/11/more-play-please-for-kindergartners-parents-ask/

Pedulla, J., Abrams, L., Madaus, G., Russell, M., Ramos, M., & Miao, J. (2003). *Perceived effects of state-mandated testing programs on teaching and learning: Findings from a national survey of teachers.* Chestnut Hill, MA: Center for the Study of Testing, Evaluation, and Educational Policy, Boston College.

Percy, W. (1991). Diagnosing the modern malaise. In P. Samway (Ed.), *Walker Percy: Sign-posts in a strange land* (pp. 204–221). New York: Farrar, Straus and Giroux.

Pressey, S. L., & Pressey, L. C. (1922). *Introduction to the use of standardized tests.* Yonkers, NY: World Book.

Rafferty, M. (1985). *Examinations in literature: Perceptions from non technical writers of England and Ireland from 1850 to 1984* (Unpublished doctoral dissertation). Boston College, Chestnut Hill, MA.

Ramstetter, C. (2010). The crucial role of recess in schools. *Journal of School Health, 80* (11), 517–526.

Ravitch, D. (2010). *The death and life of the great American school system: How testing and choice are undermining education.* New York: Basic Books.

Rothstein, R. (2004). *Class and schools: Using social, economic and educational reforms to close the Black-White achievement gap.* New York: Teachers College Press.

Sacchetti, M. (2006, October 19). More districts aim for the top on MCAS: In shift, proficient isn't good enough. *The Boston Globe.* Retrieved from

http://www.boston.com/news/local/articles/2006/10/19/more_districts_
aimfor_the_top_on_mcas/

Saulny, S. (2006, February 12). *Tutor program offered by law is going unused. The New York Times.* Retrieved from http://www.nytimes.com/2006/02/12/education/12tutor.html

Sheppard, L., & Smith, M. (1986). Synthesis of research and school readiness and kindergarten retention. *Educational Leadership, 44*(3), 78–86.

Sizer, T. (1984). *Horace's compromise: The dilemma of the American high school.* Boston: Houghton Mifflin Co.

Sparks, S. (2011, February 4). Study finds social-skills teaching boosts academics: Gains found comparable to those of strictly academic programs. *Education Week, 30*(20), 8. Retrieved from http://www.edweek.org/ew/articles/2011/02/04/20sel.h30.html?tkn=LZYFQ8ngRX/tnEt629YJn7/E0s%2BwI1hkbiAL&cmp=clp-edweek

Travers, R. (1983). *How research has changed American schools: A history from 1840 to the present.* Kalamazoo, MI: Mythos Press.

Tyler, R. (1979). Educational objectives and educational testing: Problems now faced. In *Testing, teaching and learning. Report of a conference on research on testing* (pp. 36–47). Washington, DC: National Institute of Education.

Tyre, P. (2010, November 27). As for good behavior. *The New York Times.* Retrieved from http://www.nytimes.com/2010/11/28/weekinreview/28tyre.html?_r=1&scp=1&sq=behavior&st=cse

UNICEF. (2010). *The children left behind: A league table of inequality in child well-being in the world's rich countries* (Innocenti Report Card 9). Florence, Italy: UNICEF Innocenti Research Centre.

Wolfe, T. (1987). *The bonfire of the vanities.* New York: Bantam Books.

Part III

IMAGES OF POSSIBILITY AND RECOMMENDATIONS FOR THE FUTURE

CHAPTER 9

Tensions Past, Present, and Future

Using Literature to Promote Social Awareness and Literacy in Children

Robert L. Selman and Janet Kwok

> *I want to go to the Dairy Dip with John Henry, sit down and share root beer floats. I want us to go to the picture show, buy popcorn, and watch the movie together. I want to see this town with John Henry's eyes.*

This quote by Joe comes from the children's book *Freedom Summer* (Wiles, 2001, p. 23), set in the American South just after the passage of the Civil Rights Act of 1964 that, among other changes, brought about the desegregation of public spaces. Two boys—Joe (who is White) and John Henry (who is Black)—are overjoyed at the opportunity to finally swim in a public pool together. They arrive at the pool and are crushed to discover that members of the community have destroyed the pool rather than swim in desegregated waters. The above excerpt describes a poignant moment of reflection through the eyes of Joe as he interprets this act of racism. Joe understands at last that the experiences he has taken for granted will take on a new meaning when his best friend John Henry can finally enjoy them with him.

We know that the realities of prejudice, racism, and other social problems are very challenging for us, as adults, to discuss, let alone to confront. Perhaps that is one reason why there is a growing desire among educators and parents to prevent any widening of these chronic fault lines in American society by making them more visible to even the youngest among us, our children. Yet even decades after the Civil Rights Movement began in the 1950s, educators and social

173

scientists alike are still trying to find ways to reduce old prejudices in children and prevent new ones, now by designing elementary school interventions and classroom materials and instruction that directly engage students in the understanding and awareness of these social issues.

Yet do we really expect that through explicitly teaching students in the elementary grades about prejudice and tolerance, injustice and equity, we will create a next generation of adults who will be more respectful of one another and more resistant to demagogy? Or might clumsy attempts at early antibias inoculations, despite good intentions, result in unintended, or even harmful, consequences?

Our chapter raises the following question: Is it too lofty a goal to expect younger elementary grade students to understand, let alone resolve, matters that are so difficult for the grown-ups in their community to manage? For us, it is not actually a question of should we initiate an active educational approach with an awareness of social justice as our goal so much as how we proceed in the elementary grades to help all students learn how to accomplish this. And how can we work to support the development of the cognitive, social, and emotional capacities necessary for understanding social relationships necessary to fighting against the lazy inclination toward prejudice in this world? Moreover, beyond evidence of effectiveness in the short term, what approaches will provide meaningful traction for these students throughout their lives?

This sense of purpose comes at a time when for over a decade the national educational policy climate, as characterized by the No Child Left Behind Act of 2001 (NCLB), prioritizes language and math skills and their standardized assessment. Obviously, any initiative that is not directly committed to these present educational policies faces an even greater challenge finding adequate space and time in the classroom. In response to these policies, some educators who share our priorities are using children's literature that purposefully addresses themes of prejudice and equity and their understanding as a way of reciprocally enhancing both literacy and social skills (Solomon, Watson, & Battistich, 2001).

THE VALUE ADDED OF SOCIAL AND EMOTIONAL LEARNING

What then can the promotion of social and emotional learning have to offer to a standards-anxious culture? Do the benefits of teaching children to self-regulate emotions, act ethically and responsibly, and develop empathy and compassion with their peers meaningfully help children cultivate the behaviors that are necessary for present and long-term academic as well as personal success? Toward this end, innovations in the teaching of social, civic, and moral education are propelled by the desire to promote understanding of human difference and reduce the prejudice that all too often is the response in young children to its perception (Ponitz, McClelland, Matthews, & Morrison, 2009; Zins, Bloodworth, Weissberg, & Walberg, 2004).

Among these innovations are curricula like *The 4Rs* (Morningside Center for Teaching Social Responsibility, 2010), *Making Meaning* (Developmental Studies Center, 2010), and *Voices Reading* (Zaner-Bloser, 2010),[1] which use high-quality children's literature designed not only to enhance literacy skills, but also to develop students' awareness of social issues such as the reason why discrimination is so often based on social categories like race, gender, or social class, as well as both individual and general differences in human experience.

Even as we increasingly require empirical evidence to establish the effectiveness of programs that use materials such as these to promote academic and social competencies, we must not lose sight of what we want students to be socially aware of as they are growing up, and the limits of their capacities to digest complex social issues. In other words, what metric will we use to determine a program's impact on the promotion of social awareness and the reduction of unwarranted prejudicial attitudes and beliefs?

Recently, a modest but systematic empirical exploration of the meaning that early elementary grade students make of literature that focuses on social relationships has begun to emerge in scientific journals (Banks, 1995; Bigler, 1999; Dray & Selman, 2011; Pfeifer, Brown, & Juvonen, 2007). These approaches require tools sensitive enough to evaluate the quality of young students' social, as well as reading, comprehension. This means not only their understanding of vocabulary words (e.g., *segregation, equality*), background knowledge (e.g., the history of Jim Crow laws), and factual information (e.g., Supreme Court's *Brown v. Board of Education* ruling), but also their "level" of social awareness—that is, the range of ways students construct an understanding of the social world in which they live and to which they are exposed through classroom curricula and communication.

In one application of this "constructive developmental" approach, we have reported measures that we use to assess students' developing capacity for social and ethical awareness—seen through their ability to harmoniously integrate their own needs and concerns with those of others in social situations—as reflected in their interpretations of those literary texts with themes that address the complex nature of social relationships and social conditions (Selman & Dray, 2003).

For instance, students read excerpts from *Felita* (Mohr, 1979), a chapter book (lexiled at a fourth-grade level) for children, focusing on an incident where the protagonist, Felita, a 10-year-old girl, moves to a neighborhood and struggles with social rejection. Students' level of social awareness was coded according to how well they coordinated different points of view when asked why they thought Felita is first accepted and then ostracized by "White" girls in the neighborhood to which she and her family just moved. (See also Dray, Selman, & Schultz, 2009). Recent research of ours that we discuss here builds upon this work to investigate methods to assess the meaning children make of the central themes and social issues authors raise in all children's books, such as equality versus discrimination. This is one way of gaining insight into the developmental norms and trajectories of children's social awareness, a necessary first step toward valid evaluation of the programs that attempt the promotion of social understanding, skills, and awarenesss.

DETERMINING THE EFFECT OF PROSOCIAL LITERATURE

The Strategy

In the context of the particular focus of this volume, our research is meant to provide some insights into the ways research on the meaning children make of prosocial literature can be used effectively by teachers or parents with young students. We will demonstrate how such literature, in well-practiced hands, is a rich resource, but requires guidance and scaffolding in order to help younger readers who may not be developmentally prepared to absorb the nuances of such lessons on their own. As students' comprehension across grades hopefully improves, teachers may adjust their teaching strategies accordingly to maximize a book's prosocial potential. Still exploratory at this point, the evidence that we have gathered provides a means of going forward, both in terms of practice and research directions.

Freedom Summer (Wiles, 2001), a book we used extensively for our investigation, is written at a lexical level that is accessible to the "average" third-grade reader. A picture book, its story is set during the passage of the Civil Rights Act of 1964. John Henry, a young Black boy is now able, legally at least, to swim in the municipal pool in a rural Mississippi town with his best friend, Joe, who is White and whose family employs John Henry's mother. The boys rush to the town's municipal pool, eager to finally swim together in a real swimming pool rather than a creek, but discover it has been filled with tar (ironically, by a work crew led by John Henry's older brother). The story comes to a bittersweet ending; the boys, each heartbroken in his own way, but both brave and resilient, go together to buy ice pops at the formerly segregated general store that has remained open in spite of the local assaults on desegregation. John Henry is able to enter the general store for the first time with Joe, and buys his own ice pop.

Does this book capture—and more important, communicate to the third graders of 2011—the complex emotional challenges experienced by both Black and White Americans during the desegregation of public places in 1964 by focusing on an interracial friendship of a pair of pre-adolescent boys in the American Deep South? How well can youngsters typically understand events and relationships during social upheavals that occur in far-off times and culturally unfamiliar places?

In one of our practice-based research projects, we read *Freedom Summer* to a group of predominantly low-income African American students in Grades 1 through 5, most of whom attended neighborhood elementary schools in a northeastern urban area (Hickman-Maynard & Selman, 2007). Our main goals as researchers were to assess students' comprehension of the story and their understanding of the nature of prejudice and discrimination. These are not identical, although they clearly are related. The fundamental research question within which this pilot study was conducted is: What are the developmental (referring to age) and cultural variations in how deeply and thoroughly children understand issues of prejudice and tolerance in the literature they are exposed to in school, either through reading or listening? Our research team read *Freedom Summer* to a total of 107 children from two different practice settings (in classrooms and in after-school programs), using two different strategies. The team occasionally read aloud the story to individual children (Lobron & Selman, 2007), but they generally read to students in small groups of three or four. The sample was around 50% female, predominantly Black (64.5%), 6.5% Latino, 3.7% White, 1.9% Asian, 10.3% mixed race, and 13.1% unknown.

Given our small and local pilot sample, there is little, unfortunately, we can say about the variation in cultural backgrounds of the participants in the study. In the discussion here, we will focus on variations examined across grades. We will chart, however, the next steps needed to integrate crucial contextual and cultural factors with this analysis, as research with a focus on application should, at the least, consider the impact these factors have on comprehension.

The Method

The researcher begins by eliciting students' ideas about the book's cover and taking their first impressions of it. Then the researcher gives a standardized introduction to the background of the book, emphasizing its setting in the American South during the time of the Civil Rights Movement in the 1960s when many of the students' grandparents were children. After reading, students were either interviewed or asked to write their responses, depending on their grade, age, and writing ability. In this study, we were not focused on systematic attention to or control of all factors that might influence students' performance. More modestly, we simply wanted to get a glimpse of how key themes in the book were understood and interpreted by this particular sample. We will focus on two questions that we asked each child from our project:

1. Why was the pool filled with tar so that Joe and John Henry could not swim in it?
2. Why did John Henry want to use his own nickel to buy an ice pop?

The first of these two questions is designed to capture students' understanding of the central conflict in the text, the discrimination of Whites against Blacks based on the history of American race relations: How well can students describe the events in terms of the nature and role of the historical context in the story? The second question seeks to gauge the readers' ability to take the perspective of the characters in the book toward one another against the backdrop of segregation (and desegregation): With how much complexity do students comprehend the effect that racism has on individuals and their quotidian personal relationships in society?

The first question sought to probe right to the heart of discrimination within the story: "Why was the pool filled with tar so that John Henry and Joe could not swim in it?" We wanted to know what the variation in age was for when the students begin to identify racial issues as the core reason for this "crisis" in the narrative—depicted as the filling of the pool with tar. In those responses that demonstrated some kind of awareness of racism as a motivating force, our goal was to identify the various beliefs, thoughts, and behaviors that students understood to be associated with it—such as discrimination, segregation, and prejudice—and how they were used to interpret the text. These constructs give us insight into the students' background knowledge about race relationships and the quality of the concepts they brought to bear on their interpretation of the text.

The purpose of the second question was to determine how well students would be able to use their developing perspective-taking skills to infer how a social issue, in this case racism and discrimination, affects the relationship *between* the individuals involved in the conflict. As the story proceeds and both boys feel dejected because the pool has been filled with tar, thwarting their desire to use it, Joe asks John Henry if he wants to get an ice pop (at a formerly segregated general store). John Henry says he wants to pick it out himself. Joe thinks that it is a good idea and offers to give John Henry one of his nickels, because he usually pays for both ice pops. But John Henry refuses to take Joe's money and replies, "I got my own," leaving the meaning of John Henry's final words and actions in the text open to interpretation.

In order to assess the students' understanding of how segregation, and now desegregation, affected John Henry's response to Joe, we asked: "Why do you think John Henry wanted to use his own nickel to buy an ice pop?" Thus we offered students the opportunity to place themselves in each of the characters' shoes and to re-create how the characters were feeling and what motivated them to particular behavior.

Responses to Question 1:
Becoming and Being Aware of Racism and Equality

For our first question ("Why was the pool filled with tar so that Joe and John Henry could not swim in it?"), our research objective was to identify the developmental variations in children's engagement with the text. In other words, at what grades do children begin to identify racism as the primary factor underlying the townspeople's decision to fill the pool with tar? Now, we realize that awareness of these matters does not necessarily arrive as an epiphany at any one point in one's lifetime. But, in order to get some sense of how to promote in educational contexts the awareness of sensitive topics such as racism and ostracism, we needed to determine on average the age period during which these levels of awareness appear to develop in the sample of students with whom we were working, as well as the form they take. We found that a quarter of our 154 responses from students across Grades 1 through 5 did *not* identify racism as the underlying factor. Of particular note, there were students in all grade levels, *except* Grade 5, whose responses failed to explicitly demonstrate awareness that racism was an underlying cause for the pool being filled with tar.

For this question, we found we could reliably cluster students' responses into three broad levels: (1) *Limited Awareness*, (2) *Emergent Awareness*, (3) *Developed Awareness*.[2] We want to emphasize again that by placing these responses in a leveled rubric, we are not imposing any strong or diagnostic judgment about the individual student's actual (or most competent) level of actual social awareness, neither in general, nor even the students' actual awareness of racism. Instead, we are simply judging whether and when students on average in this sample have demonstrated their awareness in the interpretation of the text as measured by their response to the questions.

In other words, if a student's response is coded *Limited Awareness*, we are simply saying that the student's response has not demonstrated or expressed the use of any racism or equity constructs to understand why the events unfolded as they did. Here are some examples of the levels we observed:

Limited Awareness Expressed: Some students, as noted, gave some explanation of pools filling that made no reference to the social issues:

- " . . . so they could walk on it" (first grader).
- "because they needed a parking lot" (fourth grader).

Emergent Awareness Expressed: Some had some facts correct, but others did not:

- Law Confusion—"Because Blacks and Whites are not allowed to swim together because it was the law" (fourth-grade boy).

Developed Awareness: And some students demonstrated the use of their knowledge of racial discrimination to explain the filling of the pools:

- "Because some of the White people who don't care for the Black people might say it's not fair because the White people always swim" (second-grade girl).
- "They just want it the way it is now so White people can do anything they want" (fifth-grade girl).

As cautioned above, please keep in mind that although we care about students as learners, with all the complexity of strengths and challenges implied, at this phase of the research process we are simply trying to understand the impact of education and experience, broadly defined, on all students through the aggregation of their responses, not the achievements of particular students.

Not unexpectedly, there were fewer responses that showed limited awareness in the upper grades than in the lower grades, and in this investigation, the proportions of such responses decrease across the age span: Nearly half of our first-grade sample demonstrated limited awareness that racism explained the filling of the pool, but only 44% of second-grade responses, 22% of third-grade responses, 18% of fourth-grade responses, and 0% of fifth-grade responses demonstrated this level of awareness. Thus, while nearly half of the students younger than third grade on their own, or even with one or two readings, had trouble identifying or articulating race as the underlying reason for the filling of the pool, progressively older students seemed to have less difficulty with this task. This should not be surprising, but it does pose a question: How do we recognize emergent awareness? Here are some additional examples of responses where students did not explicitly articulate the elements in the story that described racism, but we could infer that they had used some awareness of racism to interpret the story:

Vague Explanation: "[The pool was filled with tar] because they knew they were coming."

Power Confusion: "John Henry's brother (who, we note, was a member of the work crew in the story) didn't want him swimming with his friend, cause they're different colors."

In the first response (Vague Explanation) the student does not actually describe who the "they" who were coming were, but we can infer that this youngster probably referred to the sense that those in control of the pool did not want Whites and Blacks to swim together. The second response (Power Confusion) erroneously suggests that John Henry's brother had the authority to make the decision about who swam and who did not, but the desire to keep people of different races apart is identified as a factor in the decision. For these similar responses, which allowed us to reasonably conclude that the student believed racism was a factor in filling the pool with tar, we credited students with emergent awareness.

We did not, however, observe the same type of grade trend with respect to the *Emergent Awareness* code as we did with *Limited Awareness*. Given their age and difficulty with language, one might expect to see younger students having higher rates of responses demonstrating vague awareness than older students, but we did not find this to be the case. Not one first-grade student gave a response that was considered vague, and only one second grader did. Vague awareness, instead, seemed to be a characteristic of older children who may have been working with an emerging social awareness. Twelve percent of third graders and 7% of fourth graders who demonstrated some awareness were unable (or unwilling?) to articulate it clearly. By fifth grade, facility and comfort with social awareness likely developed to the point of clear articulation, explaining our finding that no fifth-grade response was considered vague. This finding is suggestive with respect to the educational issue of "developmental appropriateness," or the notion that developmental levels are characterized by transitions and struggling with one's changing ability is to be expected during such periods of moving to the next level. It also suggests that educational intervention in a time of emergent awareness (observed in this sample at around second and third grade) may be educationally propitious for students on the verge of advancing their understanding by building on their confusion to scaffold clarity.

We began to detect what we defined as *Developed Awareness* of racism gathering force at third grade with 42% of third-grade responses showing full awareness of racism, 58% of fourth-grade responses, and 83% of fifth-grade responses. Most of the students in our sample who demonstrated awareness that some form of racism was responsible for filling the pool with tar saw things, both literally and figuratively, as a Black and White issue. Some students, for instance, only saw color, but could not describe the relationship, such as one fourth-grade student who could say that the pool was filled with tar "because Joe was White and John Henry was Black." Other students completed the thought and gave responses similar to a fifth-grade student who said that the pool was filled with tar "because they were different colored and they"—we assume referring to the White community—"didn't want anyone different colored swimming in the same pool." Thus the most salient theme for the children was the difference between Black and White, what we as adults would call *segregation*. Articulating the reasons for these perceived differences requires *perspective taking*, the ability to understand why another person (from another "identity group") might feel a certain way in a situation (particularly if that response would be different from one's own), which children may not yet have developed, or may decide not to exercise (Selman, 2003).

Responses to Question 2: Taking the Perspective of a Friend "Back Then"

The prompt we used to gauge perspective-taking skills as applied to the text, "Why did John Henry want to use his own nickel to buy an ice pop?" proved to be an even more difficult question for the students to answer clearly and with good communicative intent. As we examine their responses, it is worth considering how young students may find it difficult to understand how societal issues of the past such as segregation would have an impact on social relationships among peers because such comprehension involves not only perspective-coordination skills that are still in development but also an awareness of how historical, cultural, and economic forces can restrict people's behavior and the relationships that are available to them.

Of the responses we collected, half of our sample across grades suggested that many of the children had demonstrated only limited awareness that John Henry's desire to use his own nickel had anything to do with desegregation and his newly granted legal right to enter the store. Another 21% demonstrated emergent awareness. Among first-grade responses, 60% demonstrated limited awareness, compared to 66% of second graders. Students begin to demonstrate greater awareness of the emergence of a desire for equity and civil rights in the story as they experience developmental changes and increase their literacy, but only slightly and mostly in Grades 3, 4, and 5.

It is important to reiterate that these limited awareness responses do not reflect these students' inability to take another's perspective or to coordinate the perspectives of the two interlocutors. These students clearly have the cognitive ability to consider another's point of view and coordinate multiple perspectives. Nevertheless, while it may be the case, as many students suggested or inferred, that Joe did not know the flavor John Henry wanted or that John Henry did not want to owe Joe money, a deeper, more contextualized, understanding of John Henry's response to Joe and his good intentions requires students to see not only how John Henry views Joe and his intentions, but also how he views the culture and context in which the two boys find themselves. It is at this point that the social awareness concepts articulated to the first question and the degree to which perspectives are coordinated to answer the second begin to come together.

Despite the fact that the majority of responses revealed little or no social (or societal) awareness, there were some students who identified desegregation as a factor behind John Henry's insistence that he use his own nickel. The majority of students demonstrating developed awareness (64%) attributed John Henry's actions to a simple desire to experience freedom where it had previously been denied, or to have the same freedom that Whites had. Responses like these included one from a fourth-grade student who said that John Henry "wanted to be like Joe. And Joe always uses his nickels, and got to go in the store. He got to do everything. But John Henry couldn't."

A few students saw John Henry's actions not only as an act of individual actualization, but also as an individual act in conversation with the views of a wider society. These students understood the intransigence of historical racism and saw John Henry's insistence on using his own nickel as a dialogue with a culture once heavily dominated by acts of discrimination. Their responses demonstrate the awareness that it is often important to assert your rights, especially when they had been denied previously, to express your own equality and place in the world to yourself and others. Such responses represented 18% of those showing developed awareness. As one fourth-grade student said, "I think John Henry might have wanted to buy his own ice cream and pay for it too. Just to prove that Blacks and Whites are the same." Some students saw John Henry's actions as an acknowledgment that desegregation laws do not alone address the issues of racism in society, as in this fourth-grade response: "Because he wants to try out everything that he can do by himself and see how people are rude and mean to him and see how they would treat him and see if they would treat him nice or [say] 'Get out of my store,' stuff like that."

While there are some children whose responses demonstrate they are very much capable of understanding the perspectives of the characters in the story in a way that applies an awareness of a desire for equality and the constraints of racism, the vast majority of elementary students in a sample of students in an urban community whom we might expect to be sensitive to these issues did not reveal such understanding. If, rather than unaware, they are in fact withholding their opinions, we need to ask why.

BEYOND ICE POPS AND PUBLIC POOLS: MAKING SOCIAL AWARENESS EDUCATION EFFECTIVE

It was over 50 years ago that John Henry and Joe grappled with a shifting social order. At about the same time, while striving to understand the racism of Nazi Germany, pioneering developmental psychologist and moral educator Lawrence Kohlberg first began to focus his developmental theory and research evidence on the value and educational importance of active and evidence-based methods of peer moral discussion and debate among the students in the classroom as a key mechanism for the promotion of social and moral literacy (Blatt & Kohlberg, 1975; Kohlberg & Mayer, 1972).

Ironically, both social change and educational reform occur relatively slowly, historically speaking. Returning to current policy directions we raised in the beginning of this chapter, after 50 years very few educational policy makers have wholeheartedly embraced these pedagogical methods in the context of moral education. The story is quite different, of course, when the concern is contemporary policies about literacy. For example, most recently, evidence of the difficulties in reading comprehension that many students at the middle school level are having has become a key empirical and practical problem to solve (Snow, Lawrence, & White, 2009), and many literacy theorists have begun to advocate for pedagogical methods that will promote more "high-quality" peer-to-peer conversation in the classroom (Larson, 2000; Mercer, Wegerif, & Dawes, 1999; Michaels, O'Connor, & Resnick, 2008).

So, in the context of high stakes testing in reading comprehension, recent researchers have (re)discovered that under current classroom conditions, teachers (and even higher education faculty) find it very challenging to lead classroom conversations that include deeply interactive discussion and debate at the late elementary and middle school grades—not only moral discussions but exchanges among peers in English language arts, social studies, and even the teaching of science (Nystrand & Gamoran, 1991; Nystrand, Wu, Gamoran, Zeiser, & Long, 2003; O'Connor & Michaels, 1996; Osborne, Erduran, & Simon, 2004).

We advocate here that this emergent movement toward a curriculum grounded in the promotion of students' capacity for quality peer discussion (exploratory, cumulative, respectful) and debate needs to start even earlier than early adolescence. It needs to permeate whole-school pedagogical processes from pre-K and beyond (Schaps, 2007), and we would advocate further that social, moral, and civic themes need to be made priority content areas across the elementary grades curriculum frameworks, nationwide, not just something done on Thursday afternoons or provided as an elective overlay. Why? Because in a mutually transformative way these are the very issues that best motivate students to want to learn to read and write as well as to assimilate academic information that has a civic and moral purpose, which will compel them to read to learn more.

LITERACY AND SOCIAL DEVELOPMENT: LEARNING TO WEAVE THE PATTERN OF RECIPROCAL TRANSFORMATION

Using discussion and debate to promote comprehension begins with an understanding of how cognitive and social developmental competencies such as perspective taking and interpersonal understanding, or conflict resolution and social awareness, affect and deepen the students' understanding of the stories they are learning how to read and understand. In response to our question, "Why was the pool filled with tar so that Joe and John Henry could not swim in it?" younger students were largely unable to express an understanding that racism was the underlying factor that led to the closing of the pool, attributing its closing instead to factors unrelated to racism, such as the need to build a road or a bridge. It was not until third grade that students were regularly able to demonstrate consistent awareness of racism's role in society and the social order. Older students were able to discuss various prejudicial attitudes, the intransigence of those who did not want to follow new desegregation laws, the ways in which intergroup and intragroup conflict served to perpetuate discrimination, as well as the stress those conflicts placed on Joe and John Henry's friendship.

Even if a student's understanding of factual historical events and the motivated actions of those people living in the past improves over time, an understanding of the meaning of these differences in "foreign" times and places must not be assumed to be part of the deeper comprehension skills of younger students. Layered books, like *Freedom Summer*, can teach different lessons at different grade levels, and to different students.

Findings such as these have significant implications for various fields of practice and research, and the links between them. Teaching is a highly sophisticated and challenging profession that requires deep disciplinary knowledge, especially where teaching controversial or uncomfortable issues such as race relations is concerned. The value of books such as *Freedom Summer* as vehicles for discussing contemporary issues of prejudice runs the risk of being reduced to mere literacy lessons that might be lost on many of the children in the class if the teacher does not understand the developmental and cultural bases of children's competencies, and is unable to help students make connections between their knowledge of the world and their experience with the text.

To aid teachers and students in the challenging task of discussing racial equality, developmental theory derived from pristine controlled research conditions spawned upstream must actively ship its evidence downstream into the classroom so that teachers might be empowered to make sound developmental choices that appropriately stimulate and scaffold student learning. Reciprocally, relevant educational issues must swim the challenging upstream waterway so usable evidence for the next generation of teachers and students can be generated.

Is it educationally appropriate, then, to deal with sensitive issues preemptively in elementary schools, or is it more appropriate to wait until fourth or fifth grade when they spontaneously emerge or erupt? Most middle school educators would not need a researcher to tell them that it is essential that these issues be addressed earlier, before students arrive in the intense peer relations of the upper elementary grades (granting that how they are presented is important), but how can these issues be broached with younger students who may not have the skills to grasp the nuances of such issues?

We realize some early elementary grade teachers may reasonably balk, cautious of the sensitivity of the themes and issues being introduced. The beauty of a book such as *Freedom Summer* is that it is a social and emotional learning resource that is effective across different levels of students' comprehension. First graders, on average, can easily engage with it as a story of the challenges of friendship; and more advanced readers, equipped with the requisite cognitive and emotional resources, can approach it as a story about the search for equities in society.

To better clarify the role educators play in these endeavors, let us think of the teacher as a weaver who is working with the warp and the woof of literacy and social awareness (Selman & Snow, 2005; Walker, 2009). First, the warp is laid down—this is the foundation of learning, where we have the mechanics of reading and writing, such as spelling and punctuation, the writing process, learning to identify letters and sounds, and to develop oral language. This is also where we have the emergent reasons for reading and writing: to know ourselves, learn about others, solve local and global problems. The teacher begins with these components in order to support literacy and help students relate the knowledge in books to the knowledge in their world.

The woof must be woven *into* the warp, not overlaid superficially. The two strands of literacy and social awareness must now become integrated. Here, there is the need for theoretical awareness on teachers' part of social development, such as understanding how students could have arrived at a range of responses to the book's theme from both developmental and cultural perspectives, as well as from each student's individuality. The teacher must also think of how to foster social development through both questions to check comprehension and absorption of messages, but also through generative activities. This act of weaving together is the translation of literacy and social awareness, when a student is able to make the jump from decoding (reading letters and words) to inference, knowing what is being said indirectly.

There is also the parallel weaving of academic rigor and ethical reflection. These achievements do not occur in spite of each other, but rather, are mutually supportive. Consider the following comments from a third-grade classroom in a rural New Hampshire school with a predominantly White and low-income student body. The discussion is animated by the reading of *Uncle Jed's Barbershop* (Mitchell, 1993), the fictitious story of an African American barber's dream of opening his business, attained at last after overcoming a number of hardships—in-

cluding the Great Depression and subsequent decades of segregation—
with dignity.

> *Student A:* I think White people should cut White people's and
>   Black people should cut Black people's hair.
> *Teacher:* You think so? Do you think they were right to have the
>   separate barbers?
> *Student A:* Yes, because the Whites were being really mean to the
>   Black people. And I think they should be treated fairly, the
>   same way.
> *Teacher:* Okay, so [Student A] thinks that it's a good thing—
>   because the White people were being mean to the Black
>   people—that way the Black people didn't have to be around
>   people who were being mean to them. Is that what you're
>   saying? So you think [segregation] is a good thing? Does any-
>   one agree with [Student A], that that was the way to solve the
>   problem?
> *Student B:* I disagree.
> *Teacher:* You do? Tell us why.
> *Student B:* I think it would be better if there weren't separate
>   barbers. Because there's one Black barber and the rest are all
>   White barbers. It's not fair; the colored can't get as many
>   haircuts, but the White can.

With which student does one side? That is hard to say, but it may
not be essential in a case like this. This interaction characterizes the
essential: the commitment required from the teacher to not only challenge her students' critical social thinking abilities but also to make
sure she, as the teacher, is fully aware of what they mean when participating in an engaging and passionate discussion (Taylor, Ross, Snow,
& Selman, 2011). To effectively use literature as both a literacy and
ethical development tool, the teacher must bear in mind not only the
promotion of the comprehension of the text, but also the awareness
each child has of the social world. The teacher must also create a safe
classroom and community so that students will feel supported, and
from this comes the development of the capacity for perspective taking and the desire for self-expression. When we are able to more fully
understand how (and why) motives and opinions may vary among
those in conversation during the same time and space, we may recognize how the pressures of a different society in a different time exert their influence. Finally, the teacher must not jump to conclusions
about what the students in her class mean by what they say. She must
have the patience to both draw meaning out of each student and facil-

itate their conversation with one another. Classrooms need to establish a norm: Asking students what they mean need not be a criticism of what they are saying. It can be a recognition of the challenges and beauty of achieving clear communication.

At the core of these processes is the use of texts that will engage students. Although this endeavor begins with reading stories about challenges faced by others beyond our community or era, this act invites the sharing of personal struggles, gradually helping students to make social justice personally meaningful. This is the beginning of a lifetime of not only reading, but also finding connections with those we know or have yet to know—the preparation for a civic and social citizen.

NOTES

1. Robert Selman is a senior author on this literacy and social awareness curriculum published by Zaner Bloser Educational Publishers, a division of Highlights for Children. *Freedom Summer,* the trade book we focus on in our research-based essay here, is used in the curriculum as an "instructional read aloud" for the second-grade curriculum as part of the social awareness theme (one of six) within this approach.

2. *Developed Awareness* does not refer to what we might expect from an adult's comprehension, but rather a solid basic awareness of what constructs like segregation denote. By studying students across grade levels and observing the nature of emergent awareness as we document it, the essentials of developed awareness become more evident.

REFERENCES

Banks, J. A. (1995). Multicultural education: Its effects on students' racial and gender role attitudes. In J. A. Banks & C. A. M. Banks (Eds.), *Handbook of research on multicultural education* (pp. 617–627). New York: Macmillan.

Bigler, R. S. (1999). The use of multicultural curricula and materials to counter racism in children. *Journal of Social Issues, 55*(4), 687–705.

Blatt, M. M., & Kohlberg, L. (1975). The effects of classroom moral discussion upon children's level of moral judgment. *Journal of Moral Education, 4*(2), 129–161.

Developmental Studies Center. (2010). Making meaning. Retrieved from Developmental Studies Center website: http://www.devstu.org/making-meaning

Dray, A. J., & Selman, R. L. (2011). Culture and comprehension: A mixed methods study of children's responses to a fictional story about interracial conflict. *Reading and Writing Quarterly, 27*(1–2), 48–74.

Dray, A. J., Selman, R. L., & Schultz, L. H. (2009). Communicating with intent: A study of social awareness and children's writing. *Journal of Applied Developmental Psychology, 30*(2), 116–128.

Hickman-Maynard, B., & Selman, R. L. (2007). Muddy waters can yield clear evidence. *Social Policy Report, 21*(2), 14–15.

Kohlberg, L., & Mayer, R. (1972). Development as the aim of education. *Harvard Educational Review, 42*(4), 449–496.

Larson, B. E. (2000). Classroom discussion: A method of instruction and a curriculum outcome. *Teaching and Teacher Education, 16*(5–6), 661–677.

Lobron, A., & Selman, R. L. (2007). The interdependence of social awareness and literacy instruction. *The Reading Teacher, 60*(6), 528–537.

Mercer, N., Wegerif, R., & Dawes, L. (1999). Children's talk and the development of reasoning in the classroom. *British Educational Research Journal, 25*(1), 95–111.

Michaels, S., O'Connor, C., & Resnick, L. B. (2008). Deliberative discourse idealized and realized: Accountable talk in the classroom and in civic life. *Studies in Philosophy and Education, 27*(4), 283–297.

Mitchell, M. K. (1993). *Uncle Jed's barbershop.* New York: Simon & Schuster Books for Young Readers.

Mohr, N. (1979). *Felita.* New York: Puffin Books.

Morningside Center for Teaching Social Responsibility. (2010). The 4Rs Program (Reading, Writing, Respect and Resolution). *Conflict resolution and diversity programs.* Retrieved from http://www.morningsidecenter.org/programs_conflict.html#4Rs

Nystrand, M., & Gamoran, A. (1991). Instructional discourse, student engagement, and literature achievement. *Research in the Teaching of English, 25*(3), 261–290.

Nystrand, M., Wu, L., Gamoran, A., Zeiser, S., & Long, D. (2003). Questions in time: Investigating the structure and dynamics of unfolding classroom discourse. *Discourse Processes, 35*(2), 135–198.

O'Connor, M. C., & Michaels, S. (1996). Shifting participant frameworks: Orchestrating thinking practices in group discussion. In D. Hicks (Ed.), *Child discourse and society learning: An interdisciplinary perspective* (pp. 6–103). Cambridge, UK: Cambridge University Press.

Osborne, J., Erduran, S., & Simon, S. (2004). Enhancing the quality of argument in school science. *Journal of Research in Science Teaching, 41*(10), 994–102.

Pfeifer, J. H., Brown, C. S., & Juvonen, J. (2007). Teaching tolerance in schools: Lessons learned since *Brown v. Board of Education* about the development and reduction of children's prejudice. *Social Policy Report, 21*(2), 3–23.

Ponitz, C. C., McClelland, M. M., Matthews, J. S., & Morrison, F. J. (2009). A structured observation of behavioral self-regulation and its contributions to kindergarten outcomes. *Developmental Psychology, 45*(3), 605–619.

Schaps, E. (2007). Community in school: The heart of the matter. In P. Houston, A. Blankstein, & R. Cole (Eds.), *Spirituality in educational leadership* (pp. 73–87). Thousand Oaks, CA: Corwin Press.

Selman, R. L. (2003). *The promotion of social awareness: Powerful lessons from the partnership of developmental theory and classroom practice.* New York: Russell Sage.

Selman, R. L., & Dray, A. J. (2003). Bridging the gap: Connecting social awareness to literacy practice. In R. L. Selman, *The promotion of social awareness* (pp. 231–250). New York: Russell Sage.

Selman, R. L., & Snow, C. (2005, May). *Understanding ourselves and each other through literacy: How social themes promote literacy learning.* Presentation given at the annual convention of the International Reading Association, San Antonio, TX.

Snow, C. E., Lawrence, L. F., & White, C. (2009). Generating knowledge of academic language among urban middle school students. *Journal of Research on Educational Effectiveness, 2*(4), 325–344.

Solomon, D., Watson, M., & Battistich, V. (2001). Teaching and schooling effects on moral/prosocial development. In V. Richardson (Ed.), *Handbook of research on teaching* (4th ed., pp. 566–603). Washington, DC: American Educational Research Association.

Taylor, T. E, Ross, T., Snow, E., & Selman, R. L. (2011). *Classroom discussions at the elementary school level: An integrative analysis of academic discourse.* Cambridge, MA: Harvard University.

Walker, P. (2009). *Teaching voices: An introduction to "Voices Reading."* Unpublished manuscript.

Wiles, D. (2001). *Freedom summer.* New York: Atheneum Books for Young Readers.

Zaner-Bloser, Inc. (2010). *Voices reading: Achievement through literacy and character development.* Retrieved from http://www.zaner-bloser.com/educator/products/reading/comprehensive/voices.aspx?id=230

Zins, J. E., Bloodworth, M. R., Weissberg, R. P., & Walberg, H. J. (2004). The scientific base linking social and emotional learning to school success. In J. Zins, R. P. Weissberg, M. Wang, & H. J. Walberg (Eds.), *Building academic success on social and emotional learning: What does the research say?* (pp. 3–22). New York: Teachers College Press.

CHAPTER 10

Creating Powerful Learning Experiences in Early Childhood: Lessons from Good Teaching

Mara Krechevsky, Ben Mardell,
Tiziana Filippini, and Howard Gardner[1]

What are the essential components of powerful learning experiences in early childhood classrooms? Of course there are baseline elements of quality: qualified teachers (secured through adequate preparation and compensation), ongoing professional development, sufficiently small class sizes and teacher-child ratios, suitable materials, and a safe environment. In our view, high-quality early childhood education entails four additional features, none of which have been sufficiently appreciated in U.S. culture: (1) the critical importance of the "group" for supporting children's and adults' learning, (2) an approach to assessment based on documenting and revisiting children's thinking and learning, (3) a focus on generative ideas that are central to one or more domains of knowledge, and (4) a rich environment that promotes inquiry and high-quality work.

In this chapter, we make the case that these four features are crucial for powerful learning for young children. First, we discuss what is often missing in early childhood education in the United States and what can be gained by addressing these features. Then we show the four features at work via analyses of two prototypical examples from the preschools in Reggio Emilia, Italy. In conclusion, we introduce a framework through which early childhood education can be authentically evaluated.

WHAT IS MISSING FROM EARLY CHILDHOOD EDUCATION IN THE UNITED STATES

Children are in groups all the time in school (or Head Start or child care). Yet schools in the United States typically focus on individual achievement and what students carry away in their own minds. Indeed, it often seems like many American educators and parents would describe the ideal teacher-child ratio as 1:1. The assumption is that knowledge is an individual attainment. This view is understandable since the value of school is typically judged by what individual students learn. Moreover many subsequent milestones, ranging from admission to selective educational programs to securing an internship or a job, are focused on the skills and achievements of a particular person. However, while desirable at times, undue emphasis on individual instruction and performance ignores the potential of the group as a rich context for learning. Small groups in particular are ideal places for inquiry, where children with similar interests can work together and teachers and children can listen carefully to each other. Small groups foster complex interactions, constructive conflicts, and self-monitoring. They catalyze the capacities to listen, collaborate, and negotiate ideas, allowing for frequent and dynamic communication. Over time, each child is recognized by others in the group as bringing a distinct perspective and way of thinking.

That said, not all groups are learning groups. As Seidel (2001) notes, "In schools we all—students, teachers, parents, and staff—are in groups and our success or failure to learn is inextricably bound to our success or failure to decipher how to learn from and with others. . . . The fact of being in the same room or building does not in itself make the group a learning group" (p. 314). The tool of documentation—the practice of observing, recording, interpreting, and sharing the processes and products of learning in order to assess and deepen learning—is a key handmaiden of effective individual and group learning. Documentation entails trying to understand when and how learning takes place through systematic observation and analysis of children's work, conversations, and strategies via notes, photographs, video, and the like. In the United States, assessment typically focuses on evaluating learning as a product ("What did the children learn?"), rather than a process ("How do the children learn?"). Americans have enormous faith in quantitative measures of performance, and are often suspicious of human observation and interpretation. But documentation blurs the line that often separates evaluating learning from supporting learning. Making learning visible in and outside the classroom can demonstrate as well as extend children's learning.

There are many purposes and ways to document learning. Making learning visible through documentation can be a way to celebrate children's competencies, aid children and adults in their reflections, and shape future contexts for learning. Documentation leads teachers to compare what they *thought* they would observe to what *really* happens and informs decisions about where to go next; this process also allows children, teachers, and often those outside the classroom to understand better the learning that takes place.

Through the close look afforded by documentation, the intellectual capabilities of young children can be identified and nurtured. Too often, early childhood classrooms lack a focus on key ideas and understandings as well as learning through play. Without a larger road map for observing children and reflecting on one's teaching, teachers fall back on basic skills (counting to 10, reciting the alphabet, identifying colors) in lieu of deeper understandings or exploration of number concepts, verbal and written communication, or the visual arts. Curriculum goals are often framed to have children "become familiar with" simple factual information and acquire basic skills (Massachusetts Department of Education, 2003) without embedding these skills in a larger social, intellectual, or cultural context. When this happens, children's abilities and their desire or willingness to explore, theorize, collaborate, and create go unrecognized.

Creating powerful learning experiences that build on the capabilities of young children can also be hindered by the physical layout and organization of classrooms. The classroom environment reflects and communicates the teachers' values and approach to teaching and learning. The physical setup and quality of materials can either motivate or inhibit learning and curiosity. Ordinary materials like paper, rocks, or glue can become extraordinary depending on how they are displayed or introduced (Topal & Gandini, 1999). Predetermined activities do not give children (or adults) the chance to pursue their own interests or encounter the unexpected. Materials presented for a specific purpose only may discourage children's exploration and the invention of stories, games, or metaphors. Even in classrooms with a wealth of materials the daily schedule tends to limit time either for open experimentation or more focused exploration in service of deeper understanding.

How schools and classrooms are judged is also an important part of the story of early childhood education in the United States. Evaluation systems can affect teaching practice positively or negatively. The question of evaluation is especially pressing because accountability often shapes the experiences children have in school. A signature of the current school reform movement in the United States is to focus accountability on outputs—in particular, the regular deployment of standardized tests that measure student achievement, generally in literacy and math. While federal statutes (consistent with the counsel of the National Association for the Education of Young Children) do not require the testing of children until Grade 3, early elementary students and kindergartners are being regularly and repeatedly tested across the country. In many schools, such testing has narrowed the curriculum and led to the reduction or even elimination of group work and long-term projects (Darling-Hammond, 2010). In too many early childhood classrooms the arts, block play, and other activities rich with potential for learning are forsaken in favor of direct instruction of academic skills so that children will be "ready for the tests" (Shepard, 2000). In New York City and Los Angeles public schools kindergartners spend more time preparing for tests than learning through play (Alliance for Childhood, 2009).

As reflected in this volume, the knowledge base of early childhood education is wide, ranging from neuroscience to developmental psychology to cultural anthropology. At the same time, there is much to be learned from good teaching. While examples of high-quality teaching exist around the world, an especially vivid example at the present time can be found in the municipal infant-toddler centers and preschools of Reggio Emilia, Italy (Edwards, Gandini, & Forman, 1998). This system of 33 schools is internationally celebrated as a hub of innovation, inspiring educators throughout the world and illuminating what excellence in early childhood education looks like.[2]

The authors of this chapter are colleagues from Reggio Emilia and Project Zero, a research group at the Harvard Graduate School of Education. For over a decade we have been collaborating on the question of how to create powerful learning experiences for children and adults in classrooms and schools (Project Zero & Reggio Children, 2001). Below we present two examples of powerful learning experiences from Reggio classrooms in order to illustrate how the four features of high-quality early childhood education mentioned above—the critical importance of the group for supporting children's and adults' learning, an approach to assessment based on documenting and revisiting children's thinking and learning, a focus on generative ideas that are central to one or more domains of knowledge, and a rich environment that promotes inquiry and high-quality work—interact with and reinforce each other in practice. We follow with an analysis of each ingredient and then offer suggestions for how these elements might be authentically evaluated.

PHOTO 10.1. Meeting

POWERFUL LEARNING EXPERIENCES: TWO EXAMPLES

Consider the following two examples of documentation from the 4- and 5-year-old classrooms at the Diana School in Reggio Emilia. In the first example children are concerned with keeping track of turns for classroom jobs. In the second example the traditional children's activity of dress-up is transported into the world of computer technology.

Conta

Every day children in the 4-year-old class recite the counting rhyme (or *Conta*) "eenie, meenie, miney, mo" in order to choose two waiters for the day who will set the table for lunch and perform other duties.

At the start of the school year, children decide the counting rhyme is the fairest way to make the selection (Photo 10.1).

Together with the teachers, Sonia and Debora, the class agrees to post photographs of the waiters on a calendar to keep a record (Photo 10.2).

Over time, several children notice that certain classmates are selected more than others. Thomas protests that he has not had as many

PHOTO 10.2. Looking at Waiter Calendar

turns as some. The children begin to suspect the selection process is not fair and share their suspicion with their teachers.

After listening carefully to the children, the teachers try to respond in a way that avoids leading to a *yes* or *no* answer. Teachers prefer to let children come to their own answer; studying the documentation will help them determine which direction will be the most generative.

Sonia asks the children, "This is something you think, but how can you prove it?" She negotiates with the children to form a small group that (1) is made up of children who volunteer or are nominated by friends, (2) is likely to work well together, and (3) represents the range of mathematical abilities in the class. The group meets for a few days, each morning giving an update on its progress to the whole group.

At first, the small group discusses the equity of *Conta*. Some think that since the count depends on where you start and your timing, people can cheat. Others continue to think *Conta* is fair. Sonia invites the children to focus on finding proof by looking through the calendar.

Thomas notes, "I'm not in the calendar. Look and see." Carlo says, "I'm there twice." Some in the group begin counting the turns different children have had. But some children do not yet have a firm sense of number and the separate pages for each month make counting difficult for them.

The number of turns needs to be represented graphically. Four-year-old Gaia explains: "Do you know why we don't know how many

PHOTO 10.3. Making a Graph

times we did it? Because if you are not able to count and you are on different pages [on the calendar], you can't tell. . . . We have to find a way that is readable for everybody."

Listening to an audio recording of the group's conversation, along with looking at their notes, helps Debora and Sonia determine what direction the exploration might take, what materials to prepare, and what questions to ask that will inform the work and keep the group on track. They decide to ask the children if they would like to go to the *atelier* (art studio) to see if there are materials that might suggest a way to solve the problem. The teachers try to choose materials that can reveal what children are thinking. The teachers prepare small photographs of each child, slips of paper with all the children's names, and small and big paper with and without grids.

The children accept the offer and return to the classroom with a large piece of graph paper and photos, which they place on the grid to represent the number of turns of each waiter. Alice suggests a way to organize the photos: "I want to put all the children's pictures, like two for me and then I don't know . . . I must count . . . " (Photo 10.3).

Alice's comment allows Gaia to organize children to carry out the

PHOTO 10.4. Displaying the Data

different tasks needed to make the graph. Over the next few days, the small group explores different ways to make the data readable to all (Photo 10.4).

When the small group presents its findings to the class, each child immediately looks for his or her own picture. Gaia explains the graph to the children, including the process the group went through to create their display.

> *Gaia:* The first picture (at the bottom) is like the name. All the others are how many turns.

But there is confusion.

> *Wisdow (to Thomas):* You have a picture so you had one turn.
> *Gaia:* Oh no, they don't understand! (Photo 10.5).

In response, Gaia finds two other ways to deliver her explanation before everyone understands. This experience builds awareness in the group that what is clear to you may not be clear to others.

PHOTO 10.5. Reading the Data Chart

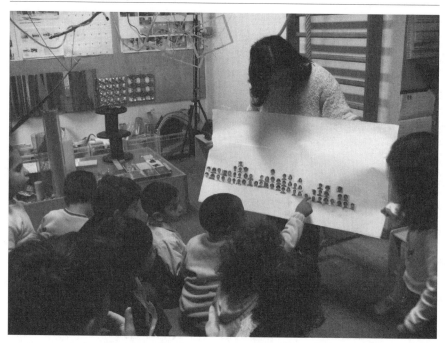

> *Gaia (to classmates):* The picture at the bottom is to explain who you are and the others are how many times you have been a waitress.
>
> *Wisdow:* I understand the misunderstanding. It's because you have used photos for both the list of kids and for the number of turns.
>
> *Gaia:* We did it that way because not everyone can read names.

Once the nature of the grid is clarified, Gaia concludes, "The *Conta* is not fair. We have to find another way." The class adopts a new selection method, prioritizing those with the fewest turns to be waiters.

The next year, the same group of children, now 5 years old, revisits the selection process and their earlier grid and chooses a different method to pick the day's waiters.

Using their new abilities to read and count, the children organize a chart with names and checkmarks to keep track of turns (Photo 10.6). Each day children negotiate who will be waiter, making sure the turns are allocated fairly.

PHOTO 10.6. Using New Skills

Observation. In this example, we begin to see the four features of high-quality early education at work. Thomas's concern could have arisen in any classroom in the world. Issues of equity and fairness are timeless. Here, effective use of the four ingredients helps teachers respond to children's concerns about a daily routine and translate them into a powerful learning experience that involves generative ideas (concepts of equity and probability), the creation of a small learning group as an especially helpful context for supporting children's thinking, the use of documentation to shape learning, and thought-provoking materials. Listening to the audiotape and looking over their notes gives teachers the idea of offering a range of materials in the *atelier* to support the children's quest to make the data understandable to themselves and to others. The recording also gives teachers insight into individual children's contributions to the group. While Gaia clarifies the need to create a graphically readable representation, she does not know how to go about it. It is Alice who helps her and the group find a systematic way to organize the data from the calendar.

Digital Dress-Up

Teachers at the Diana School often observe children at play, recording their words and gestures and noting their favorite activities.

PHOTO 10.7. Card Games

For one group of 5-year-olds, Yu-Gi-Oh! (a Japanese trading card game where characters can be combined to expand their powers using a "polymerization" card) is highly engaging (Photo 10.7).

> *Filippo: Polymerization* is a way of going round and round that unites two monsters into one really strong monster.

Simona, the school's *atelierista*, is new to teaching and eager to learn how best to support young children's learning. In reviewing documentation with her colleagues, Simona notices that children are fascinated by the idea of transformation in the Yu-Gi-Oh! play, which, Filippo explains, "is a thing in which you become what you would like to be." Why are children so captivated by things that transform themselves?

The teachers speculate that perhaps it is because children are also going through continuous change and searching for their identity.

Retaining the ideas of transformation and polymerization as generative ideas, Simona wonders if children could be engaged in an exploration of their changing identities. During the 5-year-olds' final year at school, from time to time the teachers ask the children to re-

PHOTO 10.8. Superhero Poses

flect on how they have changed since entering school at age 3. The teachers hypothesize that computers would be a good tool to support a new kind of dress-up game—where bodies can be enlarged, change shape, become powerful superheroes, or merge with their surroundings. The teachers also observe that children are very curious about how adults use the computer, often expressing the desire to have a "turn."

The play begins with Simona asking a small group of children, "Would you like to try to transform yourselves?"

> *Costanza:* With the computer!
> *Mattia:* Let's take pictures of ourselves and then let's transform them and then make ourselves speak!
> *Filippo:* We could make them like in a cartoon!

Simona invites the children to take photos of each other and download them onto the computer.

The transformation begins as soon as the children start to take pictures; many children pose as superheroes for their portraits (Photo 10.8).

PHOTO 10.9. Using Photoshop

Working in small groups, the children manipulate their images using Photoshop (Photo 10.9).

The children try things out, observe the effects, and decide what to use. They seem to be playing a collective video game—one in which they determine the setting, the characters, the plot, and the final outcome. Filippo discovers a way to clone parts of a tree, which, by mistake, he places on his face. His error becomes a source of a new power—invisibility. Mattia uses Filippo's discovery to multiply parts of his body (Photo 10.10).

Mattia: At the beginning I wanted to transform into Colossus. Then I got the idea of making a lot of heads and a lot of hands . . . I also have 1,000 brains!

Filippo: There are also 1,000 mouths. Therefore you speak differently.

Mattia: Do you know how I did this? I pushed a button and another one in the mouse. Then I pushed it over my face. Then I clicked again and a face came out.

Learning is a constant process of reflection and negotiation. When children learn in groups, they are more likely to share their discover-

PHOTO 10.10. Multiple Body Parts

ies and to see their ideas and theories as provisional. Making mistakes and changing course are integral parts of research and learning; it is important to accept them as such without worrying about them.

Simona brings two small groups together to compare their transformations. She asks the children what they might do with all the transformations (Photo 10.11).

Filippo: We could combine all the powers.
Costanza: To combine the powers to get along well.
Mattia: Yes, let's polymerize ourselves!

Back in their small group Filippo and Mattia pick up on the suggestion to combine powers. The two boys exclaim, "Now we could unite our powers! Yes! Let's polymerize ourselves! I have the power of invisibility! I have the power of all the things I've got on me. Lots of hands and lots of heads! Let's put ourselves together!"

Filippo explains, "All the transformations are real. It's just that in reality you transform with computers, not by magic."

As the year goes on, the children continue to build on their new familiarity with Photoshop. They use it to tell stories, to transform

PHOTO 10.11. Children Reviewing the Photos

images of their classroom in imaginative ways, and to share memories they would like to hold onto even after school is over.

Observation. Again, we see the four features of high-quality early education at work. Rather than dismissing—or even banning from school—the Yu-Gi-Oh! games as part of pop culture with little or no relevance to the classroom, the Diana teachers view the games as an opportunity to gain deeper understanding of children and their culture and create a powerful learning experience for their students. As in *Conta*, the small groups provide a vital context for children to share and build on each other's ideas. Reviewing documentation leads to exploring the generative ideas of change and transformation through a compelling modern-day tool—the computer.

KEY INGREDIENTS OF A LEARNING COMMUNITY

While we have seen many good early childhood programs in the United States with highly skilled teachers and plentiful resources, in our experience, examples like the two just described are rare. One reason for this is a lack of integration of the four key ingredients of powerful early childhood education. We address each of these in turn below.

Children and Adults Learning from and with Each Other to Deepen Learning

The children in *Conta* and *Digital Dress-Up* encounter other perspectives as they work together to solve problems and build understanding. In articulating their thinking to one another, they provide a window into their learning processes for each other and the teacher. Small groups are particularly hospitable for collaborative learning. In *Conta* the small group makes its thinking visible in several ways. First, the group provides concrete proof for its perception of unfairness. In order to do this, the children work to develop an accurate record of the number of times each child has served as waiter. Finally, the group presents its findings in a way that is "readable" to the rest of the class, many of whom do not yet know how to count.

Small groups are made up of children who express interest and curiosity in the topic as well as children selected by the teacher because of the usefulness of their competencies (group leadership, knowledge of Photoshop, facility with numbers or lack thereof). A pivotal move made by teacher Sonia is including children whose math abilities represent the range in the classroom, creating an awareness that counting will not be the solution for all. Members of learning groups are concerned not just with their own understanding, but also with the understanding of others. The small group shares its thinking with the class so the entire group can arrive at an informed decision that belongs to everyone.

After several mornings during which the children experiment with different systems, none of which quite work, Sonia asks the small group if they know why they have been unsuccessful. Gaia's question, "Do you know why we don't know how many times we did it? . . ." is a turning point because she understands the need to represent data that will be convincing to children not yet able to count. The teacher informs the group about histograms (a graphic display representing the distribution of data) and suggests the possibility of drawing lines. Although Sonia realizes that only a few children are ready to make meaningful use of the materials, she knows from past experience that those children will share their knowledge with their friends.

Not all of the children's ideas are accepted by the group, but the group is comfortable with the need to give and receive feedback. Self- and peer-assessment—revisiting and critiquing work—are seen as integral to the learning process. Reggio teachers pose questions and offer suggestions like, "What was your last discovery playing with the light table (or sand box, or blocks)? What ideas do you have about it?" or, "Last time you drew a bike. Would you like to try to make a bike with clay today?" At some point, the teacher may ask, "What is the difference between drawing a bike and making it in clay? Which way is easier? Which do you like more?" Before children play in an area or explore a topic, teachers sometimes ask, "What do you think you'll find out? At the end of the morning, come and let me know if you came up with a new discovery." They use words like *theory*, *discovery*, and *research* that help to make thinking visible and model the learning process. In addition, rather than responding to children's questions directly, teachers frequently refer children to each other so that children see themselves as resources of knowledge.

Ongoing Documentation for Shaping and Extending Learning

Because the Diana School *atelierista* is new to teaching young children, her colleagues suggest that she spend time observing and documenting children's "culture" in order to update the other teachers on the kinds of words, images, gestures, and other modes of expression she discovers. *Digital Dress-Up* becomes part of a yearlong reflection project on the past 3 years. Children review work from previous years to identify products that show how they have grown or what they have learned. Some children choose problems that have been difficult to solve, others choose drawings they had not been able to do previously. Looking at these products enables each child to revisit what it means to be a learner and grounds the abstract process of reflection in something concrete and meaningful.

Reggio teachers meet regularly to review documentation of children's learning in order to share perspectives, identify connections to generative ideas, and plan next steps. Sandra Piccinini, the former commissioner of education and culture for the Reggio schools, observes: "One of the most common misinterpretations is to understand documentation as a strategy to teach better what we as teachers already know. Instead, documentation needs to be a way to get to know better what the children, in their own way, already know" (quoted in Turner & Wilson, 2010, p.8). The methods used by the children in *Conta* challenge and expand teachers' understanding of 4-year-olds' capabilities.

Documentation is useful as a record or "memory" for adults as well as children. Taping children's conversations provides teachers with a record that can be reviewed with colleagues. Teachers listen not only for children's understanding of ideas, but also for the way the group functions and children participate. This kind of documentation helps to ensure that "no child is left behind." Looking back in order to move forward also characterizes the teachers' interactions with children in the classroom. Every morning children share not only the outcome of their previous day's work, but also the process they went through in their learning. The teachers in *Conta* ask the small group to choose tools and materials from the day before that have been especially useful in order to help the group maintain focus and build awareness of how they learn.

A Focus on Generative Ideas That Are Central to Domains of Knowledge

By *generative*, we mean ideas and ways of thinking that facilitate lasting understandings after less significant concepts and facts are forgotten. Generative ideas can include such diverse concepts as "science is a process of constructing and testing theories," "all measurement is comparison," "members of a group can have a say in the rules that govern them," or "ideas and feelings can be communicated through different symbol systems (drawing, numbers, Photoshop images)." Generative ideas can be taught in a variety of ways and carry through several grade levels. Reggio teachers look not only for skills like the ability to count to 10, but also for children's understanding of what numbers are for. How does the number of apples differ from the address on a house? How does the length of a table differ from a date on a calendar? Teachers devote a great deal of time to thinking about meaningful contexts so that children will understand numbers as a cultural convention that can serve different purposes.

Generative ideas are not always obvious to teachers. Early childhood teachers often engage their students in "fun activities," but these do not necessarily promote foundational knowledge or understanding in young children. When teachers develop their own understanding of generative ideas or ways of thinking—whether through conversations with colleagues, reflecting on the aims of their work, or additional study of subject matter—they can set activity goals, choose materials, and interact with children more flexibly and in ways that facilitate learning. This awareness also alerts teachers to spontaneous moments that can enhance children's understanding, even if they are outside the planned curriculum.

We get a sense of generative ideas from the two examples we have provided. In *Conta,* children develop a sense of probability—exploring the likelihood of a child getting chosen as waiter based on the current method; equity—determining whether the current method is fair to every member of the group and what should be done if it isn't; and the disposition to seek evidence for claims. *Digital Dress-Up* touches on developing and experimenting with a personal identity alone and with others and the potential of computers for creating images and transforming reality. The project is playful, yet focused on exploring and communicating ideas at the intersection of the real and the imaginary.

A focus on generative ideas with young children may be surprising to some. Yet children's engagement in *Conta* and *Digital Dress-Up* offers evidence that young children can pursue these topics with intellectual integrity (Bruner, 1960). Recognizing the capabilities of young children is *not* an invitation to push the elementary school curriculum down to preschool. Exploring generative ideas takes place not through transmission from teacher to student, but through an interactive, intergenerational process whereby children and adults learn from and with one another. Rather than following a set curriculum, teachers in Reggio explore generative ideas by preparing stimulating contexts in which children can develop and test strategies, revealing both competencies and misconceptions to be addressed.

A Rich Environment That Promotes Inquiry and High-Quality Work

The success of a learning community is contingent on teachers being able to harness children's desire to learn. As formulated by Csikszentmihalyi (1990), "The chief impediments to learning are not cognitive. It is not that students cannot learn; it is that they do not wish to. If educators invested a fraction of the energy they now spend on trying to transmit information on trying to stimulate the students' enjoyment of learning, we could achieve much better results" (p. 115). The physical environment and flexibility of the classroom schedule play a central role in engaging individuals and the group in learning with joy.

Classrooms in Reggio Emilia are set up in accordance with the teachers' images of the child and sense of children's capabilities. Teachers are constantly pondering how children learn; they are prepared to be surprised. Areas and materials are designed and presented with an eye toward inspiring creativity, facilitating exploration and connections, and engaging children in thinking about big ideas. Teachers provide media so that children can think and express ideas in multiple symbol systems. In *Conta* the small xeroxed photographs of the children's faces are an appealing way to record the children's turns as waiter. Organizational schemas like a calendar are also available and suggestive of ways to record information. When the separate pages of the calendar make counting problematic, the teacher asks the group if they want to visit the *atelier* (art studio) to see what other shapes, sizes, and types of paper they might use. Teachers carefully consider the nature, quality, and availability of these materials. The choice of different paper, colored pencils, and other high-quality art materials reflects values of beauty and high standards.

Teachers are continually aware of introducing variation to encourage children to build and express knowledge in different media. They want to make sure that children have the opportunity to revisit and revise their work alone and in a group, to compare where they started and where they ended up, and to make connections that will deepen their understanding. Time is neither rushed nor fragmented. The children in *Conta* devote several mornings to solving the waiter problem. The following year, these same children (now a year older) have greater reading, writing, and counting skills so they can modify their system for choosing a waiter. In *Digital Dress-Up* children learn enough about Photoshop so that the next time they want to enlarge or change the shape of an image, they request that tool in particular. Over time, they develop an awareness of which materials and tools (writing, clay, Photoshop) are most suitable for expressing or communicating an idea.

EVALUATION OF THE LEARNING COMMUNITY

Where would you look and what would you look for when visiting a preschool classroom to determine its effectiveness as an educational environment that supports children's learning? Certainly, the four ingredients on which we have focused are present to some extent in most early childhood settings. In almost every preschool classroom, there are opportunities for children to learn from and with one another and for teachers to record observations of children, identify topics to explore more deeply, and give thought to the choice of materials. The question is one of degree and effectiveness. How do we determine whether there are sufficient quantities of each ingredient to create powerful learning experiences and support children's learning effectively?

While parents, educators, and policy makers will approach this question in different ways, all can be informed by the following thought experiment. Imagine you are an inspector charged with the responsibility of evaluating early childhood settings. You are a critical friend, helping schools and teachers improve, but you are also ultimately responsible for ensuring that all children are provided with the best possible learning environment. We envision the inspector collecting data from a variety of contexts with a focus on the four elements of powerful learning experiences:

- A teacher-facilitated conversation (whole or small group)
- A child-directed exploration (in the block area, dramatic play, or water table)
- A structured, small-group task introduced by the inspector
- An observation of the classroom environment
- An interview with the teacher(s)

Each context could be videotaped for review by the inspector and/or teacher (see also Kane & Cantrell, 2010). Although the indicators would vary depending on the time of year, age of the children, priorities of the school system, and teacher's goals, we suggest addressing certain considerations, listed below for each context.

The Teacher-Facilitated Conversation (Whole or Small Group)

- Who is doing the talking? The teacher? A few children? How does the teacher facilitate the conversation? For example, does she refer children to other children?
- Is this a connected conversation? Are statements linked to previous ones and do ideas build off one another? Do children and adults listen to each other?
- What is the purpose of the conversation? Does the conversation involve generative ideas? Is it to share what children already know or build new knowledge? What is the quality of children's language? Are the words rich and expressive? How do children structure their sentences? Do their statements refer only to themselves or are they more decontextualized?
- Do children help each other by providing critique or explaining ideas to each other? How do they handle conflict? Are children engaged? Do they use a language of thinking and emotion, for example, employing words like *idea, theory, wonder, inspire, agree,* and *disagree*? Is there laughter and expressions of excitement and joy?

The Child-Directed Exploration (in the Block Area, Dramatic Play, or Water Table)

- What is the quality of the exploration? Given the children's ages and experiences, is the use of blocks, the water table, or play scenarios sophisticated and complex or more limited? Are the children open to multiple solutions?

- What is the quality of the children's interactions? Do they share ideas with one another? Do they have a shared goal? How do they offer and receive critique? How do they solve problems and deal with conflict?
- What is the role of the teacher? When does she step in or step out? How does the teacher respond to children's ideas and questions? How does she deal with conflict and issues of sharing, equity, or hurt feelings?

The Structured Small-Group Task Introduced by the Inspector

The inspector gives a group of children an unfamiliar, but developmentally appropriate task. For example, the inspector might ask children to pretend that a new student will be joining their class in a few days and wants to understand the daily schedule before he arrives. What is the best way to let him know? The inspector notes:

- How do the children discuss the problem? Do they listen to each other? Build on each other's ideas? Access other resources (adults or children) that can help?
- How do the children develop and carry out the plan? Do they think to put something on paper? Do they draw pictures or write words? Does the notation communicate relevant information?

The Classroom Observation

Here we recommend that both teacher and inspector fill out a short rubric or checklist evaluating the four ingredients of a powerful learning community: the presence of collaborative learning, ongoing documentation, generative ideas, and a rich environment. For example, is there evidence that teachers are documenting children's learning processes or sharing documentation back with students? What kinds and quality of materials are available and how do children interact with them? Are there blocks of uninterrupted time? Each element is rated on a scale from "not apparent" to "present with strong supporting evidence."

The Teacher Interview

Videotapes of the teacher-facilitated conversation, the child-directed exploration, and structured task along with the classroom observation checklist form the basis for the interview. For example, the inspector might share the videotapes of the teacher-led conversation and child-directed exploration and ask:

- What are the central ideas or habits of mind you were hoping children would learn? What do you think the children did learn? How do you know?
- What might you do next to deepen children's learning individually or collectively?
- What might you do in 2 weeks to make sure the learning could be extended to other contexts?

Consideration of the four ingredients in these contexts can inform how parents, educators, and policy makers evaluate the educational vibrancy of an early childhood classroom. For example, parents looking for the best educational setting for their children might observe in the block area or a whole-group meeting. During a whole-group meeting, parents could look for whether the teacher or children are doing the bulk of the talking, the number of children participating, whether comments build off each other, and connections to generative ideas. The "teacher interview" questions could be used for conversations with teachers or administrators.

For administrators and teachers, this approach suggests a possible system of supervision. For example, school or center directors could support teachers' professional growth by having conversations based on videotapes from whole-class meetings or child-led exploration in areas like blocks or dramatic play. The conversations would resemble a supportive supervisory meeting, with both teachers and administrators making observations and asking as well as answering questions. Actual footage of children at work and play would provide a shared and unmediated reference point for conversations about individual children, interactions between children, exploration of generative ideas, and next steps for learning. Teachers and directors might also complete and share classroom observation checklists in order to compare perspectives on strengths and weaknesses.

For policy makers, it is not an easy matter to craft an effective evaluation system in a nation with a staggering range of classroom populations with regard to socioeconomic background, cultural and ethnic diversity, proficiency in English, and previous experience in structured groups (see Kane & Cantrell, 2010). At the same time, policy makers have a special responsibility to evaluate early childhood settings; the decisions they make significantly affect teachers' behavior. When tests focus on discrete prereading skills, teachers worry about small gains in measurable literacy outcomes. Direct instruction of these skills increases, often at the expense of powerful learning opportunities. Blocks disappear, dramatic play is curtailed, and teachers feel they cannot make the time to follow children's interests (like exploring the fairness of organizing classroom jobs). Ironically, this shift in emphasis undermines children's opportunities to explore language and interact with print and other symbol systems in more authentic ways.

Our thought experiment suggests an evaluative framework that would direct teachers' and others' attention toward creating powerful learning experiences. While one-time observations have limitations, we are confident the indicators we describe cannot be faked. If a compelling whole-group conversation is observed, it is because children have had experience participating in such conversations. Neither can teachers fake thoughtful interviews about their teaching and children's learning. In order to prepare for such discussions, teachers need to reflect regularly on their practice, supported by documentation. If such interviews are part of an evaluation system, administrators will have a strong incentive to include this type of reflection as part of teachers' professional development. What is critical at the outset is not whether schools or centers score well on specific indicators, but rather that their consideration opens up essential conversations about supporting children's learning in powerful and compelling ways. Our hope is that teachers will leave these conversations energized, having learned something that will support their practice.

POWERFUL LEARNING EXPERIENCES FOR ALL

Early childhood is the beginning of formal learning in groups for most American children. The percentage of 3- and 4-year-olds in group settings (Head Start, family child care, community child care, and public and private preschool) has nearly doubled in the past 20 years from 40 to 78% (Barnett, Hustedt, Friedman, Boyd, & Ainsworth, 2007). With early education now embraced by politicians, business leaders, and even military officials as an important part of the national strategy to prepare children for the challenges of the 21st century (Mission: Readiness, 2009), the number of children in group settings is likely to grow.

This state of affairs adds urgency to the questions, "What should early classroom learning experiences involve?" and "How should these learning experiences be evaluated?" As we debate the nature of quality early childhood education, the work of teachers like Sonia, Debora, Simona, and their colleagues in Reggio Emilia serves as a guide. Attention to the group, documentation, generative ideas, and the environment can help provide the learning experiences all children deserve; and enlightened approaches to assessment can make this learning visible to all.

NOTES

We are grateful to Diana School educators Sonia Cipolla, Debora Iori, and Simona Spagiarri for the classroom experiences and documentation that form the basis for this chapter. Photographs were generously contributed by the Istituzione-Municipal Preschools and Infant-Toddler Centers of Reggio Emilia, Italy, and Reggio Children. We also want to thank Jie-Qi Chen, Heidi Andrade, Lisa Fiore, Mindy Kornhaber, and Tavia Mead for commenting on earlier drafts of this chapter. We dedicate our chapter to the memory of two outstanding educators, colleagues, and friends—*Janet Stork and Maggie Donovan*.

1. Order of authors was determined by a coin toss.

2. Preschools in Reggio Emilia contain classrooms with 2 teachers and 26 three-, four-, or five-year-old children. An *atelierista* (someone trained in the arts) works with the classroom teachers. There is no school director, but there is a coordinating team of 10 *pedagogistas* with a background in psychology or pedagogy that coordinates the work of several schools each. Five hours a week are dedicated to nonclassroom activities, such as professional development, planning, preparation of materials, and meetings with colleagues or parents. Children stay with the same cohort throughout their 3 years at the school. Over the course of that time, every child engages in robust long-term projects—often in small groups—which are informed by teachers' careful documentation of children's learning.

REFERENCES

Alliance for Childhood. (2009). *Crisis in the kindergarten: Why children need to play in schools*. Retrieved from http://www.allianceforchildhood.org

Barnett, W. S., Hustedt, J., Friedman, A., Boyd, J., & Ainsworth, P. (2007). *The state of preschool: 2007 state preschool yearbook*. Camden, NJ: National Institute for Early Education Research.

Bruner, J. S. (1960). *The process of education*. Cambridge, MA: Harvard University Press.

Csikszentmihalyi, M. (1990). *Flow: The psychology of optimal experience*. New York: Harper & Row.

Darling-Hammond, L. (2010). *The flat world and education: How America's commitment to equity will determine our future*. New York: Teachers College Press.

Edwards, C., Gandini, L., & Forman, G. (1998). *The hundred languages of children*. Norwood, NJ: Ablex.

Kane, T., & Cantrell, S. (2010). *Learning about teaching: Initial findings from the measures of effective teaching project.* Seattle, WA: Bill & Melinda Gates Foundation.

Massachusetts Department of Education. (2003, August). Massachusetts state social sudies curriculum frameworks. Retrieved from: http://www.doe.mass.edu/frameworks/hss/final.pdf

Mission: Readiness—Military Leaders for Kids. (2009). Ready, willing, and unable to serve. Retrieved from http://cdn.missionreadiness.org/NATEE1109.pdf

Project Zero & Reggio Children. (2001). *Making learning visible: Children as individual and group learners.* Reggio Emilia: Reggio Children.

Seidel, S. (2001). To be part of something bigger than oneself. In Project Zero & Reggio Children, *Making learning visible: Children as individual and group learners* (pp. 312–321). Reggio Emilia: Reggio Children.

Shepard, L. (2000). The role of assessment in a learning culture. *Educational Researcher, 29*(7): 4–14.

Topal, C. W., & Gandini, L. (1999). *Beautiful stuff: Learning with found materials.* New York: Sterling.

Turner, T., & Wilson, D. (2010). Reflections on documentation: A discussion with thought leaders from Reggio Emilia. *Theory Into Practice, 49*(1), 8.

CHAPTER 11

The School of the 21st Century

Addressing the Needs
of the Whole Child

Edward Zigler and Matia Finn-Stevenson

Educational failure among low-income children has been a persistent social problem. Many exemplary school reform initiatives have been developed, but the problem remains and is evident in the academic achievement gap between poor and middle-class students. Sawhill (2006) reviewed studies showing that in many respects, the U.S. educational system reinforces rather than compensates for differences in students' family background, so it is not surprising that the achievement gap persists.

The most recent national policy attempt to address the problem has been the 2001 No Child Left Behind Act (NCLB). It put the spotlight on the achievement gap, mandating that schools move to ensure that all children have a fair, equal, and significant opportunity to obtain a high-quality education. The law has various provisions to accomplish this goal, including increased student assessments, changes in academic standards and accountability, and schoolwide reforms that focus on academic content and reading. Although some aspects of NCLB have worked, the educational achievement gap continues; any effort to revise the law should adopt a holistic approach that recognizes that children's home environment impacts their education and children—and families—need various support services even before children begin formal schooling.

The importance of addressing the needs of children during their early years has been acknowledged for some time. Preceding the mandates of NCLB was the Educate America Act of 1994, which enunciated eight national educational goals. The first goal was school readiness. Alas, the law expired in 2002. Although it documented progress in helping children enter school ready to profit from the curricula, the goal of universal school readiness was not attained. Yet this benchmark is a prerequisite if we are to address the persistent achievement gap.

We say this because both the social and neuroscience research show that the early years are of critical developmental importance (Shonkoff & Phillips, 2000; Zigler, Finn-Stevenson, & Hall, 2002); studies further indicate that children who face environmental hardships such as poverty, especially early in life, are at risk for developmental delays and eventual academic failure. Indeed, wide gaps in ability have been documented before children even enter school, prompting Sawhill (2006) among others to state that the highest priority in education should be to establish a system of good-quality early care and education for children from all socioeconomic groups.

A major national problem is that we have no system in place to oversee the learning environments of young children prior to school entry. Rather, we have a mix of fragmented services, some providing part-day preschool and others all-day, year-round child care for children whose parents are working. Multiple funding streams support the programs, and a variety of provider contexts exists—individuals, public schools, nonprofit and for-profit centers, churches, and community-based organizations. Of significance is the general lack of quality that characterizes this nonsystem and the fact that the majority of preschool children attend child care programs that are of poor or mediocre quality (NICHD, 2005; Vandell & Wolfe, 2000; Zigler, Marsland, & Lord, 2009). Such environments do not promote school readiness and thus can hinder the aims of NCLB.

A national policy for universal preschool has the potential to facilitate an efficient early education and care system. Many issues have to be addressed about the governance, structure, and scope of a proposed system. In this chapter we discuss our experiences with the development and implementation of the School of the 21st Century (21C). 21C is a comprehensive school-based program that includes universally accessible preschool education and child care and several other services. The need for and rationale underlying 21C, and its adoption in schools throughout the country, illuminate some of the key issues to be considered in formulating a policy for universal preschool. As Mintrom (2001) notes, documenting already established efforts provides compelling evidence for the workability of programs as well as lessons that can help shape effective policy.

THE NEED FOR CHILD AND FAMILY SUPPORT SERVICES

Societal changes have brought on a need for a range of child and family support services in general and for the School of the 21st Century in particular. One of the most significant of the changes has been the continued increase in the number of working mothers—now the norm among the majority of families, where both parents work outside of the home. Another major change has been the dramatic rise in the number of single-parent households, due to higher incidences of divorce and parents who do not marry. Other changes in family structure have been caused by high mobility, especially in families with young children, and a lack of social capital, which refers to the dearth of adults in the lives of children and weak ties between families and their neighbors and kin (Putnam, 1995). The result has been increased isolation and alienation, with many parents raising children with little help and social support. These societal shifts, as well as two other circumstances—the large number of young children who live in poverty and increasing populations of children from low-income immigrant families—create stressful conditions under which many young children are growing up. This stress can have profound developmental and educational consequences.

Changing demographics have intensified the need for good-quality, affordable child care. The U.S. Census Bureau (2000) estimates that 65% of mothers with children under age 6 and 78% of mothers with children ages 6 to 13 are in the labor force; among mothers with infants under age one, 59% are in the labor force or actively looking for work. With their parents at work, 13 million infants and preschool children—or 3 out of every 5 children in this age bracket—are in child care. For school-age children, policy emphasis on before- and after-school programs has helped, but there remain an estimated 7 million children left home alone outside of school hours (U.S. Census Bureau, 2002).

The need for a child care system was recognized in 1971, when Congress laid the groundwork for a national child care program in the Comprehensive Child Development Act. This popular act was surprisingly vetoed by President Richard M. Nixon, responding to right-wing complaints that the system would lead to the "communal" rearing of children. Since that time, advocates have attempted in vain to create an interest at the federal level not only in establishing a system of child care but also in ensuring that there is good-quality care. At the state level there are child care licensing requirements, but often these fail to address even basic health and safety issues (LeMoines, Morgan, & Azer, 2003; Marsland, Zigler, &

Martinez, 2006). For example, the U.S. Consumer Product Safety Commission (1999) found pervasive health and safety violations in over two thirds of child care facilities, even though these facilities were state licensed. Assuming the same ratio applies to the many child care providers who operate underground with no oversight, a picture emerges of huge numbers of children experiencing poor-quality care. Such care has been linked to delayed language and reading skills and to more aggression and behavior problems (Shonkoff & Phillips, 2000). On the other hand, children in high-quality care have shown greater academic skills once they are in school, as well as fewer behavior problems (Cost, Quality, & Child Outcomes Study Team, 1999; NICHD, 2005).

In sum, the majority of young children are spending a significant part of their early development in child care settings that are not always conducive to optimal growth and school readiness. To enhance children's academic achievement, a focus on children's experiences before they enter school is paramount. In addition, what is needed is not simply additional services and more money, but the creation of an early care and education system, because the current nonsystem is difficult both to access and improve. The School of the 21st Century is an effort to establish a child care system not by creating entirely new structures, but by joining child care to the existing educational system.

THE SCHOOL OF THE 21ST CENTURY

The School of the 21st Century (21C), conceptualized in 1987, is a comprehensive approach to the provision of education and other services for children from conception to age 12. It is currently implemented in about 1,400 schools around the country. (In some communities in Kentucky and Connecticut, the program is referred to as Family Resource Centers.)

21C is a school-based child care and family support program (see Finn-Stevenson & Zigler, 1999, for a full description) that has sought to remedy the problem identified by Brauner, Gordic, and Zigler (2004): namely that the inadequate state of child care today is partially the result of the fact that early care and education are viewed as separate issues when in fact they are synergistic. The researchers further assert that to address the child care problem we need an infrastructure that combines care and education, placing educational components into child care and providing child care within the context of the educational system.

Elements of the Program

21C exemplifies efforts to use knowledge from child development research to address social policy and practice. Its goal is to improve children's school readiness and educational success. This mission is pursued along several fronts. One is to provide access to high-quality child care and developmentally appropriate preschool experiences during all the years before school entry. Another is to build parent involvement, which evidence shows is related to better school performance. A third component is support services for parents (which includes good child care). Such supports can enhance family functioning, which is ultimately reflected in the child's academic progress.

The synergy between child care and education is inherent in 21C. The program includes the following components:

1. All-day year-round child care as well as preschool education for children ages 3 and 4. We refer here to developmentally appropriate care that provides opportunities for play, social interactions, and learning. Although no specific curriculum is designated for the preschool child care component, schools are given guidance to choose curricular activities that address all developmental domains: physical, social, emotional, and cognitive.
2. Before- and after-school and vacation care for children from kindergarten to age 12. Although many school-age programs focus on academics, in 21C the emphasis is on providing children with the opportunity to choose among various types of activities, including but not limited to academic enrichment and homework. The rationale here is that children need programs with a broad framework that address overall development and the need to relax, socialize, and have fun (National Research Council, 2002).

21C also serves families with infants and toddlers. One service is home visitation, patterned after the Parents as Teachers (2006) program. In this component, parent educators visit the home to provide information to parents about their children's development as well as screen children for potential developmental or learning problems. In addition, parent meetings are held at the school to welcome families and provide social support, including referral to special services as may be needed. Parents also learn about their role in their children's development and education, with one outcome being enhanced parental involvement once children are in school (Pfannenstiel, Lambson, & Yarnell, 1996).

Among other 21C components are outreach and training to child care providers in the community; information and referral for various services families may need; and health, mental health, and nutrition education and services. In some communities, schools also provide social services and infant care in response to local needs or requests by parents. Additional components have been added over the years. Most recently, a Social and Emotional Learning (SEL) component has been added to provide schools with opportunities for mental health enhancement. This new component features The Mutt-i-grees Curriculum® (2010, 2011; see http://www.Yale.edu/21C for details), which uses dogs and dog puppets to engage children's interest in activities that promote positive behaviors.

All components are part of the 21C "umbrella" and are coordinated as a whole.

Guiding Principles of the Program

21C was conceptualized on the basis of knowledge derived from research about effective interventions, abbreviated in six guiding principles:

1. Child care is an important environment where young children grow and learn. The current nonsystem of care does not promote the optimal development and school readiness of all children. A child care system must therefore become a national priority and part of the structure of our society, as is the case with education.

2. Good-quality care should be accessible to every child regardless of ethnic or socioeconomic group. We should not accept the present two-tier system where some children receive good-quality care and others do not. Like education, child care can only be universally accessible if it is primarily a state-based system. The federal government's role is to subsidize care for children with handicaps or multiple risks, as it currently does, as well as support research, evaluation, and other efforts to build knowledge about effective services and continuously adapt best practices to keep up with children's changing needs. We should note here that the term *universal* does not imply compulsory attendance but rather universal access to good-quality, affordable care for families who need and want it.

3. Child care practices must be based on a whole-child approach that attends to all developmental pathways: so-

cial, emotional, physical, and cognitive (Zigler, Singer, & Bishop-Josef, 2004). For purposes of research, social scientists often regard each developmental domain separately, and as a society we often pay more attention to cognition. However, all aspects of growth and development are interdependent and occur simultaneously, so it is imperative to nurture all the interlocking areas. This third principle not only acknowledges that the child is a complex being, but it highlights the contributions of the child care setting to a child's developmental course. While child care may commonly be regarded as a service for parents, it is first and foremost an environment where children spend a significant amount of time. As such, its quality affects their overall growth and development.

4.   To ensure developmental continuity, parents and caregivers must work together. The importance of parent involvement is noted not only for programs for preschool and younger children, but also when children are in school (Henrich & Blackman-Jones, 2006). Parent participation is deemed so critical that it was listed as one of the now expired national education goals.

5.   Recognition, support, and appropriate pay for child care providers, since they are responsible for the quality of care children receive. This principle encompasses the need for ongoing staff training as well as upgrades in pay and benefits.

6.   A national child care system must be flexible and adaptable. Because family dynamics and needs differ, a universal system must provide a range of choices for child care. Inherent in this principle is the recognition that there are differences not only among families and children, but also among communities.

These guiding principles represent 21C's theoretical framework. The principles are used not only to provide a national context, but to shape state initiatives and guide implementation at the local level. This is an important consideration for universal preschool policy, since the ultimate success of the effort will depend on how well individual programs are implemented (Barnett, Brown, Finn-Stevenson, & Henrich, 2006). The 21C guiding principles enable each of the local schools to abide by a shared vision, but at the same time have the flexibility to be responsive to the individual community's circumstances.

Bailey (2002) also emphasized the importance of clear principles when mounting an effort. He examined federal legislation for the education of children with disabilities, noting that the Individuals with Disabilities Education Act has a set of national regulatory guidelines to ensure that certain principles shape the administration of the effort at the state level. He acknowledged that the regulations are in part controversial but indicates that without them, "we would see perhaps more cross-state variability than desired in the number and types of children served and in the nature, quantity and quality of services provided" (p. 10).

While some states have moved toward the provision of universal preschool, whether there will be national commitment to a universal preschool policy remains to be seen. If there is such commitment, many questions about how a national mandate for preschool for all children will be translated to practice will have to be answered. Two decades of experience with 21C highlight some of these questions and reveal working solutions.

LESSONS FROM THE SCHOOL OF THE 21ST CENTURY

The School of the 21st Century is now one of the largest and most comprehensive school-based, universal programs with a national footprint. The majority of 21C schools have been in operation for 2 decades, establishing the feasibility of using a public school site for preschool and other nonacademic services, as well as providing evidence that such efforts can be sustained over time. The size and longevity of the 21C program create a rich source of lessons learned that have implications for a national policy for universal preschool.

The Role of Public Schools in Child Care

The development of 21C began with the premise that a system for the care and education of preschoolers must be readily accessible in terms of cost as well as location to all families. Instead of building new facilities, a more efficient way to implement child care would be to tap into the existing educational structure. Our country has a trillion-dollar investment in public school buildings, which are supported by tax dollars and used for only part of the day, 9 months a year. By capitalizing on this investment and incorporating a child care system into schools, we would be able to increase the supply of care available to area families and lower building and occupation expenses.

The idea of using public schools for various nonacademic services is not new and is in fact inherent in the community school movement that began several decades ago and has recently enjoyed a resurgence (Dryfoos, 1994; Martin, 2003). Placing preschool care in schools was considered back in the 1970s, with proponents pointing out that schools are a resource that exists in every community. They argued that expansion of early childhood services was inevitable and that a single delivery system would prevent random development of programs (Levine, 1978).

However, opposition to the use of schools was extensive. Levine (1978) examined arguments on both sides of the debate and conducted a case study in five communities where schools provided child care. Although Levine ultimately opposed exclusive sponsorship by the schools, he saw the potential of their involvement in child care and thought it unwise for a national policy to exclude the schools.

Debate over public schools' involvement in child care has continued over the years. Lack of space, a poor track record in serving low-income and non-English-speaking children, an overburdened educational system, and presumed parental dissatisfaction with schools are some of the arguments voiced against placing child care in schools (Finn-Stevenson & Zigler, 1999). A major concern is that the elementary school environment poses "a danger that there would be a drift toward a much more regimented, scholarly curriculum than [is] appropriate" for preschoolers (Helburn & Bergmann, 2002, p. 63).

Despite the objections, increasing numbers of schools have opened their doors to very young children. The National Center for Education Statistics (2003) reported that in 2001-02, some 822,000 preschool children were enrolled in close to 20,000 schools—or 35% of all elementary schools in the United States. The momentum seems to be building as more educators and policy makers consider ways public schools can expand services for preschool children (e.g., Dwyer, Chait, & McKee, 2000; Hinkle, 2000). Other organizations in the community may work with the schools, or in some places the schools may work with community organizations. However, it is clear that schools, even if they are not the prime sponsors of preschool, are likely to become involved more in early care and education.

What the Evidence on 21C Shows

Contrary to the argument that schools are rigid, centralized bureaucracies unable to address the needs of diverse populations or young children's needs for a variety of curriculum approaches, evidence we have gathered from 21C shows that schools can provide good-quality, developmentally appropriate care. In an ongoing national study of

21C schools funded by the U.S. Department of Education, we found high-quality preschool programs as well as various practices related to good care (Henrich, Ginicola, & Finn-Stevenson, 2006). So far we have examined school districts in five states participating in the 3-year evaluation. Our findings include the following:

- The preschool programs had a mean score of 5.70 on the Early Childhood Environment Rating Scale. The range of scores on this scale is 1 to 7, with a 5 indicating good quality.
- The programs were child-centered, with teachers reporting spending an average of more than 2 hours a day on child-initiated activities.
- Staff were highly qualified. Among the teachers, the median number of years teaching preschool was 8.5 years. About 80% of the teachers had a bachelor's or master's degree in early childhood education, and the rest had a Child Development Associate credential.
- Staff turnover, another indicator of quality, was much lower than the national average, with teachers reporting a median of 7 years working in the 21C preschool program.

A study in Arkansas, where there are over 160 schools in the 21C program, clearly established the impact of the program. Arkansas is well known for its effort to address preschool education and child care needs with its Arkansas Better Chance (ABC) program where child care providers apply for state funds to offer high-quality services to children at risk. In order to determine if 21C adds value to the ABC program, the study (Ginicola et al., 2006) used results from student and program quality assessments to compare school-based preschools having both ABC and 21C services to those programs that offered only ABC services. Results indicated that, at baseline, children within the 21C/ABC programs scored the same or poorer than their ABC ONLY counterparts. However, at the end of the year, participants at 21C/ABC preschools were significantly ahead of ABC ONLY programs on all developmental indicators. There were also differences favorable to 21C/ABC preschools in the programs' quality ratings, as measured by the Early Childhood Environmental Rating Scale—Revised.

Training and Policy Guidance for 21C Schools

The high quality in 21C schools is due in part to training and assistance in implementing and maintaining quality programs provided by the 21C national office. This office, headed by Matia Finn-Stevenson, is part of the Yale University Zigler Center in Child Development and Social Policy.

To support individual school districts that are beginning the program, the 21C national office developed a training protocol and provides on- and off-site assistance. 21C technical assistance staff work intensely with the leadership in each school for about 2 years. As the schools become more proficient and implementation is underway, 21C staff assume an advisory role. Their efforts are supplemented by peer trainers. These are leaders from schools that have successfully implemented the program who are paired with their counterparts in schools that are beginning the process. Peer training opportunities also exist at the 21C National Academy, which is an annual national orientation and training conference, as well as at smaller regional events that focus on the specific needs of 21C schools in that geographic area.

Although 21C does not offer local training events, the national scope of a universal preschool policy may include this provision so preschool classroom teachers can participate. In 21C, training for early childhood teachers occurs on an individual school basis. Workshops are given in the school, and often child care providers and other early educators in the community are invited. Some school districts have established partnerships with community colleges and other higher education institutions to provide teachers with access to inservice learning opportunities. Given the increased need for teachers that a universal preschool policy would create, linkages with higher education would be essential not only to meet in-service needs, but to address existing shortages in professional preparation for early childhood careers (Maxwell & Clifford, 2006).

All of these training venues are an acknowledgment that educators cannot be expected to start and run a new program without direct guidance and support. To advance systemwide policy, we have created a School of the 21st Century National Network. The group's efforts include development of standardized professional materials and services, and procedures for working with schools with varying levels of training needs and/or those experiencing changes (e.g., an increase in the number of immigrant children). Network membership allows schools to continue to be formally affiliated with 21C after their programs are established. The network also provides a quality ladder. Schools that achieve certain quality goals can earn status as Demonstration Sites and eventually as Schools of Excellence. This and other approaches to widespread implementation have enabled us to respond to the interest schools have in starting the program as well as to maintain enthusiasm for the effort once the program is underway.

The national network thus provides form and substance to the 21C program. By the same token, a national policy for universal preschool would establish the framework for program goals and operations. State and local implementation could then proceed within established parameters so there is local control but no essential elements are disregarded.

Factors That Influence 21C Implementation

Many changes take place once 21C is implemented: Younger children are in the building, the school is open from as early as 6 in the morning until evening, year-round calendar and transportation schedules are in effect, and there is a focus on meeting more than children's academic needs. We have found in the course of working on 21C that for such dramatic changes to be accepted, the program has to be an integral aspect of the school. This means that although there are no expectations that the academic faculty of the existing school will take on responsibility for 21C (a 21C coordinator is appointed and the program has its own early childhood staff), the principal oversees the program and facilitates continuity with the rest of the school. Also, there are meetings and collaborations among the school faculty and 21C staff so everyone feels part of a team working to boost school readiness and academic success for all children the school serves.

Change is a characteristic of, and indeed, the goal of any school reform effort. With the School of the 21st Century and other programs (e.g., see Education Commission of the States, 1999; Elmore, 2000), change is unlikely to occur unless there is commitment to the effort at all levels, including the community, district, and individual schools. Change is easier when it is not imposed upon a school but is initiated from within. A locally driven approach is embedded in the design of 21C. The program provides a blueprint for action and requires schools to develop and implement services on the basis of local needs and resources. Although variations in scope of effort are noted, the majority of the schools grow to provide all of the core services of the program as well as additional services specific to community needs and desires.

Even when change is welcomed by the school, it should take place gradually to ensure actions are proceeding according to the plan. In 21C, implementation is phased in over a 3- to 5-year period. This phase-in is essential, given the numerous services that make up the initiative, but it is also important for other school-based reform efforts because it builds a strong platform for further growth (Fullan, 2001). In 21C, decisions about which services to begin with and when to add others are based on a plan of action. This is part of the initial planning process, but it remains important in later years as the program evolves and changes over time. The plan is made on the basis of an assessment of the needs of families, an inventory of services in the community, and an organizational audit to determine what strengths, resources, and capabilities the school district and individual schools have, and what else is needed to facilitate implementation. This approach provides an individualized plan that is both realistic and achievable.

Financial Considerations

Costs for comprehensive, extended-day preschool services would be prohibitive for most school districts. While 21C schools benefit from the existing management structure in the school as well as the use of space, they do not depend on local tax dollars or draw from the school budget. Rather, funding for 21C is based in part on parent fees, with a sliding scale system calibrated to family income. Federal and state subsidies support the provision of services to low-income and special needs children. (For more on the financial design of 21C, see Finn-Stevenson & Zigler, 1999, and Zigler & Finn-Stevenson, 1996.) Budget plans distinguish between start-up and operational periods. After a start-up phase of about 1 year, parent fees for child care provide core support for the operation of programs. In some 21C schools a surplus is feasible and is used to support other services for which fees cannot be assessed (e.g., home visitations), and for staff training and related activities. Some schools blend various funding streams with parent fees, integrating services without segregating the children. For example, children served by Even Start, state preschool funds for at-risk and special needs children, and Head Start are in the same classroom with fee-paying children. In some cases where there is state support for part-day/part-year preschool, parents only pay for the wraparound child care.

The blending of several public funding streams is not unique to 21C. However, we have learned from 21C that the provision of services beyond preschool, including wraparound child care, is possible with parental fees. With public funds being vulnerable to cuts during periods of budgetary shortfalls, fees provide a means to sustain operations. Public subsidies will still be needed for low-income and children with special needs. Although a new funding source dedicated to universal preschool may become a reality, funds may also be drawn from what already exists. This was pointed out by Greenberg and Schumacher (2003). They examined the use of federal funding streams, including block grants for child care and for Temporary Assistance for Needy

Families in universal preschool programs. They concluded that although states would need to make political and policy judgments to prioritize the use of these federal funds, the Child Care and Developmental Fund in particular is a potential source of support for universal preschool initiatives.

IMPLICATIONS FOR UNIVERSAL PRESCHOOL POLICY

The knowledge we have accumulated on the value of preschool and the need for universal preschool presents an opportunity to implement a national system for early care and education that would provide care and education during the early years as well as continue to provide support services during the elementary school years. We believe this system should encompass children's needs for quality child care and preschool experiences as well as support services for both children and their families. The School of the 21st Century provides an example of an efficient and effective system, using public schools. Although the final role of schools in universal preschool remains to be decided, it is clear that schools will be part of the picture in many states. 21C also proves that it is feasible to extend beyond preschool education, using parental fees to provide all-day, high-quality child care that promotes school readiness.

While the lessons about implementing preschool programs in the schools are important, so are our findings that these programs are having an impact on student achievement. Preliminary findings from the national 21C evaluation described earlier indicate that children who attended 21C preschool child care had enhanced reading and other academic skills through second grade (Ginicola et al., 2006; Henrich et al., 2006). The Arkansas 21C initiative, where programs were phased in over time, provided an opportunity to compare mature 21C sites with newer ones. The findings underscore the value added of 21C (Ginicola et al., 2006) and also point to the fact that schools with older programs were better on several academic indicators such as absenteeism and suspensions and had higher percentages of students reading at grade level (Ginicola et al., 2006). Our results are suggestive that quality early care and education for all children can contribute to reducing the achievement gap between low- and higher-income students. This desired outcome will certainly be an inherent goal of a national preschool policy.

REFERENCES

Bailey, D. (2002). *What can universal prekindergarten learn from special education?* New York: Foundation for Child Development.

Barnett, W. S., Brown, K. C., Finn-Stevenson, M., & Henrich, C. (2006). From visions to systems of universal preschool. In J. L. Aber, S. Bishop-Josef, S. M. Jones, K. T. McLearn, & D. A. Phillips (Eds.), *Child development and social policy* (pp. 113–128). Washington, DC: American Psychological Association.

Brauner, J., Gordic, B., & Zigler, E. (2004). Putting the child back in child care: Combining care and education for children ages 3–5. *Social Policy Report, 18*(3), 1–18.

Cost, Quality, and Child Outcomes Study Team. (1999). *The children of the cost, quality, and outcomes study go to school.* Chapel Hill, NC: University of North Carolina.

Dryfoos, J. (1994). *Full service schools.* San Francisco: Jossey-Bass.

Dwyer, C. M., Chait, R., & McKee, P. (2000). *Building strong foundations for early learning: Guide to high-quality early childhood education programs.* Washington, DC: U. S. Department of Education, Planning and Evaluation Service.

Education Commission of the States. (1999). A promising approach for today's schools. *Comprehensive School Reform, 1*(3), 1–7.

Elmore, R. (2000). *Building new structures for school leadership.* Washington, DC: Albert Shanker Institute.

Finn-Stevenson, M., & Zigler, E. (1999). *Schools of the 21st Century: Linking child care and education.* Boulder, CO: Westview Press.

Fullan, M. (2001). *The new meaning of educational change.* New York: Teachers College Press.

Ginicola, M., Yekelchik, A., & Finn-Stevenson, M. (2006). *Evaluation of the School of the 21st Century in Arkansas.* New Haven, CT: Zigler Center in Child Development and Social Policy, Yale University.

Greenberg, M., & Schumacher, R. (2003). *Financing universal pre-kindergarten: Possibilities and technical issues for states in using funds under the Child Care and Development Block Grant and Temporary Assistance for Needy Families Block Grant.* Washington, DC: Center for Law and Policy.

Helburn, S., & Bergmann, B. (2002). *America's child care problems: The way out.* New York: Pelgrade.

Henrich, C., & Blackman-Jones, R. (2006). Parent involvement in preschool. In E. Zigler, W. S. Gilliam, & S. M Jones, *A vision for universal preschool* (pp. 149–168). New York: Cambridge University Press.

Henrich, C., Ginicola, M., & Finn-Stevenson, M. (2006). *The School of the 21st Century is making a difference: Findings from two evaluations* (Issue Brief). New Haven, CT: Yale University, School of the 21st Century (21C) Program.

Hinkle, D. (2000). *Schools' involvement in early childhood.* Washington, DC: U.S. Department of Education.

LeMoines, S., Morgan, G., & Azer, S. (2003). A snapshot of trends in child care licensing regulations. *Child Care Bulletin, 28,* 1–5.

Levine, J. (1978). *Day care and the public schools: Profiles of five communities.* Newton, MA: Education Development Center.

Marsland, K., Zigler, E., & Martinez, A. (2006). *Regulation of infant and toddler child care: Are state requirements for centers adequate?* Manuscript submitted for publication, Yale University.

Martin, M. (2003). *Making the difference: Research and practice in community schools.* Washington, DC: National Coalition of Community Schools.

Maxwell, K. L., & Clifford, R. M. (2006). Professional development issues in universal prekindergarten. In E. Zigler, W. S. Gilliam, & S. M. Jones, *A vision for universal preschool* (pp. 169–193). New York: Cambridge University Press.

Mintrom, M. (2001). *Achieving quality in early childhood education for all: Insights from the policy innovation diffusion research.* New York: Foundation for Child Development.

National Center for Education Statistics. (2003). *Pre-kindergarten in U.S. public schools, 2000–2001.* Washington, DC: Author.

National Institute of Child Health and Development (NICHD) Early Child Care Research Network. (Ed.). (2005). *Child care and child development: Results from the NICHD study of early child care and youth development.* New York: Guilford Press.

National Research Council. (2002). *Community programs to promote youth development.* Washington, DC: Author.

Parents as Teachers. (2006). What is parents as teachers? Retrieved from http://www.parentsasteachers.org/site/pp.asp?c=ekIRLcMZJxE&b=272093.

Pet Savers Foundation, (2011). *The Mutt-i-grees Curriculum: Calm Confident and Caring Kids, Grades 4–6.* Port Washington, NY: Author.

Pfannenstiel, J., Lambson, T., & Yarnell, V. (1996). *The Parents as Teachers program: Longitudinal follow-up to the second wave study.* Overland Park, KS: Research & Training Associates.

Putnam, R. D. (1995). Bowling alone: America's defining social capital. *Journal of Democracy, 6,* 65–78.

Sawhill. I. (2006, Fall). Opportunity in America: The role of education. *The Future of Children Policy Brief.* Washington, DC: Brookings Institute.

Shonkoff, J., & Phillips, D. (2000). *From neurons to neighborhoods.* Washington, DC: National Academy Press.

U.S. Census Bureau. (2000). *Families and living arrangements.* Washington, DC: Author.

U.S. Census Bureau. (2002). *Families and living arrangements.* Washington, DC: Author.

U.S. Consumer Product Safety Commission. (1999, April). *CPSC staff study of safety hazards in child care settings.* Washington, DC: Author.

Vandell, D. L., & Wolfe, B. (2000). *Child care quality: Does it matter and does it need to be improved?* Washington, DC: U. S. Department of Health and Human Services.

Zigler, E., & Finn-Stevenson, M. (1996). Funding child care and public education. *The Future of Children, 6*(2), 104–121.

Zigler, E., Finn-Stevenson, M., & Hall, N. W. (2002). *The first three years and beyond.* New Haven, CT: Yale University Press.

Zigler, E., Marsland, K., & Lord, H. (2009). *The tragedy of child care in America.* New Haven, CT: Yale University Press.

Zigler, E., Singer, D. G., & Bishop-Josef, S. J. (Eds.). (2004). *Children's play: The roots of reading.* Washington, DC: Zero to Three Press.

CHAPTER 12

The Case for Investing in Young Children

James J. Heckman

This chapter reviews a body of research (Carneiro & Heckman, 2003; Cunha, Heckman, Lochner, & Masterov, 2006; Heckman, 2000, 2008; Heckman & Masterov, 2007) that examines the origins of inequality and analyzes policies to alleviate it. In it, I develop a case for intervening in the lives of disadvantaged children.

HOW THE EARLY LIFE OF CHILDREN AFFECTS THEIR FUTURES

Families play a powerful role in shaping adult outcomes. The accident of birth is a major source of inequality. Recent research by Cunha and Heckman (2007) shows that in American society, about half of the inequality in the present value of lifetime earnings is due to factors determined by age 18. Compared with 50 years ago, a greater fraction of American children is being born into disadvantaged families where investments in children are smaller than in advantaged families. Growing unassimilated immigrant populations in Western Europe create similar adverse trends there. Policies that supplement the child rearing resources available to disadvantaged families reduce inequality and raise productivity.

I base this argument on the following points:

- Many major economic and social problems such as crime, teenage pregnancy, dropping out of high school, and adverse health conditions are linked to low levels of skill and ability in society.
- In analyzing policies that foster skills and abilities, society needs to recognize the multiplicity of human abilities.

- Currently, public policy in the United States and many other countries focuses on promoting and measuring cognitive ability through IQ and achievement tests. A focus on achievement test scores ignores a student's full range of cognitive abilities as well as important noncognitive factors that can promote success in school and life. While cognitive abilities are important determinants of socioeconomic success, so are socioemotional skills, physical and mental health, perseverance, attention, motivation, and self-confidence. They contribute to performance in society at large and even help determine scores on the very tests that are commonly used to measure cognitive achievement.

- Ability gaps between advantaged and disadvantaged children open up early in life.

- Family environments of young children have a major impact on how cognitive and socioemotional abilities develop, as well as on a variety of other outcomes, such as crime and health.

- Family environments in the United States and many other countries around the world have deteriorated over the past 40 years. A greater proportion of children is being born into disadvantaged families, many of whom represent minority and immigrant groups.

- Disadvantage needs to be framed not only in terms of the resources available to families but also in terms of the quality of parenting available to children living in those family environments. Family environments that have little parental support for children negatively impact the outcomes of the children who are living in them. However, if society intervenes early enough, it can improve the conditions that promote the development of cognitive and socioemotional abilities as well as the health of disadvantaged children. Early interventions can promote schooling, reduce crime, foster workforce productivity, and reduce teenage pregnancy. Early interventions have high direct benefit-cost ratios and rates of return.

- Research on current programs that intervene early in the life cycle of disadvantaged children reveals that early interventions have much higher economic returns than later interventions, such as reduced pupil-teacher ratios, public job training, convict rehabilitation programs, adult literacy programs, tuition subsidies, or expenditure on police. The returns of early intervention are much higher than those found in most job training programs in the United States or active labor market programs in Europe (see Heckman, LaLonde, & Smith, 1999; Martin & Grubb, 2001).

- Because life cycle skill formation is dynamic in nature (skill begets skill; motivation begets motivation; motivation cross-fosters skill and skill cross-fosters motivation), if children are not motivated to learn and engage early on in life, it is more likely that in adulthood they will not do well in social and economic life. The longer society waits to intervene in the life cycle of a disadvantaged child, the more costly disadvantage is to remediate.
- To capitalize on this knowledge about the importance of the early years in creating inequality and in producing skills for the workforce, a major refocus of policy is required.

Unlike arguments advanced by proponents of the theory that genetics are the sole determinants of individual abilities (e.g., *The Bell Curve* by Herrnstein & Murray, 1994), the research summarized above establishes the power of socioemotional abilities and an important role for environment and intervention in creating abilities (Almlund, Duckworth, Heckman, & Kautz, 2011; Borghans, Duckworth, Heckman, & terWeel, 2008; Heckman, Stixrud, & Urzua, 2006). High-quality early childhood interventions foster abilities and attack inequality at its source. They also boost the productivity of the economy.

ENRICHING EARLY ENVIRONMENTS CAN PARTIALLY COMPENSATE FOR EARLY ADVERSITY

Interventions that enrich the early environments of disadvantaged children demonstrate causal effects of early environments on adolescent and adult outcomes and provide powerful evidence against the genetic determinism of Herrnstein and Murray (1994). Enhancements of family environments improve child outcomes and affect both cognitive and noncognitive skills. Noncognitive skills—personality factors, motivation, and the like—are an important channel of improvement (Almlund et al., 2011; Heckman, Malofeeva, Pinto, & Savelyev, 2010). The most reliable data come from interventions that aim to substantially enrich the early environments of children living in low-income families.

The HighScope Perry Preschool Program, an intensive, high-quality preschool program, is one of the most studied of such interventions (Schweinhart, Montie, Xiang, Barnett, Belfieldand, & Nores, 2005).

It provided 2.5-hour classroom sessions each weekday for 30 weeks, as well as a weekly 90-minute afternoon home visit by the teacher. Fifty-eight randomly selected children of African American descent who came from high-poverty households were participants in this program. They were followed long after the interventions ended—through the age of 40—and compared to a similar randomly selected untreated cohort. The results of the study demonstrate substantial positive effects of early environmental enrichment on a range of cognitive and noncognitive skills, schooling, achievement, job performance, and social behaviors. Additional data from David Olds's Nurse-Family Partnership Program (2002) and from noncontrolled assessments of Head Start and the Chicago Child-Parent Centers programs confirm these findings. The estimated rate of return (per dollar of cost) from those attending the Perry Program is 7–10% (Heckman, Moon, Pinto, Savelyev, & Yavits, 2008). This rate of return (which is actually an underestimate because it does not take into account the economic returns to health and mental health) is higher than the return from investing in the stock market (prior to its recent meltdown) and suggests that society can benefit substantially from early childhood interventions.

Important to note are some points that are raised by these studies: that skills beget skills and capabilities foster future capabilities. Because all capabilities are built on the foundation of capacities that are created in early life, early mastery of a range of cognitive, social, and emotional competencies makes learning at later ages more efficient and therefore easier and more likely to continue. That is why early intervention is much more effective than later-life remedial programs such as public job training, adult literacy services, prisoner rehabilitation, and education programs for disadvantaged adults. In fact, even in studies in which later intervention shows some benefits, the performance of disadvantaged children in these is still behind the performance of children who experienced interventions in their preschool years. The returns to investment are highest for those who received early supports and lowest for those who did not receive them.

Furthermore, it has been found that the advantages gained from effective early interventions are best sustained when they are followed by continued high-quality learning experiences. Due to dynamic complementarity, or synergy, early investments must be followed by later investments if maximum value is to be realized. Remedial interventions for disadvantaged adolescents who do not receive a strong initial foundation of skills face an equity-efficiency trade-off. They are difficult to justify on the grounds of economic efficiency and generally have low rates of return (Cunha & Heckman, 2008; Cunha, Heckman, & Schennach, 2007). The evidence in the recent research literature supports the economic efficiency of early initial investment that is sustained. The optimal policy is to invest relatively more in the early years. But early investment must be followed up to be effective. Later remediation for early disadvantage is possible but to attain what is accomplished by early investment is much more costly. If society intervenes too late and individuals are at too low a level of skill, later investment can be economically inefficient. Middle-class children receive massive doses of early enriched environments. Children from disadvantaged environments generally do not.

PRACTICAL CONSIDERATIONS IN IMPLEMENTING EARLY CHILDHOOD PROGRAMS

A variety of practical issues arise when implementing early childhood programs.

Who Should Be Targeted? The returns to early childhood programs are the highest for those who in their early years have the least resources and supports.

It should be noted that the proper measure of disadvantage is not necessarily family poverty or parental education. Available evidence suggests that the quality of *parenting* is the important scarce resource. The quality of parenting is not always closely linked to family income or parental education. Those born into disadvantaged environments receive less stimulation and child development resources than those from advantaged families. Measures of risky family environments should be developed that facilitate efficient targeting.

What Types of Programs Are Most Effective? Programs that target the early years seem to have the greatest promise. The Nurse-Family Partnership Program (Olds, 2002), the Abecedarian Program (Campbell, Ramey, Pungello, Sparling, & Miller-Johnson, 2002), and the HighScope Perry Program (Schweinhart, et. al., 2005) —all high-quality programs for children that offer supports for families—have been evaluated and show high economic returns. Programs with home visits affect the lives of the parents and create a change in the home environment that supports the child long after center-based interventions end. Programs that build character and motivation that do not focus exclusively on cognition appear to be the most effective.

Who Should Provide the Programs? In designing any early childhood program that aims to improve the cognitive and socioemotional skills of disadvantaged children, it is important to respect the sanctity of early family life and to respect cultural diversity. Community support needs to be generated to create effective and culturally sensitive programs.

Who Should Pay for the Programs? One could make the programs universal to avoid stigmatization. However, universal programs would be much more expensive and create the possibility of deadweight losses, whereby public programs displace private investments by families. One solution to these problems is to make the programs universal but offer a sliding fee schedule by family income to avoid deadweight losses.

Will the Programs Achieve High Levels of Compliance? It is important to recognize potential problems with program compliance. Many successful programs alter the values and motivations of the child. Some of these changes may run counter to family values. There may be serious tensions between the needs of the child and the acceptance of interventions by the family. Developing culturally diverse programs will help avoid such tensions. One cannot assume that there will be no conflict between the values of society as it seeks to develop the potential of the child and the values of the family, although the extent of such conflicts is not yet known.

SUMMARY

About 50% of the variance in inequality in lifetime earnings is determined by age 18. The family plays a powerful role in shaping adult outcomes that is not fully appreciated in current policies for skill formation around the world. Current social policy directed toward children focuses on improving cognition. Yet more than cognition is required for success in life. Gaps in both cognitive and noncognitive skills between the advantaged and the disadvantaged emerge early and can be traced in part to adverse early environments. There is a growing percentage of children in the United States, as well as in many other countries, who are born into adverse environments, measuring adversity by the quality of parental environments. The problem of rising dropout rates is not due mainly to defects in public schools or to high college tuition rates. It is due to lack of skills created in the early years. Late remediation strategies designed to compensate for early disadvantage (such as job training programs, high school classroom size reductions, convict rehabilitation programs, adult literacy programs, and other active labor market programs), while sometimes helpful, often earn low or negative returns. Remediation in the adolescent years can repair the damage of adverse early environments, but it is costly.

Prevention is much less costly. Social policy, therefore, should be directed toward the malleable early years when the base of skills is formed. Any proposed program should respect the primacy of the family. Policy proposals should be culturally sensitive and recognize the diversity of values in society. To effectively do this, resources should be mobilized to produce a menu of programs from which parents of young children can choose.

REFERENCES

Almlund, M., Duckworth, A. L., Heckman, J. J., & Kautz, T. (2011). Personality psychology and economics. In E. A. Hanushek, S. Machin, & L. Wößmann (Eds.), *Handbook of the Economics of Education*. Amsterdam: Elsevier.

Borghans, L., Duckworth, A. L., Heckman, J. J., & terWeel, B. (2008). The economics and psychology of personality traits. *Journal of Human Resources, 43*(4), 972–1059.

Campbell, F. A., Ramey, C. T., Pungello, E. P., Sparling, J., & Miller-Johnson, S. (2002). Early childhood education: Young adult outcomes from the Abecedarian Project. *Applied Developmental Science, 6,* 42–57.

Carneiro, P., & Heckman, J. J. (2003). Human capital policy. In J. J. Heckman, A. B. Krueger, & B. M. Friedman (Eds.), *Inequality in America: What role for human capital policies?* (pp. 77–240). Cambridge, MA: MIT Press.

Cunha, F., & Heckman, J. J. (2007). *The evolution of uncertainty in labor earnings in the U.S. economy.* Unpublished manuscript, University of Chicago (under revision).

Cunha, F., & Heckman, J. J. (2008). Formulating, identifying, and estimating the technology of cognitive and noncognitive skill formation. *Journal of Human Resources, 43*(4), 738–782.

Cunha, F., Heckman, J. J., Lochner, L. J., & Masterov, D. V. (2006). Interpreting the evidence on life cycle skill formation. In E. A. Hanushek & F. Welch (Eds.), *Handbook of the economics of education* (pp. 697–812). Amsterdam: Elsevier.

Cunha, F., Heckman, J. J., & Schennach, S. M. (2007). *Estimating the technology of cognitive and noncognitive skill formation.* Unpublished manuscript, Department of Economics, University of Chicago; Paper presented at the Yale Conference on Macro and Labor Economics, May 5–7, 2006 (under revision, *Econometrica*).

Heckman, J. J. (2000). Policies to foster human capital. *Research in Economics, 54*(1), 3–56.

Heckman, J. J. (2008). Schools, skills, and synapses. *Economic Inquiry, 46*(3), 289–324.Heckman, J. J., LaLonde, R. J., & Smith, J. A. (1999). The economics and econometrics of active labor market programs. In O. Ashenfelter & D. Card (Eds.), *Handbook of labor economics* (Vol. 3A, pp. 1865–2097). Amsterdam: Elsevier.

Heckman, J. J., Malofeeva, L., Pinto, R. R., & Savelyev, P. (2010, revised). *The effect of the Perry Preschool Program on cognitive and noncognitive skills: Beyond treatment effects.* Unpublished manuscript, Department of Economics, University of Chicago.

Heckman, J. J., & Masterov, D. V. (2007). The productivity argument for investing in young children. *Review of Agricultural Economics, 29*(3), 446–493.

Heckman, J. J., Moon, S., Pinto, R. R., & Yavitz, A. Q. (2008). *The rate of return to the Perry Preschool Program.* Unpublished manuscript, Department of Economics, University of Chicago.

Heckman, J. J., Stixrud, J., & Urzua, S. (2006). The effects of cognitive and noncognitive abilities on labor market outcomes and social behavior. *Journal of Labor Economics, 24*(3), 411–482.

Herrnstein, R. J., & Murray, C. A. (1994). *The bell curve: Intelligence and class structure in American life.* New York: Free Press.

Martin, J. P., & Grubb, D. (2001). What works and for whom: A review of OECD countries' experiences with active labour market policies. *Swedish Economic Policy Review, 8*(2), 9–56.

Olds, D. L. (2002). Prenatal and infancy home visiting by nurses: From randomized trials to community replication. *Prevention Science, 3*(2), 153–172.

Schweinhart, L. J., Montie, J., Xiang, Z., Barnett, W. S., Belfieldand, C. R., & Nores, M. (2005). *Lifetime effects: The HighScope Perry Preschool study through age 40.* Ypsilanti, MI: HighScope Press.

Supporting Children's Education and Care

Putting Into Practice What We Know

Beverly Falk

What the best and wisest parent wants for his own child, that must the community want for all of its children. Any other ideal for our schools is narrow and unlovely; acted upon, it destroys our democracy.

—John Dewey, *The School and Society*, 1900/1915

In the preceding chapters of this book, the authors have shared understandings about how children learn, noted dangers posed by 21st-century challenges, and described practices and policies that enhance the optimal development of all children. Together they make a powerful case that there is tension between what we know about how to effectively nurture children and what we provide for children's education and care. In this concluding chapter, I offer recommendations for how to bridge this gap so that children can be supported in accordance with their developmental needs and taught in the ways that they learn.

STRENGTHENING EARLY EDUCATION AND CARE: TRANSFORMING OUR KNOWLEDGE INTO ACTION

The research is clear that children's cognitive growth is integrally connected to their physical, social, and emotional development, and that optimal growth in all of these areas is dependent on being healthy and secure—physically, emotionally, and economically. Optimal growth is also supported when children feel connected to the people in their lives; when they and their families have access to quality supports from prebirth through early childhood and beyond; when they are able to go to safe schools that provide a broad, challenging, and engaging curriculum; when assessment of their learning is designed to capture authentic evidence about what matters most and used to support their progress toward those goals; and when school accountability systems take responsibility not only for monitoring learners' progress but also for ensuring that they are provided the resources and opportunities needed to learn (Association for Supervision and Curriculum Development [ASCD], 2007; Darling-Hammond, 2010; Ravitch, 2010; Rothstein, 2010).

For young children, this specifically means providing quality cognitive stimulation; rich language environments; and the facilitation of social, emotional, and motor development in the context of good physical care and warm affective relationships. Such quality, caring environments improve social and intellectual competence and the ability to take advantage of subsequent learning opportunities. These qualities of care and education are important for all children, but particularly critical for those who, because of poverty, have limited access to resources and, as a result, are more likely to be at risk in the area of academic success and, ultimately, for realizing their human potential (Bowman, Donovan, & Burns, 2001; Bransford, Brown, & Cocking, 1999; Bredekamp & Copple, 1997; Falk, 2010; Shonkoff & Phillips, 2000).

Coherence is needed between policies, practices, and resource allocation to ensure that these support the "whole child." Specifically, the principles and goals described below can be a guide for future action.

Provision of High-Quality Early Care for All Children

Affordable programs for children and their families at all points of the developmental spectrum are needed. Universal pre-K is a good start but greater attention also needs to be paid to the development and education of children in the entire birth through age 5 span, a critical period that profoundly affects lifelong learning. Research suggests, for example, that 2 years of a quality program give more benefits than just a single year (Perkins-Gough, 2007), so we need to consider universal programs for 3- as well as 4-year-olds. Also, importantly, we need to consider how to make quality care available to all families from prebirth through toddlerhood, such as in the full-service programs described by Zigler and Finn-Stevenson in Chapter 11 of this book.

A caring society cares for its children. Families of all income levels need supports—such as prenatal care, maternity/paternity leaves, and preventive measures against such environmental influences as violence and substance abuse. They also need affordable options for child care, early education, and after-school care. Such initiatives require a coordinated infrastructure that reduces the fragmentation of existing policies and programs (Bowman et al., 2001; Schumacher, Hamm, Goldstein, & Lombardi, 2006; Shonkoff & Phillips, 2000).

Attention to the Full Range of Early Development in Programs for Children

In early care and other educational settings, attention needs to be paid to the full range of factors that impact the health and well-being of children, with special emphasis placed on reducing the disparities that lead to the skill gap evident at school entry in children from high-poverty and/or minority backgrounds. Closing this gap, often referred to as the "achievement gap" but more accurately framed as an "opportunity gap" (Ladson-Billings, 2006), will entail marshaling a full range of resources, comparable to those currently focused on literacy and numeracy, to translate "the knowledge base on young children's emotional, regulatory, and social development into effective strategies for fostering: (1) the development of curiosity, self-direction, and persistence in learning situations; (2) the ability to cooperate, demonstrate caring, and resolve conflict with peers; and (3) the capacity to experience the enhanced motivation associated with feeling competent and loved" (Shonkoff & Phillips, 2000, p. 387). These emphases on aspects of development that might appear to some to be nonacademic are actually critical for academic success and need to be present in educational settings in early child care, pre-K, kindergarten, as well as throughout the childhood years.

Implementating High-Quality Teaching, Curricula, and Assessment Practices

Teaching practices, curricula, and assessments used in educational settings need to be guided by what is known about children's thinking and learning processes. Special attention needs to be given to teaching approaches that enable children—from different cultural and linguistic backgrounds, at different developmental levels, as well as those who have different learning styles and strengths—to learn and to experience a rich, experiential, "thinking" curriculum.

Analyses of teaching in the countries where students do well on international assessments (e.g., Finland, Canada, Singapore, China, Japan) offer insights about how to deliver an effective and appropriate education for all children. These countries have broad social safety nets for their citizens that include supports for early learning and care. They have leaner standards than those in the United States; fewer topics taught more deeply each year; a greater focus on inquiry, reasoning, and application of knowledge rather than mere content coverage; and a thoughtful sequence of expectations based on developmental learning progressions within and across domains. Children are not expected to read in kindergarten and teachers don't focus on the lower order rote skills (memorization of information, simple operations based on formulas or rules, or filling out short-answer and multiple-choice worksheets) that often dominate in urban schools serving predominantly low-income children (Darling-Hammond, 2010). High-performing countries do not emphasize this type of learning because they know that educational settings and materials that focus narrowly on academics at too early an age and that emphasize skills over meaning at the expense of other developmental areas—all in the name of preparing children for standardized tests—limit children's capacity to learn for genuine understanding and, ultimately, their potential for serious intellectual work.

High-performing countries also do not make either-or choices about teaching approaches. They generally do not pit content against skills nor do they mandate curricula and pacing schedules—practices that are used widely in the United States, especially in communities that have high percentages of poor and minority children. Rather, many high-performing countries offer guidance through standards, which provide teachers and students with direction, while at the same time allowing for flexibility in teachers' approaches and children's paces of learning. They focus on skill development in meaningful contexts that support children to construct their own understandings and solve complex problems (Darling-Hammond, 2010).

Teaching strategies, like those used in the high-performing countries just described, are informed by multiple forms of observational and performance assessments that reveal many different kinds of knowledge and many ways that children learn (National Association for the Education of Young Children & National Association for Early Childhood Specialists in State Departments of Education, 2003; National Association of School Psychologists, 2005). In addition to being used to guide curriculum, they are also used for evaluation of student progress. This system of student assessment is enhanced by an accountability system that examines the quality of instruction children receive (based on articulated standards of practice) as well as the resources the system provides (based on articulated standards for opportunities-to-learn) (Darling-Hammond, 2010).

Support for Teacher Development

A substantial investment in the education of teachers needs to be at the heart of the effort to promote better learning (Bowman et al., 2001; Darling-Hammond, 2005, 2010; Tucker, 2011). Because research strongly suggests that teacher quality is the single most important factor that determines the quality of children's educational experiences and the quality of the outcomes of those experiences (National Commission on Teaching and America's Future, 1996), to make sure that all children receive quality education and care, attention needs to be paid to ensuring that all educators have high-quality preparation and support. For those who work with young children, this means having a specialized education related to early childhood. As it now stands, there is a huge gap between this goal and the level of preparation that typifies early childhood educators.

Progress toward achieving a high-quality teaching force for children of all ages, however, will require an investment in supports to improve the recruitment, preparation, induction, ongoing professional development, and compensation of those who want to work in the field. Of particular importance are: recruitment of high-quality candidates into the profession; support for the professional preparation of teachers in schools of education that place strong emphasis on teaching about how children learn and that offer field-rich experiences so that teacher candidates get lots of experience in how to apply theory to practice; high-quality leadership in all educational settings that provide guidance focused around a powerful vision of teaching and learning; and incentives for professionally trained and experienced educators to work and stay working in communities of highest need (Darling-Hammond, 2010; Tucker, 2011).

Respecting Notions of What Counts as Research

Research initiatives on how children learn have influenced the ways that teachers teach. Continued study of how children learn, especially in authentic contexts, will no doubt lead us to ever more effective practices. Likewise, research on effective teaching has led to enhanced understandings about how children learn. Particularly helpful is research from the *inside* of classrooms, often conducted by teachers themselves, documenting teaching that is responsive to how children learn and that is effective with learners who have different cultural, linguistic, and learning-style backgrounds. This kind of research has a powerful potential to reveal the complexities and nuances involved in teaching (Cochran-Smith & Lytle, 2009; Falk & Blumenreich, 2005, 2012; Hatch & Pointer Mace, 2006; Schumacher et al., 2006).

Educating the Public About Children's Learning and Development

Preparing children to meet the challenges they will face as citizens of the future requires public support for high-quality education. To garner this support, we need to develop better understandings among the public about what "high quality" means. Prevailing beliefs about teaching that contradict what research shows about the ineffectiveness of isolated skill and drill practices, one-size-fits-all teaching, and the overuse or misuse of high-stakes testing need to be countered with clear and accessible explanations of what quality education and genuine accountability look like. Images of practice need to be disseminated to make visible how children acquire and demonstrate skills and content knowledge immersed in literacy-rich, active, purposeful, *joyful* learning environments that are culturally sensitive, that nurture children's social-emotional as well as cognitive development, are supportive of their interests and needs, and use assessment and accountability measures as part of a feedback loop for continuous improvement. Additionally, public consciousness needs to be raised about the huge percentages of children growing up in poverty in the United States and the toll that this takes on their learning and development. A citizenry informed about all of these matters is essential for closing the gap between what exists and what needs to be done to improve children's learning (ASCD, 2007; Bowman et al., 2001).

TOWARD A BROADER VIEW OF QUALITY EDUCATION AND CARE

The research literature on development and learning is unequivocal that the quality of care and teaching children receive in their very earliest years is critical to ensuring that they experience productive and fulfilling lives. There is also consensus that "quality" is signified by the degree to which relationships between children and their caregivers are responsive to the active nature of the child and the full range of each child's social, emotional, physical, as well as cognitive needs.

Much work still needs to be done to translate these understandings into practice. But from what is known about practices in other countries, it is clear that accomplishing this goal is indeed possible. The need to do it is economic, political, social, and moral: A healthy and just society needs to provide all children with opportunities to prepare not only for economic independence in their adult lives, but to engage constructively with others and to experience personal fulfillment and success.

If we as a nation are truly serious about educating *all* of our children toward these goals, we need to provide them with equitable access to the full range of supports that are needed to achieve them. "Now more than ever, high-quality education for all is a public good that is essential for the good of the public" (Darling-Hammond, 2010, p. 328). Work toward this goal has to begin by recognizing that education cannot be viewed in a vacuum. Efforts to improve education must go hand in hand with efforts to address the conditions of poverty—lack of quality health care, housing, and employment opportunities—that place so many young children at a disadvantage before they ever set foot in a school.

In the context of this overarching and compelling need, our challenge as a nation is to focus on teaching children in the ways that they learn; assessing them about what matters most; recruiting great teachers as well as providing them with respect and supports for their preparation, induction, and ongoing development; ensuring adequate resources for early care and school environments; investing in and using research about effective teaching and learning; and communicating knowledge about development and learning so that the public is well armed to defend and support childhood.

These challenges are critical to our collective well-being. We owe it to our children to embrace them. We must not settle for anything less.

REFERENCES

Association for Supervision and Curriculum Development. (2007). *The learning compact redefined: A call to action.* Washington, DC: Author.

Bowman, B. T., Donovan, M. S., & Burns, M. S. (Eds.). (2001). *Eager to learn: Educating our preschoolers.* Washington, DC: National Academy Press.

Bransford, J. D., Brown, A. L., & Cocking, R. R. (Eds.). (1999). *How people learn: Brain, mind, experience, and school.* Washington, DC: National Academy Press.

Bredekamp, S., & Copple, C. (1997). *Developmentally appropriate practice in early childhood programs.* Washington, DC: National Association for the Education of Young Children.

Cochran-Smith, M., & Lytle, S. (2009). *Inquiry as stance: Practitioner research for the next generation.* New York: Teachers College Press.

Darling-Hammond, L. (2005). Teaching as a profession: Lessons in teacher preparation and professional development. *Phi Delta Kappan, 87*(3), 237–240.

Darling-Hammond, L. (2010). *The flat world and education: How America's commitment to equity will determine our future.* New York: Teachers College Press.

Dewey, J. (1915). *The school and society.* Chicago: The University of Chicago Press. (Original work published 1900)

Falk, B. (2010). Supporting the education and care of young children: Putting into practice what we know. In M. Fullan, A. Lieberman, A. Hargreaves, & D. Hopkins (Eds.), *Second international handbook of educational change* (pp. 933–952). New York: Springer.

Falk, B., & Blumenreich, M. (2005). *The power of questions: A guide to teacher and student research.* Portsmouth, NH: Heinemann Press.

Falk, B., & Blumenreich, M. (2012). *Listening for their stories: What we can learn from teachers inside the urban classroom.* New York: The New Press.

Hatch, T., & Pointer Mace, D. (2006). Making teaching public: A digital exhibition. Retrieved from http://www.tcrecord.org/makingteachingpublic/.

Ladson-Billings, G. (2006). From the achievement gap to the education debt: Understanding achievement in U.S. schools. *Educational Researcher, 35*(7), 3–12.

National Association for the Education of Young Children & National Association for Early Childhood Specialists in State Departments of Education. (2003). Early childhood curriculum, assessment, and program evaluation [Online joint position statement]. Retrieved from www.naeyc.org/about/positions/pdf/pscape.pdf

National Association of School Psychologists. (2005). NASP position statement on early childhood assessment [Online document]. Bethesda, MD: NASP. Retrieved from www.nasponline.org/information/pospaper_eca.html

National Commission on Teaching and America's Future. (1996). *What matters most: Teaching for America's future.* New York: Author.

Perkins-Gough, D. (2007). Giving intervention a Head Start: A conversation with Edward Zigler. *Educational Leadership, 65*(2), 8–14.

Ravitch, D. (2010). *The death and life of the great American school system: How testing and choice are undermining education.* New York: Basic Books.

Rothstein, R. (2010). How to fix our schools (Economic Policy Institute, Issue Brief #286). Retrieved from http://www.epi.org/page/-/pdf/ib286.pdf

Schumacher, R., Hamm, K., Goldstein, A., & Lombardi, J. (2006). *Starting off right: Promoting child development from birth in state early care and education initiatives.* Washington, DC: Center for Law and Social Policy.

Shonkoff, J. P., & Phillips, D. A. (Eds.). (2000). *From neurons to neighborhoods: The science of early childhood development.* Washington, DC: National Academy Press.

Tucker, M. (2011). *Standing on the shoulders of giants: An American agenda for education reform.* Boulder, CO: National Center on Education and the Economy. Retrieved from http://www.ncee.org/wp-content/uploads/2011/05/Standing-on-the-Shoulders-of-Giants-An-American-Agenda-for-Education-Reform.pdf

About the Editor
and the Contributors

Barbara Bowman is one of the founders of Erikson Institute, serving as its president from 1994 to 2001, and currently the Irving B. Harris Professor of Child Development. A past president of the National Association for the Education of Young Children, she is chief early childhood education officer for the Chicago Public Schools and a former consultant to Secretary of Education Arne Duncan. Among the many honors she has received are the Voices for Illinois' Children Start Early Award; Chicago Association for the Education of Young Children Outstanding Service to Children Award; Harold W. McGraw Jr. Prize in Education; and the National Black Child Development Institute Leadership Award.

Nancy Carlsson-Paige is a professor of early childhood education at Lesley University. She is the author or coauthor of five books and has written numerous articles on media violence, conflict resolution, peaceable classrooms, and global education. An advocate for policies and practices that promote children's well-being and encourage skills and attitudes that further peace and nonviolence, her most recent book is called *Taking Back Childhood: A Proven Road Map for Raising Confident, Creative, Compassionate Kids* (Plume, 2009).

Delis Cuéllar is a research associate at the Center on Teaching and Learning in the College of Education at the University of Oregon. Former positions include a postdoctoral appointment at the National Institute for Early Education Research at Rutgers University and an assistant professorship at Humboldt State University. Her research encompasses issues of bilingualism, parent involvement, and literacy development.

Linda Darling-Hammond is Charles E. Ducommun Professor of Education at Stanford University where she has launched the Stanford Educational Leadership Institute and the School Redesign Network. She has also served as faculty sponsor for the Stanford Teacher Education Program. She is a former president of the American Educational Research Association and member of the National Academy of Education. Her research, teaching, and policy work focus on issues of school restructuring, teacher quality, and educational equity. From 1994 to 2001, she served as executive director of the National Commission on Teaching and America's Future, a blue-ribbon panel whose 1996 report, *What Matters Most: Teaching for America's Future*, led to sweeping policy changes affecting teaching and teacher education. Among Darling-Hammond's more than 300 publications are *Preparing Teachers for a Changing World: What Teachers Should Learn and be Able to Do* (with John Bransford, for the National Academy of Education, winner of the Pomeroy Award from AACTE); *Teaching as the Learning Profession: A Handbook of Policy and Practice* (co-edited with Gary Sykes), which received the National Staff Development Council's Outstanding Book Award for 2000; and *The Right to Learn: A Blueprint for Schools that Work*, recipient of the American Educational Research Association's Outstanding Book Award for 1998.

Beverly Falk is a professor and the director of the Graduate Programs in Early Childhood Education at the School of Education, The City College of New York. She has served in a variety of other educational roles: as a classroom teacher; a public school founder and director; district administrator; consultant to schools, districts, states, and national organizations; and associate director of the National Center for Restructuring Education, Schools, and Teaching at Teachers College, Columbia University. She has been a fellow at the Carnegie Foundation for the Advancement of Teaching and is founding editor of *The New Educator*, a quarterly, peer-reviewed journal. The author/co-author/editor of many publications and books, her most recent work includes *Teaching the Way Children Learn* (Teachers College Press, 2008) and *Listening to Their Voices: What We Can Learn From Teachers Inside the Urban Classroom* (New Press, 2012).

Tiziana Filippini is a *pedagogista* for the municipality of Reggio Emilia, Italy. She is responsible for the Pedagogical Coordination Team at Scuole e Nidi d'Infanzia, Istituzione del Comune di Reggio Emilia, and coordinates professional development activities for teachers and *atelieristas* of the Reggio Emilia infant-toddler centers and preschools. A founding creator of the original *Hundred Languages of Children* exhibit, she is a curator of the new exhibit, *The Wonder of Learning: The Hundred Languages of Children*.

Matia Finn-Stevenson holds positions as both research scientist at the Yale University Child Study Center and associate director of Yale University's Edward Zigler Center in Child Development and Social Policy, where she is director of the School of the 21st Century program. She has conducted extensive research in child development and work-family life issues, with a current focus on examining the impact of demographic and other changes on schools and on the involvement of schools in child care and family support programs. The author or coauthor of numerous publications, she has been an advisor/consultant on domestic policy issues to staff and members of the White House, U.S. House of Representatives, U.S. Senate, Connecticut legislature, state departments of education, foundations, and school districts.

Eugene García is vice president for Education Partnerships at Arizona State University. A former senior officer and director of the Office of Bilingual Education and Minority Languages Affairs in the U.S. Department of Education from 1993 from 1995, he served as dean of education at both Arizona State and the University of California–Berkeley, and as chair of the 2006–2009 National Task Force on Early Education for Hispanics. Among his extensive publications are his most recent books: *Teaching and Learning in Two Languages* (Teachers College Press, 2005) and *Early Education of Dual Language Learners,* edited with E. Frede (Teachers College Press, 2010).

Howard Gardner is John H. and Elisabeth A. Hobbs Professor of Cognition and Education at the Harvard Graduate School of Education. He also holds positions as adjunct professor of psychology at Harvard University and senior director of Harvard Project Zero. His numerous honors include a MacArthur Prize Fellowship in 1981, honorary degrees from 26 colleges and universities, and selection by *Foreign Policy* and *Prospect* magazines as as one of the 100 most influential public intellectuals in the world. The author of 25 books translated into 28 languages, and of several hundred articles, Gardner is best known for his theory of multiple intelligences, a critique of the notion that there exists but a single human intelligence that can be adequately assessed by standard psychometric instruments.

Roberta Michnick Golinkoff is the H. Rodney Sharp Professor of Education, Psychology, and Linguistics and Cognitive Science at the University of Delaware. She has held the John Simon Guggenheim Fellowship and the James McKeen Cattell prize for her research on language development. A fellow of the American Psychological Association and the American Psychological Society, she is the recipient of the APA Distinguished Service Award and the Urie Bronfenbrenner Award for Lifetime Contribution to Developmental Psychology in the Service of Science and Society. An associate editor of *Child Development,* her extensive publications include *Play = Learning: How Play Motivates and Enhances Children's Cognitive and Social-Emotional Growth* (Oxford, 2006); *Celebrate the Scribble* (Crayola, 2007); and *Einstein Never Used Flash Cards: How Our Children Really Learn and Why They Need to Play More and Memorize Less* (Rodale, 2003).

Todd Grindal is a doctoral candidate at the Harvard Graduate School of Education where he studies the impact of public policies on young children and children with disabilities. He is involved in a number of research projects, including the development and analysis of a comprehensive meta-analytic database of early childhood interventions sponsored by the National Scientific Forum on Early Childhood Program Evaluation. Prior to his doctoral studies, Todd worked as a teacher and school administrator at the high school level in Florida and at the elementary school and preschool levels in Washington, DC.

James J. Heckman is the Henry Schultz Distinguished Service Professor of Economics and Public Policy at the University of Chicago. The author of over 280 articles and several books, he has received numerous awards from all over the world, including the 2000 Nobel Prize in Economic Sciences. He directs the University of Chicago's Economics Research Center in the Department of Economics and the Center for Social Program Evaluation at the Harris School for Public Policy. Additionally, he is professor of Science and Society in University College Dublin, and a senior research fellow at the American Bar Foundation. His recent research focuses on inequality, human development, and life cycle skill formation, with a special emphasis on the economics of early childhood.

Christina Hinton is a doctoral candidate at Harvard University, where she works on issues at the nexus of neuroscience and education. In addition to being a primary author and editor of the Organization for Economic Co-operation and Development's (OECD) Learning Sciences and Brain Research project—*Understanding the Brain: The Birth of a Learning Science*—she also worked for the United Nations Children's Fund (UNICEF), specializing in early childhood care and education. She lectures internationally on implications of neuroscience research for education.

Kathryn Hirsh-Pasek is the Stanley and Debra Lefkowitz Professor in the Department of Psychology at Temple University where she serves as the director of the Infant Language Laboratory. A fellow of the American Psychological Association and the American Psychological Society, she is an associate editor of *Child Development* and a consultant to and member of numerous boards and organizations. She is the recipient of many awards, including the American Psychological Association's Bronfenbrenner Award for Lifetime Contribution to Developmental Psychology in the Service of Science and Society. Her research in the areas of early language development and infant cognition, funded by the National Science Foundation and the National Institutes of Health and Human Development, has resulted in 11 books and over 100 publications, including the award-winning *Einstein Never Used Flashcards: How Children Really Learn and Why They Need to Play More and Memorize Less* (Rodale Books, 2003).

Mara Krechevsky is a senior researcher at Project Zero at the Harvard Graduate School of Education. For over 25 years she has investigated the educational implications of the theory of multiple intelligences and the Reggio Emilia approach to education. Currently the director of Making Children Visible: Documenting the Power of Children's Minds, a research collaboration with five Boston-area schools, she is the author of *Project Spectrum: Preschool Assessment Handbook* (Teachers College Press, 1998); a coauthor of *Making Learning Visible: Children as Individual and Group Learners* (ReggioChildren, 2001); and a general editor of the three-volume series *Project Zero Frameworks for Early Childhood Education* (Teachers College Press, 1998).

Janet Kwok is a doctoral student at the Harvard Graduate School of Education where she is studying the measurement of how adolescents understand the choices available to them and the motivations behind the actions that they take.

Terrence J. Lee-St. John is a Ph.D. candidate in the Educational Research, Measurement, and Evaluation department at Boston College. He has served as an educational policy data analyst at City Connects: Optimized Student Support (Boston College) since 2008.

George Madaus is the Boisi Professor of Education and Public Policy Emeritus at Boston College. He has been a visiting professor at the Harvard Graduate School of Education and at St. Patrick's College, Dublin. A recipient of the 2003 American Educational Research Association (AERA)/ACT E. F. Lindquist award for distinguished research, he is a past president of the National Council on Measurement Education and has been a fellow at the Center for Advanced Studies in the Behavioral Sciences. Currently, he is the vice president of AERA Division D, an AERA Fellow, and a member of the National Academy of Education.

Ben Mardell is an associate professor in early childhood education at Lesley University and a researcher on the Making Learning Visible Project at Project Zero at the Harvard Graduate School of Education. A teacher and researcher with infants, toddlers, preschoolers, and kindergartners for 25 years, he is the author of *From Basketball to the Beatles: In Search of Compelling Early Childhood Curriculum* (Heinemann, 1999); *Growing Up in Child Care: A Case For Quality Early Education* (Heinemann, 2002); and a coauthor of several Making Learning Visible publications.

Sonia Nieto, who has taught students from elementary school through doctoral studies, is Professor Emerita of Language, Literacy, and Culture at the School of Education, University of Massachusetts, Amherst. Her research focuses on multicultural education, teacher education, and the education of

Latinos, immigrants, and other students of culturally and linguistically diverse backgrounds. She has written many journal articles, book chapters, and several books, including *Affirming Diversity: The Sociopolitical Context of Multicultural Education* (5th ed., Allyn & Bacon, 2008, with Patty Bode); *The Light in Their Eyes: Creating Multicultural Learning Communities* (10th ed., Teachers College Press, 2010); and *Language, Culture, and Teaching: Critical Perspectives* (2nd ed., Routledge, 2010). In addition to serving on several regional and national advisory boards that focus on educational equity and social justice, she has received many academic and community awards, including four honorary doctorates.

Valerie Polakow is professor of Educational Psychology and Early Childhood at Eastern Michigan University. Her scholarship, which documents the lived realities of those who have been shut out from early childhood education, from K–12 education, and from postsecondary education, gives voice to those whose rights have been violated by poverty, race, and gender discrimination. She was a Fulbright scholar in Denmark and is the recipient of several honors, including the 2010 Distinguished Contributions to Gender Equity in Education Research by the American Educational Research Association. She is the author/editor of seven books, including the award-winning *Lives on the Edge: Single Mothers and Their Children in the Other America* (University of Chicago Press, 1993) and *Who Cares for Our Children: The Child Care Crisis in the Other America* (Teachers College Press, 2007).

Aisha Ray is senior vice president for Academic Affairs and Dean of Faculty at Erikson Institute. Her areas of research include cultural and situational contexts of child development, early childhood professional development, father-child relationships in urban communities, and early childhood services for immigrant children and families. A senior research associate at the University of Pennsylvania's National Center on Fathers and Families, she has served as consultant to numerous organizations.

Jessa Reed is a graduate student in developmental psychology at Temple University. She has worked as a research assistant at the Yale Child Study Center's Developmental Disabilities Clinic. Her current research focuses on how an arts-enriched preschool pedagogy can foster school readiness skills and how maternal responsiveness scaffolds and promotes early verbal learning in young children.

Robert L. Selman is the Roy E. Larsen Professor of Education and Human Development at the Harvard Graduate School of Education where he served as chair of the Human Development and Psychology area for several years. He is also a professor of psychology in the Department of Psychiatry at the Harvard Medical School and senior associate at the Judge Baker Children's Center. His research focuses on the child's developing capacity to coordinate points of view, develop interpersonal negotiation strategies, and become aware of the personal meaning of risk in the context of social relationships and the larger culture. He is a fellow of the American Educational Research Association and the recipient of the Association for Moral Education's Kuhmerker Award for career contributions.

Jack P. Shonkoff, M.D., is the Julius B. Richmond FAMRI Professor of Child Health and Development at the Harvard School of Public Health and Harvard Graduate School of Education; professor of pediatrics at Harvard Medical School and Children's Hospital, Boston; and founding director of the Center on the Developing Child at Harvard University. He chairs the National Scientific Council on the Developing Child, a multiuniversity collaboration whose mission is to bring credible science to bear on policy affecting young children; and he cochairs the National Forum on Early Childhood Policy and Programs, a multiuniversity collaboration of leading researchers in policy and program effectiveness and implementation. In addition to serving on the editorial board of several scholarly journals, he has chaired the National Academy of Sciences' Board on Children, Youth, and Families and headed an Academy blue-ribbon committee that produced a landmark report in 2000, *From Neurons to Neighborhoods: The Science of Early Childhood Development*. His more than 150 publications include nine books and two coedited editions of the *Handbook of Early Childhood Intervention* (Cambridge University Press, 1993, 2000).

Edward Zigler is Sterling Professor of Psychology Emeritus at Yale University. The first director of the U.S. government's Office of Child Development (now the Administration on Children, Youth, and Families), he was also chief of the U.S. Children's Bureau and a member of the national planning committees of the Head Start, Follow Through, and Early Head Start programs. The founder and now Director Emeritus of the Edward Zigler Center in Child Development and Social Policy at Yale University, he created the School of the 21st Century model, which has been adopted by more than 1,300 schools in 20 states. He has authored, coauthored, or edited over 800 scholarly publications and more than 35 books and is the recipient of over 100 awards and many honorary degrees.

Index